INVITATION TO ECONOMICS

Wk 1 - Chapt 1, 2, 3 + 7
2   4, 10, 11, 12, 13, 16 + 17
3   5, 6, 7, 8 + ⑨
4   9   8 + 6
5   18, 19 + 20

INVITATION TO ECONOMICS
Macroeconomics and Microeconomics

SECOND EDITION

James Eggert
University of Wisconsin, Stout

Bristlecone Books

Mayfield Publishing Company
Mountain View, California
London • Toronto

Library of Congress Cataloging-in-Publication Data
Eggert, Jim, 1943-
    Invitation to economics: macroeconomics and microeconomics /
    James Eggert.-2nd ed.
        p.   cm.
    "Bristlecone books."
    Includes index.
    ISBN 0-87484-993-4
    1. Economics.   I. Title.
HB171.E345 1991
330-dc20   90-46314
                                 CIP

Manufactured in the United States of America
10 9 8 7 6 5

Bristlecone Books
Mayfield Publishing Company
1240 Villa Street
Mountain View, California

Sponsoring editor, Gary Burke; managing editor, Linda Toy; copy editor,
Mary George; text and cover designer, Jeanne M. Schreiber; production
artist, Jean Mailander; illustrator, Willa Bower; photographs by Jim Eggert;
cartoons by Robert Cavey. The text was set in 10½/13 New Century
Schoolbook and printed on 50# Butte des Morts Smooth (recycled paper) by
Banta Company.

Preface

The purpose of *Invitation to Economics*, Second Edition, is to provide, in an engaging and relevant style, the essentials of macroeconomics and microeconomics. *Invitation to Economics* is decidedly *not* encyclopedic in scope, yet it does present the basic economic principles both in theory and, through a variety of examples, in application.

There are three areas of emphasis. First, I try to give the reader a solid grounding in the meaning of a "market economy." As governments of Eastern Europe (and elsewhere) begin to evolve genuinely free-market, capitalist economies, it is important for students to understand precisely what this means and to learn some of the market's great advantages as well as its built-in shortcomings. (In particular, I've outlined "three tragic flaws of pure capitalism" in Chapters 4 and 5.)

Second, I've tried to expand and integrate the treatment of environmental and ecological considerations while offering the student a workable context in which to examine and account for "neighborhood effects" locally, nationally, and internationally. Ecological degradation is, in fact, one of market capitalism's tragic flaws. Points of view, both pro-growth and anti-growth, are then summarized at the conclusion of Chapter 7, and global implications are examined in Chapter 20.

Finally—this time on the microeconomic side—immediate status is given to the indifference-curve/budget-line approach in consumer theory and also to its counterpart, the equal-product curve in production theory. In teaching beginning microeconomics to non-majors, I've found this approach provides an uncommonly reliable method for helping beginning students understand the "ins and outs" of building a specific supply/demand market from scratch. In addition, to disarm the reader's anxiety about pure, abstract presentations, I've used non-intimidating, concrete illustrations. For the most part, these examples involve the economic odyssey of a Mr. Chester Olson, who, like an actor who has been given parts in a play, weaves in and out of the chapters on microeconomics in a variety of producer and consumer roles.

As students make their way through *Invitation to Economics,* I hope to encourage their curiosity. Indeed, my objective will have been achieved if this book stimulates and, in a friendly way, prods students to dig deeper into economic principles and issues—to the point where they might feel truly confident to actively participate in the political and economic debates of the day.

Warm thanks go to Bob Eggert—father, friend, and fellow economist. Thanks also go to Paul Barkley, Emil Haney, Lou Tokle, Dave Liu, and Marty Ondrus, who took the time to read the manuscript and offer helpful suggestions on various sections. In addition, I extend special thanks to Jim Pinto, colleague and author of the *Study Guide* and the end-of-chapter questions in the book. In addition, I appreciate the helpful suggestions from Gary Burke, publisher of Bristlecone Books, and Mary George, manuscript editor. Pat Eggert, my wife, made especially helpful comments from start to finish. And, of course, much of the credit for this book goes to all my "Intro Econ" students over the past two decades, whose individual and collective contributions have helped make this a better book in ways that would be difficult to measure.

Contents

Sequences for Alternative Emphasis

To my father,
Robert J. Eggert

PART 1
The National Economy

1

What Is Economics?

What Is Economics?

Unfortunately, there is no single or simple answer to this question. In the most basic sense, economics is the study of how individuals or communities survive and reproduce using scarce resources. Indeed, this definition could apply to all life forms as they pursue their successful evolution over time. Using this approach, we might, for example, examine "bumblebee economics," "bluebird economics," or the complex interrelationships of a biological community, such as a prairie or rain forest.[1]*

Of course, most of our emphasis in this book will be on human societies, in which economics originally meant *household management*. Still, the **economic problem** is the same: how best to use scarce resources. Household resources may include a family's money, time, working and living space, and so on. Of course, our human objectives are much more complicated than simple survival. People have a wide variety of economic desires, including (among other things) general comfort, financial security, interesting diversions, recreational pursuits, and health care. In fact, the economic wants of most households or individuals appear for all practical purposes to be *unlimited*.

*Notes appear on pages 321–325 in the back of the book.

We are also different from other animals in that we are able to make *deliberate choices* as to how our limited resources will be used. Thus, a basic definition of economics might go something like this: *economics is the study of how an individual or a household chooses to use limited resources to best meet its unlimited wants.*

Now let's extend our view from the household economy to the national economy. The basic economic problem is still the same: the nation's resources are limited. Our material demands, however, tend to be unlimited, and the nation must learn how to best organize its resources to satisfy its material wants. Unwise use of resources—whether by consumers, businesses, or governments—can bring about such unfortunate results as unemployment, inflation, poverty, and (in extreme cases) hunger or starvation. The study of economics can help us understand how we can avoid the mismanagement of national resources.

National Resources

What exactly then are our *national economic resources?* The first and primary resource is **labor:** the millions of men and women in the U.S. labor force (the doctor, the farmer, the butcher, the assembly-line worker, and so on). Labor is the *human* element in the production process.

The next national economic resource is **land.** Our land resources include every natural resource above, on, and below the soil. Air is a land resource, as is farmland and the mineral ores and petroleum in the crust of the earth. Land resources are distinguished by the fact that we cannot make more of them. The earth has only so much topsoil and so much oil. Once the topsoil is destroyed[2] and the oil is burned up, they will be gone forever.

The third national resource is **capital.** Many people think that "capital" means money. You often hear people say, "I need to raise (so much) capital for my new project," but what they are actually referring to is financial capital. To the economist, however, *capital* means the physical tools that help workers produce goods and services. In other words, *capital goods* are human-made, can be reproduced or replaced, and tend to increase the productivity of labor.

What are some examples of capital goods? The typewriter that I use is a capital good. It is a tool that increases my output; it's human-made (unlike land resources); and, once it wears out, I can replace it. The pen that you wrote your last check with is a capital good, and so is the car that gets you to work or school. In fact, all machinery, tools, buildings, plants, and equipment are capital resources. Now you can see that there is much more to the meaning of capital than just plain money. Obviously, capital goods are very important in determining the nation's level of wealth and economic growth.

Finally, we come to that elusive resource called **management.** The manager is quite special in our economy; managers coordinate and organize all other resources in order to produce and market the products and services that people want, thereby creating a *profit*. In earlier days, the manager was called an "entrepreneur"; we think, as examples, of Henry Ford and Andrew Carnegie as large-scale managers personifying this scarce resource. Perhaps the days of the great manufacturing entrepreneurs are over, but whether you are talking about the bakery down the street or Sony or General Motors, some one person or group of people must still coordinate and manage resources to produce saleable products and services.

Asking Questions, Making Choices

Thus, labor, land, capital, and management are the four major resources available to produce the goods and services that people need and want in our economy. To define a working economic system, however, we must ask further questions; for example, *how does an economic system determine what is to be produced?* What will our economic output consist of, and who will determine its composition? Will our economy produce bombs and tanks, or hospitals and homes? Small cars, large cars, or bikes and trains? Gas, oil, or solar heat? Who or what will decide for us? Of course, different economic systems will provide different answers to these questions. Leaders in Cuba or China determine what is to be produced in a somewhat different manner than they do in the United States or Brazil.

In addition, there are other important questions to ask, such as *how does the economic system decide who gets the output?* Why are incomes, goods, and services distributed in the ways they are? Throughout world history, dividing up the economic pie has often been a very controversial question. Will our economic system give a majority of the output to a few "super rich" families, will it try to divide the pie up more equally, or will the economic distribution fall somewhere in between? The uneven distribution of incomes and wealth often results from differences in education, intelligence, skills, work habits, monopoly power, geography, family background, luck, and political or social savvy. More equal incomes, on the other hand, are usually regulated by government policies, such as minimum-wage laws, progressive taxation, subsidized education, and welfare assistance.

And finally, there is the question *how will these goods be produced?* At first glance, the answer might seem to be a purely technical one. Building an automobile, for example, is a problem for the engineer. And yet we know there are really many ways to produce a finished automobile. Ideally, we want to build efficiently, using abundant, low-cost resources in place of scarce, high-cost resources. Assembling that car one way in preference to another returns us to the question of *allocating* resources. Choosing the correct production techniques (conserving the scarce resources and using the abundant ones) is as much an economic problem as it is a technical or engineering problem. Economics is therefore the science (or art) of making choices—of choosing the best way to organize our limited resources to meet our material needs.

Finding Answers

The method by which an economic system answers these questions varies from time to time and from country to country. In fact, there are three basic systems for organizing economic resources.

The first is called *tradition*. The decision makers in a **traditional economic system** answer these questions by saying, "We will organize our economy in the way we have always organized it," by following age-old patterns determined by a complex culture that has evolved over thousands of years. Tools and houses are constructed as they were always constructed. Junior goes into the same trade as dad, while the daughter's life will be very much like her mother's. Output is allocated by custom, with few changes over the years and only minute trial-and-error improvements over the centuries; it's a system that is predictable, predetermined, and relatively static.

Economics by tradition certainly has some advantages: there may be less conflict, and there are probably few expectations that cannot be met. But as an economic system, it is likely to offer a relatively low standard of living, at least as we in the industrialized world would define it. If you feel that having more choices moves you closer to the "good life," then the traditional economic system is probably not for you.

Yet we certainly have elements of tradition in our so-called "modern economy." For example, my own father is an economist, and he was once a teacher, as I am now. Many instructors still use a lecture method that dates back to Plato in ancient Greece, even though some critics think that the lecture technique should have been discarded with the invention of the computer. Whether the critics are correct or not, contemporary education certainly adheres to very traditional methods of conduct and even ritual. Women, too, have become more aware of the extent to which their lives are determined by social and economic traditions. Discrimination on the basis of sex has eliminated a large proportion of our population from the competition for highly productive and professional jobs, and our economy has lost a potentially vast economic force. You can probably think of many more examples of how tradition weaves in and out of our supposedly "modern" economy.

The second method of organizing economic resources is the **command system,** which is characterized by the allocation of resources, incomes, prices, and so on, by a centralized authority (in other words, a dictatorship). The command system invites no questions: either you follow orders, or you take the consequences. This system is often the offspring of a despotic political system; they frequently go hand-in-hand. The economy of Cuba is a good example, as was that of ancient Egypt under the Pharaohs.

European democratic socialists believe, however, that we can have a planned, state-directed economy without dictatorship. The combination appears to be difficult, yet democratic state planning has been approximated in Scandinavia and Japan. The U.S. economy, too, has some elements of economic command. Our military services, for example, work on this principle, as does the government allocation of goods during wartime. When price-wage controls are in effect, we have a perfect example of government command. Furthermore, almost all government laws on economic affairs (including our tax system) constitute direction from above. By and large, however, our private enterprise system cannot really be called either a command or a traditional system.

What we have in the United States is the third mode of economic organization: a *market economy*. A relatively recent phenomenon, the **market system** motivates people by offering economic incentives and rewards within a process of exchange. Instead of government direction, decisions on resource use are made by millions of independent individuals and institutions striving to do what is best for themselves or their businesses. Here, the economic mule moves by carrot instead of stick. A market economy is indeed a system of carrots.

If the command system is centralized, the market system is decentralized. A market economy churns out prices in countless markets of supply and demand; these prices, in turn, *act as guidelines* in a new round of economic decisions. It is a competitive, interdependent, self-regulating system.

From a recent historical perspective, the market system appears to be "the economy of choice" in terms of its capacity to bring about modernization, to broaden economic opportunity, and to improve a nation's standard of living. In eastern Europe, for example, such countries as Poland, Czechoslovakia, Hungary, and East Germany are rejecting political dictatorship and command economics and are apparently moving toward democracy and a production/distribution system more in tune with a decentralized market economy. Thus, many of the large-scale, twentieth-century experiments with command economics are currently being phased out or abandoned outright.

Economic Sacrifices

Another way of looking at economics is to examine sacrifices—what economists call **opportunity costs.** What does this mean?

Let's say that you have spent half an hour reading this chapter. By spending this time reading, you have given up doing a number of activities you could have enjoyed. When you use up one of your resources (an hour of time, a dollar, etc.), the cost to

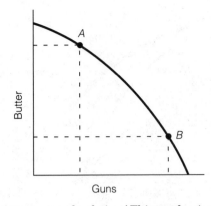

FIGURE 1-1   A society must make choices! This *production-possibilities curve* represents the various choices that society can make about military versus consumer spending. Possible combinations along the curve include a lot of butter (consumer goods) and few guns (military goods) at point *A* or a small amount of butter and a large amount of guns at point *B*.

you is really the opportunities that you have forfeited. That hour is gone forever, and so are the alternative activities you might have enjoyed. Sometimes we hear the question, "If you had your life to live over, would you do it any differently?" If you answer yes, then you are referring indirectly to your opportunity cost.

Although this explanation of opportunity cost is somewhat philosophical, the economic concept is often more concrete. Economists look at the sacrifices that must be made when the economic resources of land, labor, capital, and management are used. If, for example, we commit our resources to producing 10 million automobiles, then these resources *cannot* be used for such alternative goods and services as housing or mass transit. Thus, the economist (unlike the businessperson) is interested not only in monetary costs but also in what is going to be sacrificed when resources are put to use.

The idea of looking at economic costs as sacrifices can be seen quite dramatically if we look at Figure 1-1. We can assume that point *A* represents an economy much like our own; it has directed most of its total resources toward the production of "butter" (private consumer goods) and fewer resources toward "guns" (military expenditures). As we move away from zero on either the "guns" or "butter" axis of this graph, we are producing more and more of that good. Thus, point *B* represents a country that has chosen to produce more military goods than consumer goods (as the United States did during World War II).

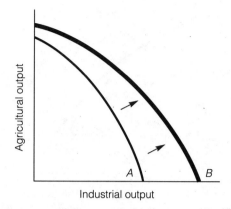

FIGURE 1-2 *Economic growth* is reflected by an expanding production-possibilities curve (from an early developmental stage, represented by curve *A*, to a stage of increased production, represented by curve *B*). Here, China's economic growth favors industrial output over agricultural output.

Given the fact that a country has only so many total resources, it is forced to choose some mix on the line (or curve) between guns and butter. This line or curve is called the **production-possibilities curve.**

Our production-possibilities curve therefore represents all the various choices open to society regarding consumer versus military production. With our limited resources, we may opt to produce more butter (*A*) *or* guns (*B*), but note that we cannot have large amounts of both goods—there are simply not enough total resources! In fact, to move from point *A* to point *B* means that the production of butter *must be sacrificed* to get more guns. Stating this opportunity cost a little differently, economists sometimes say, "There is no such thing as a free lunch."

The *true cost* (opportunity cost) is the measure of what is sacrificed. Thus, we might view the true economic cost of a large defense buildup as all the desirable things that *might* have been produced or accomplished if the resources had been applied to the production of peace-time goods and services. Or, the true economic cost of having so many automobiles is that the resources used to manufacture them are not available to produce mass-transit systems (see Figure 1-3).

Now let's take a look at another production-possibilities curve. The one in Figure 1-2 represents a less-developed country like China.

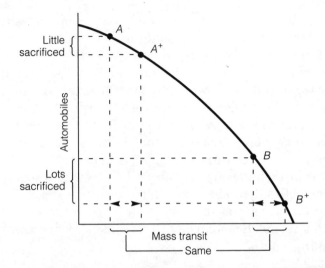

FIGURE 1-3 *Law of increasing costs:* note the *small* sacrifice *(opportunity cost)* of automobiles when mass transit increases from *A* to *A*⁺, compared to the *large* sacrifice of automobiles that results when mass transit increases from *B* to *B*⁺. The amount of increase in mass transit is the same in both cases.

Curve *A* represents the country at an early stage of development, when it has more agricultural potential than industrial potential. The expanding production curve *B* represents this country after some economic growth has occurred. The country in this example has chosen the kind of economic growth that tends to favor industrial output over agricultural output. This is a typical pattern for economic development throughout the world.

The Law of Increasing Costs

Finally, there is an additional piece of information we can gather by examining a production-possibilities curve. Take a look at Figure 1-3.

Assume for a moment that the United States is producing a lot of automobiles and few mass-transit systems; the country is therefore operating at point *A*. Now suppose that the United States decides to put more of its resources into mass transit, so that production moves down the curve a little way from *A* to *A*⁺. Note how much additional mass transit there is in relation to the relatively *small* amount of sacrificed automobiles. If, however, the United States is producing a lot of mass-transit systems (operating at point B) and wants even more mass transit, the country gains the *same* amount as before (A to A^+) when it moves from B to B^+. Note the difference in the real cost of obtaining that extra mass transit: the number of sacrificed automobiles *is much larger*. We might say, then, that as the United States moves to higher levels of mass transit, the opportunity costs of squeezing out yet *more* mass transit becomes greater and greater as more and more automobiles have to be sacrificed. Obviously, when a country is producing almost all mass transit, it has few interchangeable resources left to switch from producing automobiles to producing even more mass transit. Thus, the sacrifice (or cost) must be very high to gain these additional trains, buses, etc. Economists call this phenomenon **the law of increasing costs.**

The Economist's Concerns

Let's return to our original question: what is economics? We might answer this question by simply saying that economics is "what economists study." Most economists, in fact, are not too concerned with such broad generalizations as "studying how to best allocate resources to meet our unlimited wants." They are more interested in the specific economic problems of society, such as unemployment, inflation, balance of payments, economic stagnation, and pollution. So we could say that economics is "the study of how our society solves economic problems."

Alternatively, we could view economics as "the study of goals"—how a society moves closer to specific economic objectives. These economic goals are more or less universal; most countries (capitalist, socialist, and communist) are striving to achieve them.

The primary economic goal that seems to be universally desired is *a decent material standard of living for all citizens,* and much economic activity is directed toward this goal. But exactly what steps or intermediate goals lead to such a "successful economy"?

The first objective is *full employment.* Nations would like to see all, or nearly all, of their available resources being used. Men and women out of work or idle machines and factories can result in great economic suffering and social instability. It is foolish for resources to go unused when the means to correct the situation are available. How we move an economy toward full employment will be explored later in the text.

The second goal of an economic system is *price stability.* Rapid price increases—what is commonly called *inflation*—have the undesirable effect of grossly distorting income distribution. The victims include savers, lenders, and people on fixed incomes; while these groups lose, others (including borrowers and speculators) win. At its best, mild inflation is merely irritating, if it is accompanied by full employment. At its worst, however, inflation invites panic buying and can lead to the eventual collapse of a monetary system.

Conflicts arise in pursuing various economic goals, as they do in pursuing price stability and full employment. For example, when there is high unemployment, there is frequently lower inflation; however, if there is high inflation, almost everyone is working. As a society struggles to achieve one economic objective, it sometimes loses its grip on another.

The third goal of most countries is *economic growth.* Respected critics argue that the United States is presently "overdeveloped" and believe that we would benefit by not adding any more to our economic affluence. And yet most Americans, and most other people in the world, seem to desire higher and higher levels of output and consumption. They feel concerned when the total economic output fails to rise; if output drops, alarms are sounded throughout the government and business sectors of the economy. Furthermore, in the poorest two-thirds of the world, economic stagnation may mean hunger and possible starvation.

A fourth goal of most nations is the desire for a *quality environment.* Mounting evidence of the massive pollution problems that face our small planet compels economists to regard the environment as a major economic issue. But, again, potential conflicts can arise in pursuing these economic goals concurrently. For example, strong enforcement of antipollution laws may slow down economic growth and, within some industries, increase unemployment.

A fifth goal of an economic society is to move toward a *fair distribution of income.* However, the absolutely equal distribution of income is not the economic goal of a nation. Perfect equality would be unrealistic and probably undesirable because it would destroy healthy economic incentives. On the other hand, most economists would agree that a system that allows a large number of its citizens to live in debilitating poverty while others enjoy immense wealth is certainly unfair. What then can we do about a grossly unequal system?

Generally accepted methods of moving toward a more equal distribution of income include government taxation and redistribution of income (welfare, food stamps, Medicare, etc.), as well as the enforcement of equal opportunity in education and job procurement. If the government becomes, as some have suggested, "the employer of last resort," then it will have an even greater impact in this area. Although some people disapprove of government intervention, the policies and programs just mentioned are at least some ways of breaking down the natural, social, and institutional inequalities that operate in all societies.

The sixth and final goal of most societies is *economic freedom*. Like the goal of fair income distribution, economic freedom is sometimes difficult to define precisely. To many people, economic freedom thrives in a decentralized, free-enterprise system in which workers choose occupations suited to their skills and experience. By this definition, twentieth century America may be one of the most "free" economies in the world. Yet critics might ask what meaning economic freedom has for a consumer who has no income. Indeed, what does occupational freedom mean to an unskilled person in a high-unemployment area? How realistic would our "freedom of enterprise" be if you or I were to attempt to compete with IT&T, Proctor & Gamble, or the Ford Motor Company? The *ideal* of economic freedom is therefore often diluted by income inequalities, by barriers imposed by large, concentrated industries, and by restrictive policies and regulations of government. But compare the United States with other countries, and it's clear that the U.S. economy would score quite high in meeting the objectives of economic freedom.

Take a moment now to think about these six goals in relationship to yourself. How does the nation's economic performance—in terms of freedom, price stability, employment, growth, fairness, and the environment—affect *you?* Does the national economy help or hinder your effort to create your own personal "successful economy"? You can see that whether we like it or not, we are all connected to the larger national economy.

It is now time to take a more intimate look at some of the specific characteristics and inner workings of the complex system we call the U.S. economy.

Questions for Thought and Discussion

1. How are economic freedom and political freedom related?
2. Chapter 1 lists several goals for any economic system. In what kind of a world or society would we live if we met all of these goals? Explain in detail.
3. Why would an equal distribution of income in a society be unfair to some individuals?
4. Why isn't money an economic resource?
5. Why isn't the production-possibilities curve shaped like a straight line?

2

The U.S. Economy

It would not be unusual if someday someone from a foreign country asks you: "What is the U.S. economy like? What makes it tick?" How would you answer that person? How would you try to portray its broad outlines and significant characteristics?

Markets and Prices

We learned in Chapter 1 that the U.S. economic system is basically a **market economy.** Now let's amplify this important idea. A *pure market economy* is self-regulated, interdependent, and competitive. Self-regulation takes place when supply and demand operate for every good and service that has economic value. There is a market for welders and secretaries, for wheat and bread, for toothpicks, tractors, and teachers. Each of these markets is constantly interacting with hundreds of others. This process churns out prices (or wages), and these price signals modify other markets and influence economic decisions. Let's look at an illustration.

We will begin by assuming that there is a shortage of milk; and, as a consequence, the price of milk goes up. In a market economy, buyers and sellers note this signal (high milk prices) and then respond in various ways. First, the existing dairy farmers demand more cows and farmland so that they can expand their operations and increase their profits. Soon, higher profits in milk production begin to attract more farmers into the dairy industry.

This growing number of farmers begin to demand more milking machines and silos. Stainless steel for milking machines and cement for silos are diverted into farming and away from other industries. Milking-machine manufacturers try to out-bid steel-pipe manufacturers for the available steel. Plumbers now find that steel pipes are simply priced too high; they soon discover that low-cost plastic pipes can do the job almost as well. Suddenly the plastic industry has a need for new people and raw materials: chemists and petroleum. The many readjust-ments—both large and small—that could take place because of a milk-price increase are almost endless. Note that in this example no economic dictatorship tells people what to do; every-thing takes place automatically in response to price signals in the marketplace.

In reality, our neat system of supply and demand is often not allowed to regulate itself. The government, reacting to economic special-interest groups, is often responsible. For example, when the federal government imposes price-wage controls, we find that prices are no longer flexible. If prices are not allowed to move upward or downward, these economic signals are thwarted. Shortages and black markets develop where the demand for certain products is great. We can see something similar happening when city governments impose rent controls. When rents are artificially low, a greater quantity of rental property is demanded than is supplied, leaving many frustrated demanders. Other examples of market regulation by government include farm subsidies, minimum-wage laws, and tariffs on imports and ex-ports. Whenever the government interferes with the free movement of prices, market efficiency is usually reduced.

Specialization

The U.S. economy can also be described as **specialized.** Just about every worker specializes. A worker can specialize in program-ming computers, making handmade furniture, fixing cars, or tightening a bolt on an automobile assembly line. If we did not specialize, many of us would be forced to become self-sufficient—like the original settlers of the American frontier—and we would undoubtedly undergo a reduced standard of living.

Why does output increase when workers specialize? Some people, of course, simply have *natural abilities* in some specialties. Also, the more we work at our particular job, the faster and generally more efficient we become. We learn to use shortcuts and special tools to increase our productivity. The assembly-line operation is a good example of how *specialization* and *division of labor* can create greater output than a system of nonspecialized workers.

Specialization can be worthwhile, even when an individual has superior skills in several areas. For example, Jim is a good plumber and a good mechanic. Bob is a plumber and a mechanic as well. However, Bob is almost a genius at fixing cars, whereas Jim is just average. Their skills as plumbers are about equal, but Bob is a little better here, too. Even though Bob has an *absolute advantage* in both skills, he has a *comparative advantage* only in mechanics; that is, Bob's advantage is *much greater* than Jim's in mechanics, but not in plumbing. Jim is not as good in either skill, but *his disadvantage is smaller* in plumbing. We therefore say that Jim has his comparative advantage in plumbing. If Jim and Bob lived in a town that had room for only one plumber and only one mechanic, the economy of the town would be more productive if Bob worked as the mechanic and Jim concentrated on plumbing. In short, specialization brings about higher output in almost all situations.

Some economists feel, however, that we, both as individuals and as a society, are overspecialized, despite the gains from comparative advantage. One drawback of specialization is that we become highly dependent on our specialists. What would happen if the truck drivers and railroad workers (only about 1 percent of the labor force) went on strike at the same time? Our economy would be paralyzed within a week. If the strike lasted a month, we might face starvation and panic. The slender threads of economic interdependence can easily be broken in a complex economy such as ours.

There is also some evidence that overspecialization on the assembly line and in menial jobs takes its psychological toll:

> The man whose whole life is spent in performing simple opera-
> tions which the effects to are, perhaps, always the same, or very
> nearly the same, has no occasion to exert his understanding or to
> exercise his invention....He naturally loses, therefore, the habit of
> such exertion and generally becomes as stupid and ignorant as it
> is possible for a human creature to become.

Adam Smith wrote this in his book *Inquiry into the Nature and
Causes of the Wealth of Nations* in 1776. Even today, we see
some people rebel against overspecialization. Sometimes we
read, for example, of individuals or families moving from the
cities into the country to set up "homesteads" where they can
operate partially self-sufficient farms with little specialization. Often they build their own homes, make their own
clothes, and grow some of their food, as most of our nation's
farmers did generations ago. Even though their material standard of living is usually lower than average, they take great
pride in their work and seem quite happy with their newly found
independence.

Finally, there is evidence that many people—even those
with specialized jobs—would like to rely less on the services of
others. Home gardening, for example, seems to be fairly common;
"do-it-yourself" remodeling has always been popular in this
country. These trends seem to defy the laws of comparative
advantage and specialization. Still, by and large, we remain
primarily specialists, operating within an interdependent and
highly specialized American economy.

Self-Interest

If much of our productivity and efficiency comes from specialization and division of labor, the motivation to do all this work
comes from **self-interest.** Why do some people go into dirty coal
mines or get up early on a cold winter morning to work on an
outdoor construction site? Why does the barber cheerfully cut
your hair even when he or she isn't feeling so hot? Why does
General Motors make Chevrolets? Why do some companies go
to all the trouble of creating a "better" fast-food hamburger
or paper diaper? There is no economic commander-in-chief
telling them what to do, and they don't do these things because

of tradition. They perform their jobs *because it is in their own self-interest to do so.* Economists call this self-interest **income maximization;** others call it "just trying to make a living." Whatever it's called, it is the motor of our capitalist economic system. Things get done because each individual group or institution is constantly trying to enlarge its base of income, consumption, or profit.

The self-interest of businesses is to maximize profits. The self-interest of workers is to maximize income. And finally, the self-interest of consumers is to maximize their material satisfactions from limited incomes.

Surprisingly enough, out of this very "self-centered" economic turmoil, the society as a whole benefits! In *The Wealth of Nations,* this is what Adam Smith meant by the *"invisible hand"* when he said that each individual (or business) pursuing his own interest is "led by an invisible hand to promote the end which was not part of his intention."

It was not the intention of the diaper company to make it easier for parents to take care of their babies. The company's purpose was to make a profit. Therefore, the company had to make something society wanted. This is where paper diapers came in. If the company did not make a product society wanted, it would be eliminated by the laws of economics. You might recall this ad from the Sun Oil Company; it has a refreshing honesty about it:

> These days, I need all the friends I can get. This is a tough business I'm in. You really have to hustle to make a buck. And right now I need the bucks. I'm due for a new wrecker. A new car. And my wife's screaming for an avocado refrigerator. That's why, when you drive into my station, I'm going to come out smiling. I'm going to wash your front window. Your back window. Now to be honest, I'm not really crazy about having to work this hard, but I need that new wrecker, the new car, and like my wife says, what's an avocado kitchen without an avocado refrigerator? Try me; I can be very friendly.

Of course, not everyone is interested in maximizing his or her income. Henry David Thoreau once said, "None can be an impartial or wise observer of human life but from the vantage ground of what we should call voluntary poverty."[3] And in his thought-provoking article, "Four Reasons for Voluntary Poverty,"[4] James Park explains that income maximization can lead to exploitation, pollution, compromises on personal freedom, and a tacit support of militarism (through taxes). Readers will have to decide for themselves whether voluntary poverty is a desirable path to follow. It seems safe to say, however, that if a majority of workers and businesses renounced income or profit maximization, the U.S. economic system would be radically different from what it is today.

Private Ownership

Another notable characteristic of the American economy is **private ownership.** If we were living under a socialist instead of a capitalist system, then the means of production—the businesses, factories, capital, and other resources—would be largely publicly owned.

The debate over **socialism** versus **capitalism** has been going on for years. Unfortunately, opinions are too often based on emotion rather than on factual information. Many people, for example, are convinced that socialism implies a political system that is totalitarian, ruthless, and nonlibertarian. The truth is that political despotism may thrive in a capitalist state (South Africa) as well as in a socialist one (Cuba). Again, the major difference between the two systems is that socialist businesses are owned and controlled publicly, whereas capitalist businesses are owned and controlled privately. To say much more is to confuse the issue.

Now let's consider the term "communism." How does it differ from capitalism and socialism? According to Karl Marx, the production-distribution philosophy of communism is, "From each according to his ability, to each according to his need." Surprisingly, our most "communist" institution is the family. In most conventional family living situations, members receive an approximately equal distribution of goods and services. Consumption is based on "need" instead of on productive effort; an infant, for example, doesn't work for its formula. Pure communism has been approximated by a few comparatively small groups (the Shakers and some North American Indian communities are examples), but on a national scale it doesn't appear to be as workable as the varieties of socialism and capitalism.

Competition

Another characteristic of the U.S. economy is **competition.**
According to proponents of the capitalist system, competition
allows the most intelligent and skillful to prevail in a "dog-eat-
dog" battle for survival. This is a virtue, they say, because in a
system where only the fittest and strongest come out on top, the
economic organization itself will remain strong and healthy.
Producers must make a cheaper, better product than their rivals, or they will find themselves out of business. A competitive
economy is like a grandscale pro-football game where, according
to the late Green Bay Packer Coach Vince Lombardi, "Winning
isn't everything; it's the only thing." It should be noted that some
people feel this kind of "competition" may be unhealthy. Educa-
tor George Leonard, for example, writes[5]

> The . . . argument for hot competition all the way down to nursery
> school is that competition makes winners. The argument is, at
> best, half true. It makes nonwinners, too—generally more
> nonwinners than winners. And a number of studies indicate that
> losing can become a lifelong habit.

What is perhaps even more interesting is a businessman's
reaction to the suggestion that this kind of competition creates
more problems than it solves. Leonard continues

> I once spoke to a group of top-ranking industrialists in a seminar
> session and argued that hot competition is far from inevitable in
> the future. As my argument developed, I noticed a look of real
> anxiety on some of the faces around me. One industrialist finally
> spoke up, "If there is to be no competition, then what will life be
> all about?" We would probably be appalled to discover how many
> people in this culture have no notion of accomplishment for its
> own sake and define their own existence solely in terms of how
> many other people they can beat out.

Thus, to beat out your opponent and to build a better
product than your rival are common ways of defining competition. Economists, however, define it somewhat differently. A
good example of a competitive industry in the United States is
farming, with tens of thousands of producers who usually don't
care about what the other producers are doing! In *pure competition,* there are really *no differences* between the sellers' products. For example, grade A milk is generally the same throughout the dairy industry. We never see advertisements claiming

that Farmer Jones's milk is better than Farmer Brown's. Another characteristic of competition is that no seller is big enough to set prices or to control the market. A competitive industry is the *least concentrated* of all industries. (In contrast, a monopoly is the most concentrated.)*

Obviously, to be a producer in a truly competitive industry is to operate at a disadvantage. For example, the farmers' inability to control prices and their low rate of return on investment are problems that have plagued U.S. agriculture for decades. Even though competition may mean "hard times" for sellers, it usually gives consumers the lowest possible price. Furthermore, the more sellers there are, the more potential choices the buyer has. Competition is therefore a kind of "consumer's price insurance policy."

Since real competition can be threatening to businesses, we see all kinds of efforts to do away with it. Sellers can sometimes lessen competition by eliminating other sellers, by erecting barriers to new firms attempting to enter the field, and by making products slightly different from those of other sellers in the industry. Keep in mind that even though a decentralized competitive market is a traditional American "ideal," it is a rare sight on our economic landscape.

To summarize, we can say that industry is *purely competitive* if it has the following characteristics:

- A large number of sellers of the same product
- No single seller with any control over price
- Easy entry into the industry
- Low profits in the long run
- No rivalry among sellers

Monopolies

Now let's look at the other extreme. If competition allows consumers the widest potential choice, a monopoly seller has total control over its specific economic kingdom. If you are a consumer and want the goods, you must buy from the monopolist. A **monopoly** is, in short, a *one-firm industry*.

*For a more detailed analysis, see Chapters 13, 14, and 16.

Are there any good examples of monopolies in the United States? Well, your local telephone company has an effective monopoly on local telephone service. The government, too, holds a legal monopoly on first-class mail. The companies that sell you electricity and natural gas are also monopolies. We call them **natural monopolies** because the market is too small to accommodate more than one seller. If, for example, your local utility already has electric power lines leading to your home, it would obviously be inefficient (and also very costly) for another firm to install other power lines. Consumers tolerate natural monopolies, but what protects the consumer from profit-maximizing utilities? The answer is government regulation. Although natural monopolies are legally protected, their prices and rates are subject to review by public commissions.

There are other monopolies, however, that operate without any restrictions. Imagine a small town with just one drug store or only one dentist. We call this kind of market a **regional monopoly.** We can't say these are pure monopolies, because there may be another dentist or drug store 20 miles away. Yet for the retired residents of that town or for people with no convenient transportation out of town, the one dentist or drug store becomes an *effective* monopoly. In such a situation, the buyer is, from an economic perspective, at the mercy of the seller. Did you ever have the nightmare that your car breaks down in the middle of nowhere and you discover there is just one garage within 50 miles? Perhaps you can imagine the owner of the garage rubbing his hands together as his tow truck brings your car in. Unregulated monopolies can be bad news!

We can also see monopolistic behavior among the big industrialists. American Tobacco, Standard Oil, and Alcoa Aluminum were considered monopolies at one time. Others, such as General Electric and Westinghouse during the late 1950s, simply agreed among themselves to set prices on certain products and then behaved as if they were a single monopoly. This arrangement is called a **cartel.**

However it occurs, such monopolistic behavior is illegal under the Sherman Antitrust Act of 1890, Section 2 of which reads

> Every person who shall monopolize, or attempt to monopolize, or combine or conspire with any person or persons ... shall be deemed guilty of a misdemeanor.

The antitrust laws were written in an attempt to reverse the natural tendency for industries to become more concentrated. The big often get bigger. Indeed, if one firm begins to dominate a market, there is a tendency for that firm to attempt to eliminate (or merge with) rivals.

Let's review the conditions for a monopoly:

- Only one seller (one choice for the consumer)
- No close substitutes for the product sold by the monopolist
- Great barriers of entry into the industry
- Usually higher prices (unless regulated) than in a competitive market

The one industry that fits all these conditions but still is not ordinarily considered a monopoly is the public school system. Some economists point out that the public school monopoly contains many of the undesirable features of an industrial monopoly (a no-choice situation, high costs, lack of innovation, etc.). Not only do consumers (students) have no alternative, but they also *must* "consume" the "service" whether they want to or not. Not to do so means stiff penalties under the compulsory-attendance laws. To make things more difficult, a child often cannot get out of going to school even if he or she knows the required material. Would less compulsion and more choice make for a better public school system? Many educators and economists think that some alternative system is worth a try.

Milton Friedman, for one, has suggested a **voucher system** in which parents would be allowed to choose the kind of schooling they would like for their children. It would be something like the GI Bill for veterans. (No one, for example, tells a student on the GI Bill that he must go to a military academy.

The student can go to any accredited school.) Under this system, you might choose to use your educational vouchers for a public school, a private school, or even an apprenticeship. "Voluntary organizations—ranging from vegetarians to Boy Scouts to the YMCA—could set up schools and try to attract customers."[6] Minnesota is, in fact, currently experimenting with a modified voucher system; other states are also considering it.

Oligopolies

We have not yet mentioned the most prevalent type of industrial structure in the American economy. It's not competition, and it's not monopoly. Economists call this type of industry an **oligopoly,**[*] an industry dominated by a few firms. Think of almost everything we buy—automobiles, steel, aluminum, processed food, appliances, gasoline, etc. The companies that dominate each of these industries can often be counted on one hand.

Other major characteristics of an oligopolistic industry include:

- Emphasis on *nonprice competition* (advertising, product differentiation, styling, service, etc.)
- *Price leadership* (usually by the largest firm)
- Very difficult (because of barriers to entry) for outsiders to compete with established firms
- *Limited choice* for buyers between a few suppliers

Look carefully at the pyramid (Figure 2-1) to see how oligopoly fits between competition and monopoly in respect to market concentration. The oligopolistic industries are quite concentrated. Indeed, they are closer to a monopoly than they are to pure competition.

One of the major features of the oligopoly is *entry barriers*. What if you decided to start a rival company in the automobile industry? What difficulties would you encounter? For one thing, you would need millions and millions of dollars just to build one assembly plant, and even if you built it, you would still be left with a massive marketing problem. You would have to convince

---

[*]For a more detailed analysis of an oligopoly, see Chapter 17.

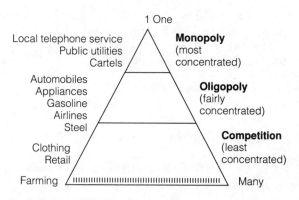

FIGURE 2-1 *Market-structure pyramid:* the upper-most point is *monopoly*—the most concentrated type of market; the base represents the thousands of suppliers that make up a *competitive market structure. Oligopoly* lies in between these two extreme market structures.

a large number of dealerships to handle your product. Even if you did that, why would people go out of the way to buy *your* car? They probably wouldn't, at least until you had established a name for yourself. This might take years and additional millions for advertising—and still would not include the high cost of financing annual model changeovers. Indeed, potential investors would probably consider your undertaking doomed to fail. Even large corporations that manufacture similar products (such as farm machinery or air frames) would hesitate to plunge into such a hazardous venture. The economic barriers are simply too great.

Well, what has happened to our model of the American economy? We began by saying that it was a competitive market economy, regulated by supply and demand. Although these concepts are still operational within our economy, we are nevertheless forced to modify some of our traditional viewpoints:

"But aren't we now saying that most of the production in the U.S. economy is dominated by oligopolists?"

"Yes."

"And didn't you say that it's very difficult for a newcomer to invade oligopolistic markets because there are so many barriers?"

"Yes."

"Then, whatever happened to the so-called 'free-enterprise ideal'?"

"To be truthful, it's not easy to find. We do see it in local service and retail, in some innovative small-scale manufacturing (such as computer software), and above all, in the *supply-demand determined industries,* such as farming, and the buying and selling of financial securities (stocks, bonds, etc.)."

"Supply and demand. I've heard that before. Can you go into more detail?"

"Sure. Please read on."

Questions for Thought and Discussion

1. In early August of 1990, Iraq invaded Kuwait and within a matter of days, the price of a barrel of oil increased by roughly 50 percent. Assume that this magnitude of price remained the world market price for a year or two, list as many repercussions in the U.S. economy as you can. Include major impacts and subtle ones as well.

2. Why do economists use a "pure market economy" model if such a market does not really exist?

3. Does Adam Smith's concept of the "invisible hand" mean that a person does not have choices and is predestined to behave, as Smith stated, "to promote the end which is not part of his intention"?

4. What is so "natural" about a natural monopoly?

5. Why is the pyramid that economists use to explain the levels of market concentration shaped the way it is?

3

Supply and Demand

You can hardly open up a magazine or newspaper without hearing someone refer to supply and demand: "Lower (or higher) food prices are a result of the supply and demand for farm commodities."..."The U.S. housing market depends on the supply and demand for money."..."The future world-energy situation can be understood through supply and demand." I even heard someone say, "Economics is really nothing more than understanding supply and demand." An exaggeration? Yes, but not by much. So what does it all mean?

The Demand Curve

Let's begin with the **demand curve.** To *demand* something means more than just to have a desire for a product; it implies that you want that product *and* have the money to buy it. As an example, your *effective demand* for a hamburger will be made evident only when you actually go out and buy one.

Economists are also interested in how many hamburgers people demand at different prices. By observing the quantity Q of goods bought at a variety of prices P, they can work out what is called the *demand curve*. Let's look at an example.

Suppose that the price of sweet corn is $5 a bushel. Let's say that people buy 5 bushels at that price. If we lower the price to $4 a bushel, then they will buy, say, 10 bushels. As we continue to lower the price, observe how much more corn people will buy:

Price P ($)	$5	$4	$3	$2	$1
Quantity Q (bu)	5	10	20	30	40

This information, in turn, can easily be graphed (see Figure 3-1).

At lower prices, greater quantities are demanded. This makes sense, doesn't it? For example, when your local grocery store lowers the price of certain vegetables, you will usually buy more of those vegetables. Behind this simple economic law, however, is some fairly complicated reasoning; let's look at what's involved.

One reason people buy more when the price goes down is that, in our example, regular buyers of corn now find that their *real incomes* have gone up slightly. Consider the Smiths—a family who likes to buy and eat lots of corn. Their *money income* has remained unchanged (the Smith's take-home pay of $500 per week is still the same), but the lower price of corn has increased their **purchasing power** (their real income). Lower corn prices mean that the Smith family can buy more of *all* goods, including corn, with their $500 weekly income. It's as if the Smiths were given a small income raise when they walked into the grocery store and saw that corn was marked down from, say, $0.50 to $0.12 an ear. Their greater real income probably means that they will purchase more of the other items they like too, such as canned tuna; but for now we are just interested in the fact that they can buy more corn. This is called the **income effect.**

The second reason people buy more when the price goes down is that they gain more total satisfaction if they buy a larger quantity of a low-priced product instead of a relatively high-priced substitute. For example, tuna and hamburger are substitute goods: they both provide protein for family meals. If they were the same price last week but tuna is much cheaper this

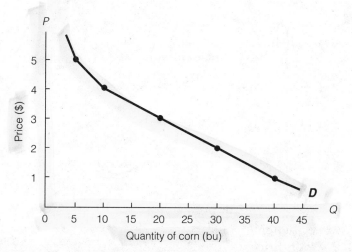

FIGURE 3-1 The *demand curve* shows that if the price of corn decreases, consumers tend to demand greater quantities of corn. This negative, or *inverse,* relationship between price and quantity gives the demand curve its downward-sloping appearance.

week, consumers gain in total satisfaction by substituting the lower-priced tuna for the higher-priced hamburger. This is called the **substitution effect.**

Both the income effect and the substitution effect contribute to the economic law illustrated in our example: as the price decreases, the quantity demanded increases. Sometimes economists refer to this as the **law of downward-sloping demand,** because the demand curve does slope downward (as you can see in Figure 3-1). A downward-sloping demand curve demonstrates the *inverse* relationship between price P and quantity Q.

Shifting Demand

Now let's look at the demand curve from the eyes of a businessperson. As we have seen, the demand curve itself is a useful tool that shows at a glance what quantities of a product will be sold at different prices. But businesses would like to take this one step further. A business wants to see the demand curve for its product *shift to the right,* which means that even *more* of a product can be sold at the *same* price. Look, for example, at Figure 3-2; note that the new expanded demand curve D_1 shows

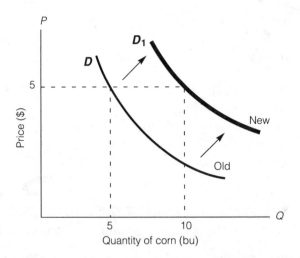

FIGURE 3-2   *Shifting demand:* at $5 a bushel, a greater quantity of corn (10 units) is demanded on the new demand curve D_2, compared to a lesser quantity of corn (5 units) demanded on the old demand curve D_1. If such increases take place at other prices, then the new demand curve appears to shift to the right, as indicated here.

greater quantities demanded at any given price than the old demand curve D shows.

Surely this is good for businesses—to sell more goods at a given price. But what causes the demand curve to shift? It is not a change in price, because when the price of a good changes, we simply move along a stationary demand curve D (see Figure 3-1).

What about advertising? Yes, it is commonly acknowledged that the purpose of advertising is to shift the demand curve for a product to the right and to expand its market by increasing the number of customers who buy the advertised product. Indeed, anything that brings about a broader base of potential customers will shift the demand curve to the right. For example, when the United States recognized the People's Republic of China and trade between the two countries was legalized, a new market for U.S. products, ranging from aspirin to computers, suddenly opened up.

What else might shift the demand curve? Suppose that canned peas are considered a **substitute product** for canned corn. What would happen if the price of peas suddenly went up from $0.50 to $2 per can but the price of corn remained at $0.50 per can? The demand for *corn* would increase! On the other hand, if canned green beans (another substitute for corn) went down in price from $0.50 to $0.25, the demand for corn at $0.50 a can would decrease. The businessperson watches very carefully to see what happens to the price of substitute goods, because this can greatly influence the demand for his or her product. In summary, then, the higher the price of a substitute good, the greater the shift in demand for the product that remains low in price.

If, however, two products are *complementary,* it can work the other way around. Cameras and film are **complementary products.** The demand for cameras tends to go down (the demand curve shifts to the left) if the price of film goes up. Businesses, therefore, must keep a wary eye on what is happening to the prices of those goods that "go with" their products.

Changes in *tastes* and *fashion* also cause demand curves to shift to the right or left (forward or backward). Also, a *new use for an old product* shifts the demand curve to the right. A backward shift usually occurs when *incomes* decrease; when incomes increase, demand shifts forward. There can be exceptions, however. People in a poor family who consume lots of macaroni, for example, may experience an increase in income and *reduce* their demand for macaroni. Under these conditions, macaroni is considered an **inferior good.** Most goods, however, are what we call **normal goods;** an increase in income brings about an increase in the demand for normal goods.

In a free and decentralized market, a demand curve is never stationary for very long. It gets battered around like a ship in a stormy sea. An environment of rapidly changing incomes, tastes, and prices of substitute or related goods makes it all but impossible to accurately predict the behavior of the demand curve. In the more controlled markets of oligopolistic industries, the power of advertising can make demand curves more manageable and predictable than they would be in a pure market.

The Supply Curve

We now turn our attention to the **supply curve,** which shows what quantities of their products suppliers would like to provide at different prices. For example, you might ask Farmer Brown, "How much corn would you want to *supply* to the market if the

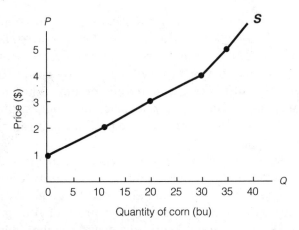

FIGURE 3-3   The *supply curve* shows that if the price of corn increases, farmers tend to supply greater quantities of corn. This positive, or *direct,* relationship between price and quantity gives the supply curve its upward-sloping appearance.

price of corn were $5 a bushel?" Brown might reply, "At $5 a bushel, I'd supply 35 bushels." Next, you could ask what quantities he would produce at $4 a bushel, at $3, and so on. Let's say Brown gives you the following information:

Price P ($)	$5	$4	$3	$2	$1
Quantity Q (bu)	35	30	20	12	0

Based on this information, the supply curve S can be graphed as shown in Figure 3-3.

We can see that Farmer Brown's supply curve is *upward-sloping:* the *higher* the price, the *more* he wants to supply; the *lower* the price, the *less* he's willing to supply. In fact, at the price of $1 per bushel, Brown does not want to supply any corn at all! Other farmers will probably respond in much the same way, so we could ask *all* corn growers our supply question. Instead of one individual farmer producing 35 bushels at $5 each, we may find out that all corn growers will supply 35 million bushels at $5 a bushel, 30 million at $4, and so on. The curve will have the same original shape, regardless of the quantities involved.

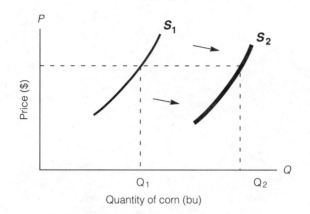

FIGURE 3-4 *Shifting supply:* when a greater quantity of a good is supplied at different prices, the supply curve shifts to the right (from S_1 to S_2).

Remember how the demand curve in Figure 3-2 shifted back and forth? The supply curve can shift, too, as shown in Figure 3-4. A rightward shift in the supply curve means that a larger quantity will be supplied at a given price. This increase in supply can take place when *more suppliers* move into the market. If businesses move out of the industry, the supply curve often shifts to the left.

Perhaps the major reason for an increase in supply is *technological advancement.* Good examples include Henry Ford's introduction of the automobile assembly line and the development of new and improved hybrid corn seeds. Shifting the supply curve to the right (through technology) has often resulted in lower prices and the creation of mass-consumption markets. Try drawing a simple market curve under conditions of fixed (nonshifting) demand (downward-sloping) and supply (upward-sloping); then shift the supply curve to the right, and see what happens to the product price.

What else can cause a shift in the supply curve? If the *costs of production* (for example, labor costs) go up, then the supply curve will usually shift backward (to the left). In addition, certain industries, such as farming, must always contend with supply changes caused by the *weather;* extreme weather conditions can have a great impact on food commodity supply and, hence, on food prices. And so it goes. The supply curve, like the demand curve, is buffeted about by a number of unpredictable forces.

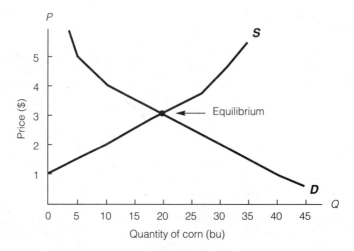

Figure 3-5   At the point of market equilibrium, the supply curve crosses the demand curve. The quantity demanded equals the quantity supplied only at the *market equilibrium price.*

Market Equilibrium

Now we're ready to take one more important step. We have enough information to combine the supply and demand curves to form a *market.* Carefully examine Figure 3-5, a corn market created by putting our demand and supply curves in Figures 3-1 and 3-3 together on the same graph. This gives us a visual representation of what quantities of corn demanders will buy at different prices and of what quantities of corn suppliers will sell at different prices. Note that there is *only one price* at which the quantity supplied is equal to the quantity demanded; this is called the **equilibrium price.** According to the graph, that price will be $3 per bushel (unit) of corn. At $3 a bushel (unit), suppliers will want to offer 20 bushels of corn and demanders will want to buy the same quantity. No other price will "clear the market" in a similar way.

Indeed, what will happen if the price of corn is something other than the equilibrium price? To answer this question, imagine a large warehouse: on one side, we have corn suppliers; on the other, corn demanders. In the middle is the auctioneer (who is not aware of the true equilibrium price). Just to get things started, the auctioneer shouts out in a hearty voice, "Five dollars a bushel!" Can you see what will happen? At $5, the suppliers

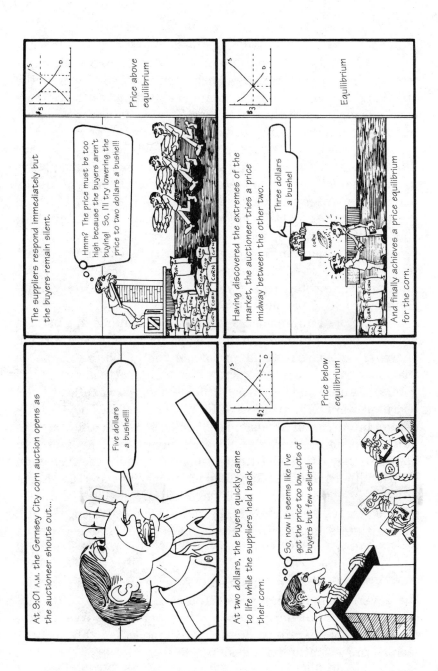

will want to sell 35 bushels, but the demanders will only want to buy 5 bushels (see tables on pages 30 and 34). Something is wrong. The price is too high! A surplus of corn is piling up in the suppliers' corner, while the demanders sit tight. An oversupply of corn begins to glut the warehouse. The auctioneer realizes his mistake and has no alternative but to lower the price.

Now, however, he goes to the other extreme. He yells out, "Two dollars!" Now what happens? The glut quickly disappears as the quantity of low-priced corn is eagerly bought up by demanders. After the dust settles, we find many frustrated demanders wanting large amounts (30 bushels) of $2 corn, but suppliers are unwilling to provide more than 12 bushels at that price. Again, something's wrong! The frustrated demanders start to put pressure on the auctioneer to raise the price again. After more trial and error, he arrives at the final price (the equilibrium price) of $3 per bushel.

In the *free* (unimpeded) *market* in our example, the price of a bushel of corn had complete freedom to move to equilibrium. However, in the real world, prices may not be so free. Suppose that the corn farmers (who are only a small fraction of the total voters) organize and form a political lobbying group called CORN (Corn-growers Organization to Raise Net Profit). They quickly obtain hundreds of thousands of dollars, which they just as quickly spend on dinners and other favors for legislators. In addition, they use their leftover money to finance the reelection of "friendly" candidates. When legislation comes up regarding a **price support** for corn (sometimes called a **price floor**), the lobby is hard at work to get a favorable vote. After considering the bill, the legislators pass it with votes to spare. CORN is able to report back to its members that from now on the government will support corn prices!

What exactly does this mean? A price support means that the government will guarantee the corn farmers a unit price *above* the equilibrium price. In other words, the free-market forces will not operate while the price support is in effect. Let's look at this situation in a graph.

In Figure 3-6, we see exactly what effect this government interference will have. If the price support is $5 per unit, then 35 units will be supplied but only 5 units will be demanded. Clearly, the government will be compelled to buy up the *surplus*

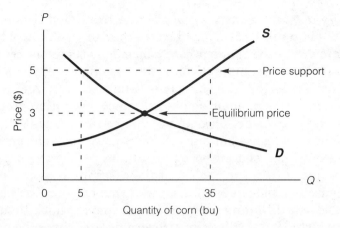

FIGURE 3-6 The *support price* (for example, $5) of a bushel of corn is a price, established by the government, that is higher than the market equilibrium price ($3) of a bushel of corn.

of corn (the difference between these two quantities) at $5 per bushel—a profitable deal for CORN! Its members can produce more corn than they would have produced at the equilibrium price and receive a higher support price for it. The corn market is stabilized, and their prices are guaranteed.

Of course, it's a bad deal for almost everyone else. As consumers and taxpayers, you and I will pay more for corn ($5) and get less (only 5 units), while we also pay more in taxes to provide these government *subsidies* to the corn growers. In addition, we will be paying even more taxes to finance the storage of the surplus. In many similar examples in American industry (especially in agriculture), the taxpayers' money artificially raises prices and impedes free-market forces. This happens because when it comes to legislative support, special-interest groups speak with a "shout," while consumers (and taxpayers) with no special lobbyists speak in a "whisper."

Now let's reverse the situation. What if the government establishes a lower price for a bushel of corn than the equilibrium price? The government would in effect be telling the corn growers, "You cannot legally charge more than $2 for a bushel of corn." This $2 price is called a **price ceiling.** What effect would this government intervention have on the corn market? Like our warehouse example earlier, the lower price will *generate greater* *quantity demanded than supplied.* The frustrated demanders want to bid up the price, but the government won't allow these prices to rise. A permanent corn *shortage* is therefore created. What, then, is the rationale for a price ceiling?

Sometimes the government will impose price ceilings on certain key items in an attempt to slow down inflation. But just as our example predicts, sooner or later, consumers will begin to experience shortages. In time of war, however, shortages already exist; then the purpose of a ceiling is to prevent prices from "going through the roof." In the cases of necessary items (food, gasoline, fuel oil, etc.), a price ceiling may not be enough. Often, so-called **black markets** are created in which the price of a product is bid up illegally. (Never underestimate the power of the market!) When black markets develop, one potential solution is to allocate scarce commodities, using *ration tickets* or *stamps.* Rationing, however, needs an expensive bureaucratic support system, and black markets in ration tickets or stamps may develop. No matter how they are handled, price ceilings usually turn out to be political nightmares.

Shifting Supply and Demand

Even if we assume that government price interference has been abolished, prices *still* may change due to shifts in supply and demand. For example, as shown in Figure 3-7, after a period of wartime economic austerity, a rapid increase in the supply of a product can come about when new suppliers enter the market or when the industry experiences some rapid technological advancement. This increase will shift the supply curve to the right (from S_1 to S_2). The equilibrium price will eventually decrease due to competition, and emergency measures to handle the shortage will no longer be necessary.

On the other hand, if the supply curve shifts to the left, prices will rise. This is what happens when, for example, bad weather reduces the supply of a farm commodity. If the demand curve remains stationary, the price of the product will increase.

Remember, though, that demand often is not stable for very long either. Recall that demand curves can move backward or forward for the following reasons:

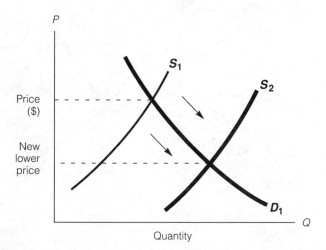

Figure 3-7   When the supply curve shifts to the right from S_1 to S_2 (with no change in demand), the equilibrium price is reduced.

- Changing incomes
- A change in the price of a substitute or complementary good
- A change in taste
- Advertising
- A change in the number of buyers

What will happen to the equilibrium price if there is an increase in the demand for a product? Figure 3-8 shows us. You might find it interesting to examine the commodities page in the business section of your daily newspaper. See how rapidly the prices of corn, wheat, soybeans, and other commodities can change on a daily basis because of shifts in supply and demand.

Elasticity

Another important idea associated with demand is **price elasticity.** Let's consider a practical example. A restaurant owner charges $5 for a top-quality small pizza. Not long ago she was asking people if the price should be raised to $6. Of course, nobody knew for sure, but some did know enough to ask her, "Approximately how many *fewer* pizzas would you sell if you

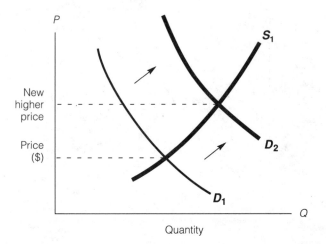

FIGURE 3-8   When the demand curve shifts to the right from D_1 to D_2 (with no change in supply), the equilibrium price is increased.

raised the price by $1?" They felt the answer to this question would help them get an idea of the pizza's price elasticity. It would be nice, for example, if the owner could increase the price without losing any customers. On the other hand, the owner could lose a great deal of customers. Two possible demand curves for these small pizzas are shown in Figure 3-9.

Although the demand curves in (a) and (b) are downward-sloping (remember our law of downward-sloping demand?), the curve in (a) is much flatter than the curve in (b). To put it another way, the demand curve in (b) is much steeper than the curve in (a). If (a) represents the demand curve for small pizzas, would it be wise to raise the price? Probably not. Economists would say that this is an **elastic demand curve** (the quantity demanded is *very responsive* to a change in price). In (a), even with a small change in price, we see the quantity of pizza demanded decline rapidly to less than one-half of what it was. Almost any business intending to raise its price would rather have a demand curve like the one in (b), because it can increase the price of its product without losing much quantity demanded. Economists call this an **inelastic demand curve** (the quantity demanded is *not very responsive* to a change in price).

What kind of products have inelastic demand curves? One example of an **inelastic good** is table salt. If salt is $0.30 a box but then doubles in price, people will still demand about the same amount of salt. However, if the mortgage interest rate

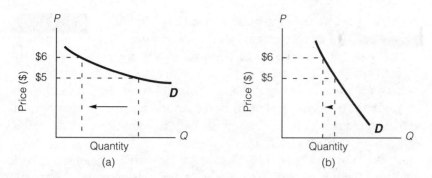

FIGURE 3-9 In graph (a), a $1 increase in price (from $5 to $6) reduces the quantity demanded by a considerable amount. This demand curve is *elastic*. In graph (b), the same $1 price increase reduces the quantity demanded by only a small amount. This demand curve is *inelastic*.

doubles from, say, 7 to 14 percent, there will be a drastic reduction in the number of homes demanded. New housing is therefore an example of an **elastic good.**

Let's examine a few other examples. Gasoline and toy balloons are inelastic goods. The prices on both of these items could be increased substantially, and in the short run, demand would not be greatly reduced. Can you see a pattern that might allow you to predict the degree of elasticity of a product? Why are some goods sensitive to a change in price, while others are not? Some general principles for determining inelastic demand might include the following:

- It's a necessary good (gasoline, heating oil, prescription drugs, telephones).
- It's a small part of the person's budget (toy balloons, soda pop, paper clips).
- There are few substitutes (insulin, light bulbs, diamond rings).

Note that table salt meets all of these criteria. No economic good, however, is inelastic at *all* prices. If we walked into the grocery store and discovered that the price of salt was not $0.30 or $0.60 a box but $10 a box, the quantity demanded would certainly be affected! In this case, you would probably learn to eat your food with less salt (or use a salt substitute), and your favorite restaurant would sell you small salt packets instead of putting a salt shaker on the table.

Let's get back to the pizza restaurant. The relative **elasticity of demand** for the pizzas will depend mainly on how many substitutes (both direct and indirect) are available. A *direct substitute* would be a Pizza Hut restaurant down the street; an *indirect substitute* might be cooking a pizza at home. If the restaurant owner happens to be a monopolist and people regard eating pizzas out as a "necessity," then a price increase more than likely will benefit the business.

Is there any way that the owner can affect the elasticity of demand for her pizzas? Yes, if she can convince people that she has a truly unique, superior, and "necessary" product. Note the words "if she can convince people"; she does not necessarily have to have a better or different product.

Advertisers for Bayer aspirin, for example, have convinced people that their product is truly different. Most druggists say that "aspirin is aspirin," but by convincing headache sufferers that Bayer is superior, the company has successfully made its demand curve *more inelastic* than it would otherwise have been; hence, the company is able to charge a higher price than most of its competitors.

Our theory still does not enable the restaurant owner to determine whether the demand for her pizzas is elastic or inelastic. The only way to know for sure is to actually raise the price and see what happens to sales (*total revenue*). We can say with some accuracy that if you increase the price and the total revenue goes up, the demand between these two prices is inelastic; if you increase the price and the total revenue is reduced, the demand is elastic. Let's call this the *businessperson's definition of price elasticity*.

Note that the demand in Figure 3-10(a) is *inelastic*. It should be apparent that the lower-price total revenue (price multiplied by quantity) is quite small. To tell for sure, simply compare the area that represents total revenue at the lower price (the area inside the thicker black lines) with the shaded area of total revenue at the higher price. By raising the price in the inelastic example, total revenue is increased. This is, of course, what the restaurant owner wanted to happen when she raised the price of her pizza. Note what would have happened if demand had been *elastic*. In Figure 3-10(b), we see that the increase in price *reduces* the quantity demanded so much that the total revenue

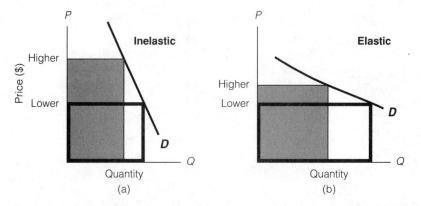

FIGURE 3-10 In graph (a), demand is *inelastic:* increasing the price tends to increase total revenue. The shaded block, which represents total revenue, is somewhat *larger* than the total area within the thicker, black lines. In graph (b), demand is *elastic:* increasing the price tends to decrease total revenue. The shaded block is somewhat *smaller* than the total area within the thicker black lines.

(shaded area) becomes smaller compared to the area inside the thicker black lines (lower-price total revenue).

A final point to remember: if you are a businessperson, it might be in your best interest to lower prices, particularly if your demand curve is elastic. A lower price on an elastic demand curve will generate so much more business that total revenue will go up. In addition, expanding the scale of business operations will often lower the *unit cost of production* (the cost of manufacturing one unit of the product). After World War I, Henry Ford combined these two ideas (an elastic demand for cars plus mass-production efficiencies) and reaped a personal fortune of over a billion dollars. It pays to know about elasticity!

Now let's take a moment to review what we have learned about this subject. Elasticity is basically a measure of how much the quantity demanded responds to a change in price. An *elastic curve* is very responsive to price variations; an *inelastic curve* is not very responsive.

Elasticity can also be determined by observing what happens to total revenue (or total sales) when the price changes. If total revenue goes up when we raise the price, we have *inelastic demand.* If total revenue goes down, we have *elastic demand.* If you find your-self confused about what happens to total revenue

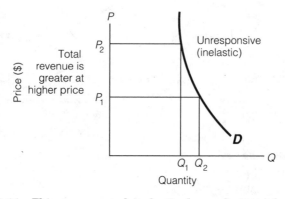

FIGURE 3-11   This exaggerated inelastic demand curve clearly shows a higher total revenue (larger rectangle) at the higher price than at the lower price.

when the price is changed, simply sketch an exaggerated demand curve (either very flat or very steep) and see what happens to total revenue when the price goes up or down (for example, see Figure 3-11).

So far, so good, but we still do not know how to determine the precise *degree* of elasticity. For example, both salt and gasoline are inelastic goods, but which is *more* inelastic?

Let's suppose that the President of the United States determines that gasoline supplies may be threatened and decides that it is in the national interest to reduce the nation's consumption of gas by 15 percent. There are, of course, different ways to handle this situation. First, he might ask drivers to reduce their consumption voluntarily. If this doesn't work, he could establish a gasoline-rationing system. We know, however, that this kind of rationing invites black-market counterfeiting and requires an expensive bureaucracy to make it work.

The third and probably the quickest way to reduce consumption would be to raise the price of gasoline to the consumer via a tax increase. But how much would the total price of a gallon of gas have to go up in order to reduce by 15 percent the quantity of gasoline demanded? Would a 15-percent increase in price do the trick, or a 30-percent increase, or perhaps even a 75-percent increase? This question leads us to our most exact definition, the *economist's definition of price elasticity*.

To measure the precise value of a product's elasticity, we divide the percent change in price into the percent change in quantity demanded:

$$E_p \text{ (coefficient of elasticity)} = \frac{\text{Percent change in quantity demanded}}{\text{Percent change in price}}$$

If this ratio is greater than 1, it is elastic; if this ratio is less than 1, it is inelastic. For example, if we find out that the price of a gallon of gas must increase by 30 percent to reduce gasoline consumption by 15 percent, then the exact elasticity of a gallon of gas would be:

$$E_p = \frac{15\%}{30\%} = 0.50$$

Since this ratio is less than 1, it's inelastic. If the President had known beforehand that the coefficient of elasticity for gasoline was 0.50, he would have known exactly how much gasoline prices would have to increase before consumption would decrease by the desired amount.

As another example, let's assume that the demand for pizzas is very elastic. The restaurant owner goes ahead and raises the price of a pizza by 20 percent anyway and discovers that the quantity of pizza demanded goes down by 80 percent. Under these conditions, what is the elasticity of demand? Using our formula, the answer would be:

$$E_p = \frac{80\%}{20\%} = 4.0$$

This ratio is greater than 1, so the demand is elastic.

In the real world, you may never know the exact elasticity of a product. It may change over time, or it may be one value in a lower price range and a totally different value in a higher price range. Still, the most successful businesspeople seem to have an uncanny instinct for elasticities and how they affect revenues and profits.

Now what about you? What products do you buy? How elastic or inelastic are they to you? If the price of your favorite newspaper or magazine were raised considerably, would you still buy it? Would you buy your favorite hamburger or pizza if the cost went up 20 percent or 30 percent? These are the kinds of interesting economic questions we can all ask ourselves.

In summary, we have come a long way in understanding the inner workings of an individual market. We have discovered how supply and demand operate and how the natural forces of the market drive prices toward an equilibrium price. We have also seen what happens when these natural forces are impeded by price supports and price ceilings. We now know that the supply and demand curves shift in response to a variety of economic forces and also know how such information can be of value to consumers, businesspeople, and government.

So we've learned quite a bit about single markets; but what about the vast interconnections between these single markets and the overall economy? What about the massive amounts of money, goods, and resources flowing in and out of millions of interrelated household and business markets? How does all this fit together to form an economic system? We are now ready to find out.

Questions for Thought and Discussion

1. How could the concept of elasticity be used to establish government policy?

2. Do the concepts of supply and demand apply only to conventional private production and private consumption? Or can they be applied to "nontypical" areas of consumption, such as prostitution, drugs, crime, etc? Explain.

3. Does the existence of an equilibrium price and an equilibrium quantity mean that all suppliers and demanders are willing to produce and consume at that point of balance? Why or why not?

4. When someone would rather pay a high price than a low price for a good, does this mean that the law of demand does not hold? Explain.

5. Why do we need the concept of "elasticity" when we can just look at the slope of the demand curve to determine how price affects quantity demanded?

4

Businesses and Households

We are now ready to take a larger view of our economy. In this chapter we will enlarge our "economic vision" to include not only the single supply-demand markets discussed earlier but also the major economic institutions of businesses and households that give life to these individual markets. Instead of using an economic "microscope" to focus on a particular market, we now need a pair of "wide-angle binoculars" to help us see the broad outlines of our large and complex economy.

Let's begin with an analogy. The operation of our economy is something like the operation of an automobile. The performance of both depends on two vital flows. On the one hand, gasoline (the automobile's primary operating "resource") flows from the gas tank through the carburetor into the cylinders where, on combustion, it produces power to run the car. On the other hand, a circulating flow of lubrication oil travels around and around to various parts of the engine, reducing friction in the bearings and pistons. Take away either of these two flows and the automobile will soon stop functioning.

Economic Flows

Our economic system also depends on two vital flows. The first is the flow of *money,* which economists consider a kind of "lubricating agent" because it makes economic exchange simpler and smoother. Money flows through resource markets (land, labor, capital), into the pocketbooks of householders, and then back into the markets for goods and services, bubbling up in the business sector. This continuous circulatory stream of money flows on and on, unless the economic system breaks down.

The second vital flow is of *real things*—actual goods and services, plus the physical land, labor, and capital needed to produce them. Real things also flow through the markets, pushed on by monetary impulses in response to levels of supply and demand, and eventually become used up or consumed.

It's a fascinating system. Let's look at a graphic representation of our economy. In Figure 4-1, which is commonly called the **circular flow diagram,** the clockwise flow is money. Starting, for example, in the upper left corner, we find dollars flowing out of businesses (expenses) into the resource markets. There, these dollars are translated into the demand for land, labor, and capital.

When the resources are sold to the business sector, the so-called "expense dollars" are suddenly translated into *incomes* for the households. These dollars then flow out of the households into the markets for goods and services; we look at these same dollars and now call them *expenditures*. Demand then stimulates supply in the product (goods and services) markets. As payments are made for corn, car repairs, or bicycles, the dollars become *sales* for businesses, providing them with working capital to start another round of productive flow. And the cycle begins all over again.

It sounds like a simple, foolproof system, doesn't it? The chance of a breakdown does exist however. For example, there is no guarantee that the *money supply* of the amount of total spending will be correct. If the money supply is too low, the economy may slow down because there is not enough currency to make basic transactions. On the other hand, too much money will create an inflationary situation in which "too many dollars chase after too few goods." Similar problems can arise when there is also too little or too much spending.

Whose responsibility is it to regulate these economic flows? The responsibility lies primarily with the **government sector.** Along with the business and household sectors, government plays an important role in the operation of our economic system.

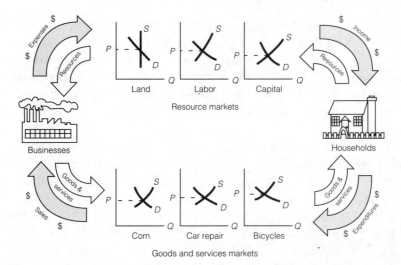

FIGURE 4-1 This *circular-flow diagram* is a simplified version of a market economy. Note that the two major economic sectors (businesses and households) are connected by flows and markets—the resource markets (land, labor, and capital) and the goods and services markets.

(We will have much more to say about government in Chapter 5.) For now, however, let's take a close look at the **business sector.** How do we define a "business"? How are businesses organized? How effectively do they operate in a capitalist setting?

The Business Sector

There are approximately 20 million businesses in the United States. The majority of them are small retail or service businesses and other single-owner operations, including farming. Operating these small enterprises often means overworking "Mom and Pop" to keep the business going. To make things worse, small businesses frequently end in bankruptcy. (Three out of five new businesses fail before the third year of operation!)

Now let's play a little game. Assume that you have carefully considered the odds and have decided to plunge into a new business. You might try to write, publish, and market your own book, for example. Or perhaps you would like to manufacture computer software or run a candy store. A repair service is another possibility. For our purposes here, though, let's assume you go into manufacturing.

Of course, the first question is, "What are you going to make?" You don't want to compete with a large, oligopolistic industry because you would have to overcome too many economic barriers to enter the market (see Chapter 2). Obviously, you want to develop a new or improved product. You may also wish to select something that can be manufactured by one or two people.

One day you read in *The Wall Street Journal* that the sale of cat food has quadrupled in the last decade. You begin to think

> "Yes, about half my friends have cats, and you know, their cats always want to be let in or out. Why couldn't I make an entrance-exit device to let cats enter or leave the house whenever they want. It would have to be designed so that heat is not let out, and it would have to be easy to install. . . ."

You convince yourself that you can make a go of it and begin to work on a prototype. By the end of the year, you have your cat-loving friends trying out your new invention—KITTYOUT.

Now you need to think about the business end of your operation. You have several options. You may decide to set up what is called a **single proprietorship.** The proprietorship is perhaps the most simple type of business organization. It can be started up with a minimum of red tape; no charters or extensive reports are needed. "A good deal," you say to yourself—until you find out some of the disadvantages. If you decide to expand your small operation later, you may find that no one wants to loan you any money. You try the local banks; they smile pleasantly and say, "We're sorry." The Small Business Administration (an agency of the federal government) also lends a kindly ear but tells you that the enterprise is still unproved: "Please come back when sales and earnings are more stable."

You can also face the disadvantage of **unlimited liability,** which means that if things go badly, your creditors can sue you not only for your business assets but also for your personal assets. Your child's educational fund could be liquidated as a result of a bad business decision!

But business is going OK for now, and your major worry at present is finding the financial capital to expand. You begin thinking of alternatives, and one comes to mind: a partner. You invite a friend (or relative) to join you and form a **partnership** in order to provide additional financial capital as well as a helping hand. There is now, however, more red tape. A partnership is a legal entity, and if your partner leaves you (or dies), you usually have to start all over. Plus, you are still faced with the problem of unlimited liability.

Nevertheless, let's assume that you and your partner are not worried much about the liability problem; current sales are excellent, and you both are becoming intoxicated with visions of unlimited profits. Expansion is the only thing on your minds. You ask yourselves, "How should we expand?"

You might, for example, elect **vertical expansion.** Perhaps you have been purchasing supplies from a local sheet-metal shop, and you now decide to buy the shop out. By expanding vertically, you are *taking over another stage of production.*

Or, instead of taking over the early stages of manufacturing, you might go to the other extreme of marketing the product and set up your own shops to sell KITTYOUT. Until now, you have been selling your cat doors to a regional distributor, who, in turn, sells them to established retail shops. (In the larger economy, the oil industry is a good example of vertical expansion. It often owns or controls almost all stages of production: oil wells, pipelines, refineries, and, of course, distribution through local service stations.)

Another option is **horizontal expansion.** This means *doing more and more of the same operation.* You might buy out the competition, or you might set up a small-scale factory in another location. Either way, your expansion activities would concentrate on the assembly stage.

Another choice open to you is expansion by **diversification**— bringing out one or more additional products. They may be related to your original product, or they may be totally different products. For example, you might decide to manufacture an improved cat or dog house, or even a DOGGYOUT (based on the same design and engineering principles used in your successful KITTYOUT).

Many large American corporations diversify so widely that there is often little or no relationship between their products. A business that expands through buying or merging with *unrelated* businesses is called a **conglomerate.**

Why would a company diversify—especially in the direction of an unrelated conglomerate? Some economists say that broad diversification is more often than not a personal "power trip" or an exercise in financial empire building. Another answer is that large-scale, diversified companies can more efficiently disperse their overhead (the continuing costs of running the business) over all operational phases. A small company for example might not have sufficient resources to afford a business economist, a market researcher, or an advertising division, but the large parent company can afford these important marketing aids and provide such assistance when it is needed. Diversification is also a kind of "insurance policy" against a sudden shift in demand away from a single-product line such as vinyl recordings (replaced by tapes and compact discs) or cigarettes (consumption reduced due to health concerns). And, undoubtedly, there have been numerous cases of diversified mergers or leveraged buyouts (LBOs), often financed by so called "junk bonds," that have forcefully dislodged an inefficient management team and improved the performance of the weaker company.[7]

There can, however, be a darker side to the trend toward mergers and leveraged buyouts. Giant companies often operate with a kind of cold, insensitive detachment. Owners of these mega-businesses fixate on short-run rates of return or on selling off assets. They can play with the fates of factories and employees with the calculated ruthlessness of a chess player, doing whatever is necessary to win the game. Economist Ernest Mandel captures this feeling of absentee ownership in his prophetic piece, "Where Is America Going?":

> They retain ultimate power—the power to open or to close the plant, to shut it in one town and relaunch it 2000 miles away, to suppress, by one stroke of their pens, 20,000 jobs and 50 skills acquired at the price of long human efforts.[8]

But we've gotten a little ahead of ourselves! Our KITTYOUT business is still only a partnership—not a large conglomerate. The major question facing our enterprising partnership is still, "How can we best grow?"

At this stage of development, the answer to this question is probably to form a **corporation.** Among the major advantages of a corporate form of ownership are the new opportunities that are available for obtaining financial capital. A corporation, for example, can sell *equity* (ownership) stock as well as float corporate bonds. In addition, obtaining a loan from established financial institutions (banks, credit unions, etc.) is often easier for corporations than for unproven single proprietorships or

partnerships. **Limited liability** is another advantage of the corporate form; the debts of the corporation are "limited" by law to extend only to the corporate assets—not to the assets of the owners (as in a proprietorship or a partnership).

You and your partner therefore hire a lawyer to draw up a charter, and various friends and relatives buy into your little company. Thus, KITTYOUT, INC. (Incorporated), joins the ranks of the approximately 3 million corporations that exist in the United States. However, your little company is not yet in the "big time," and it probably never will be. As we discussed in Chapter 2, it is extremely difficult to become a major industrial company in an American industry.

To get an idea of just how big some of these giant companies can get, imagine a list of 3 million corporations, with the larger companies up at the top and the smaller ones at the bottom. If we were to tally up the assets of the 200 largest corporations at the very peak of this list, we would discover that this small group of companies (less than one-tenth of 1 percent) own over *50 percent* of all manufacturing assets in the country! These corporations indeed dominate the mainstream of American business.

In our KITTYOUT example, we have looked at the different forms of business enterprises and noted some of their advantages and disadvantages. However, we have not yet examined the inner workings of a business. How do businesses combine their resources to produce goods and service? What rules, if any, do they follow to achieve the best results?

Diminishing Returns

One well-known law of economics that businesses must be aware of when they combine resources is the **law of diminishing**

returns. What exactly is this law all about? It's best to explain it with a simplified illustration.

A few years ago, I helped a neighbor, a farmer we'll call Chester Olson, bring in his hay. Chester has just one tractor, one hay baler, and one hay wagon; we call these his **fixed inputs.** His **variable input** is labor: he can choose to work by himself or with any number of hired hands. Chester told me that if he works by himself, he can bring in only 2 loads of hay per working day. He brings in so few loads because he has to bale the hay, pick it up off the ground, stack it on the wagon, unload it from the wagon into the barn, and then climb up into the hot, sticky hay and stack it neatly—a big job for one man!

If I help Chester, the total output per day goes from 2 to 5 loads. My additional contribution, sometimes called the **marginal physical product** (MPP), is 3 full loads of hay above what Chester can bring in by himself. Because a second person (myself) increased *per worker output,* we can say that Chester is in a stage of **increasing returns.** But if we add a third person (Steve), we find that total output goes up only 1 additional load to make 6 total loads. With Steve added to the production force, total output goes up, but at a *diminishing rate.*

Beginning with Steve (the third person), we have therefore reached the **point of diminishing returns.** Why did it begin with Steve? Is he lazy? Definitely not. If Chester or I had been that third person, the same thing would have happened. The reason diminishing returns begins with Steve is because Chester has a *fixed set of machinery* for us to work with. If Chester had additional equipment—perhaps just one more hay wagon—that third person might give us a lot more loads. When we speak of diminishing returns, we therefore must assume that *all inputs except one are fixed.*

How will this knowledge of diminishing returns help Chester make decisions concerning the number of people to hire? Can we automatically assume that Chester shouldn't hire that third person? If Chester is a good businessperson, he should take a careful look at how much extra money the third person's extra loads of hay will bring and compare it with the cost of hiring him. To illustrate, if the value of an additional load is $50 and Chester has to pay Steve only $20 to bring in the load, then it *would* be profitable to hire Steve despite the law of diminishing returns. The general rule is to *keep hiring people as long as the*

Law of Diminishing Returns

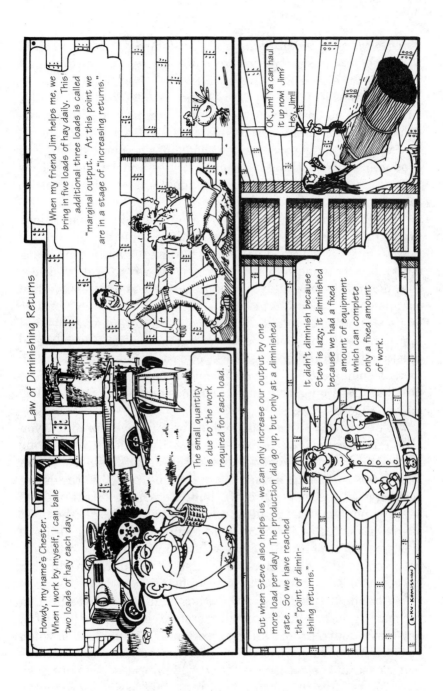

value of the marginal product (the additional hay) *is greater than the cost of producing that product* (the extra wages Chester must pay to get the additional hay).

Chester has it quite easy. Outside of keeping his old baler running, all he has to worry about are diminishing returns, the price of hay, and the cost of hiring an extra hand. Imagine, however, the complex decisions that must be made during the production of something as complicated as an automobile. How would you go about finding the ideal mix of resources to manufacture a car?

Perhaps the best way to build a car might be to simply give an engineer the following proposal: "Here is my design; tell me how to build it!" A good engineer, however, should come back with more than one solution: "Here is one way to build your car that is almost completely mechanized; here is another method that is more labor intensive (uses more human labor)." The engineer may go on to tell you many other different ways to build approximately the same car. The bumpers might be made of plastic or steel; the engine block, of cast iron or aluminum. In fact, an engineer may give you an entire book describing different possible techniques that meet your design specifications. How do you choose?

The answer, of course, is that for any given product, you *should choose the lowest-cost technique.* If you don't, your rivals may—and then you might find yourself out of business! When businesses choose the lowest-cost technique, note that the entire economy will become more efficient. Returning to the idea of supply and demand, the ideal approach is to conserve the most scarce resources and use the most abundant ones. If a resource is scarce, its supply will be low; if it is in demand, the resource will command a high price. In trying to minimize production costs, businesses will naturally avoid using that scarce resource.

Abundant resources on the other hand, tend to cost less in the marketplace. A business will therefore choose these plentiful, low-cost resources more and more often. It's a simple idea when you think, for example, of how much more low-cost plastic is being used in the place of relatively high-priced steel or wood. Consumers, in turn, benefit from relatively low-cost products.

In summary, *low cost equals economic efficiency.* This constant drive to lower cost is indeed one of the most remarkable and beneficial characteristics of a capitalist economic system.

Ironically, it is one of the most destructive aspects of our economic system as well. Why is this so?

Pollution

The drive to operate businesses at the lowest cost possible has also contributed to the pollution problem. Take, for example, Gary, Indiana. If you have ever driven past the steel and oil production complex in Gary, you probably had to close your car window. The air is often unbearably dirty. Why do these companies pollute the air? Do they want to increase the death rate and the incidence of lung disease? Obviously not. They pollute the air and water for a simple reason: it's cheaper to pollute than not to pollute.

Of course, in almost every such case, there is a technology available that will reduce pollution to reasonably low levels. However, if they can get away with it, why shouldn't producers attempt to push the clean-up costs onto society (that is, make them *social costs*) instead of paying these costs themselves? Thus, in a strange way, our capitalist system tends to *reward* polluters: the more pollution you can get away with, the lower your costs and, hence, the greater your profits. In a few instances, when short-run profit making is pushed to an illogical extreme, the attitude and actions of a company can be difficult to believe:

> "Profit-ability" was the 1970 slogan for Union Camp, a company whose paper-bag plant helps make the Savannah River one of the foulest sewers in the nation. The executive vice-president of the company, answering Nader's Raiders' charge that his firm was dangerously depleting groundwater supplies, replied, "I had my lawyers in Virginia research that, and they told us that we could suck the state of Virginia out through a hole in the ground, and there was nothing anyone could do about it." Union Camp's director of air and water protection noted for the benefit of *The New York Times* that "it probably won't hurt mankind a whole hell of a lot in the long run if the whooping crane doesn't quite make it. . . ."[9]

Fortunately, most businesses today cannot operate with such total disregard for the environment. Nonetheless, the short-run pressures to keep costs down continue to create problems in a capitalist economy. In fact, this is what we might now call "the first tragic flaw of capitalism": in the great drive to be efficient producers, which lowers production costs and generally benefits the consumer, we have simultaneously provided an irresistible temptation to pollute. What can be done about this problem?

In theory, the economic remedy is quite simple: force producers to pay *all* production costs. *Neighborhood effects*—passing pollution costs on to society at large—should not be tolerated. Perhaps the easiest way to enforce this rule is to impose a pollution tax. The government would be saying, in effect,

> Until now, you have behaved as if the air and water were a free resource—a free trash can that never fills up—but from now on, you will have to pay a pollution tax for the use of that trash can. In fact, we will make the tax so high that it might be more profitable for you to buy your own garbage cans and collect your pollutants yourself.

A more direct approach to the pollution problem is to state maximum levels of pollution (as the government has done with automobile emissions). Yet there are drawbacks to the various methods of pollution control, as you probably know if you have recently purchased a car. Prices rise, and in some cases, short-run economic "efficiency" may be sacrificed.

Still, why shouldn't producers—and, ultimately, the consumers of steel, chemicals, or paper (or any product from a high-pollution industry)—assume the *full* costs of production, even the pollution clean-up costs? If we are truly concerned about minimizing the degradation of our environment (including not only the visible pollution but also the invisible poisons, such as pesticides, radioactive materials, mercury, etc.), then perhaps we ought to act now—not for ourselves so much as for future generations. Paying the extra price in the short run may well turn out to be a good investment in the long run.

The Household Sector

The other major sector in our economy is the **household sector.** If the business sector organizes resources and supplies goods and services, what economic role does the household sector play?

Households are in a pivotal position in our economy. On the one hand, they *supply resources* to businesses (land, labor, capital, management); on the other hand, they are consumers of goods and services. About 100 million household units purchase roughly two-thirds of the total U.S. economic output each year. In what form do households receive their income?

Looking at the statistics, we find that approximately three-quarters of the national income flowing to resource suppliers is in the form of wages and salaries. Interest represents about 10 percent of the total, corporate profits and proprietorship incomes are roughly 8 percent each, and rent income makes up the remainder.

Once the money is in our pocketbooks, what do we do with it? Americans spend about 80 percent of their income, and personal taxes take approximately 15 percent. The remaining amount, roughly 5 percent, is saved. (Americans are not known to be great savers!) On the average, households spend about 54 percent of their money on services (household operations, financial services, health, transportation, education, recreation, restaurant services, etc.); 32 percent on nondurable goods (food, clothing, gasoline, etc.); and only about 14 percent on durable goods (anything with a useful life of over a year). Columnist George Will vividly reminds us that there has been a dramatic shift away from durable goods, which, over the years, has brought about a fundamental change in American industry:

> ...golden arches, not blast furnaces, are becoming the symbols of American enterprise. Today McDonald's has more employees than U.S. Steel. This "once great industrial giant" used to make big locomotives, big Buicks. Now it makes Big Macs."[10]

Then why are services such a large part of the average family budget today? Part of the answer is that it takes more and more repair and maintenance services (and more skilled individuals) to match the quantity and complexity of the durable goods and components of modern housing and transportation. More important, perhaps, is the great increase in the *cost* of professional services (medical, dental, educational, legal, etc.). The prices of durable goods, on the other hand, have been rising relatively modestly; in fact, some product prices have even gone down in the past couple of decades (radios, televisions, computers, pocket calculators). Service costs, in turn, have increased mainly because of relatively low productivity. Let's look at this idea a little more closely.

Productivity is how economists measure the *useful output gained over a standard amount of input* (such as an hour of a worker's time). For example, a 60-word-per-minute typist is twice as productive as a 30-word-per-minute typist. Let's assume that a decade ago a factory employed 50 people and turned out 100 radios a day. By utilizing labor-saving technology, that same factory today might produce 500 radios with only 10 people, demonstrating a dramatic increase in worker productivity. Why did the factory mechanize? It was forced to do so to offset the higher and higher costs of labor. In addition, it was able to mechanize without great difficulty, because it is relatively easy to adapt technology to an assembly-line operation. Such mechanization helps to keep product prices lower than they would be without it.

Consider Helen, the fourth-grade school teacher. Helen provides an important service to society, but she finds it very difficult to increase her productivity. There she stands in front of her class of 28 students, as her grandmother did (in a one-room schoolhouse) 50 years before her, but Helen feels the school board must increase her salary to match inflation and higher wages throughout the economy. As long as wages continue to rise but productivity remains relatively low or unchanged, households must pay proportionately more for schooling, medical and dental care, government operation, and other services.[11] Some economists feel that without substantial increases in productivity, it will be very difficult to eliminate inflation in our current economic environment, particularly in the service industries. (There are, of course, other factors that contribute to inflation, which will be examined in detail in Chapters 8 and 9.)

Another observation can be made about households. Look around you. You will note with some interest (or perhaps some resentment) that some households receive very large incomes and others receive relatively small incomes. Why are some wages high and others low? To answer this question, we must refer again to the economics of supply and demand.

Both supply and demand must work for us if we are to enjoy high wages. This means that the supply of people with your particular skill must be low and the demand for your skill must stay high. High salaries for doctors, for example, are not so much a matter of great skill or life-saving capability as they are a result of a relatively low supply of doctors and the high demand for medical services. If there were millions and millions of doctors in the United States, their average wage could conceivably fall below that of a skilled automobile mechanic. In fact, back in the 1930s, the American Medical Association fought hard to keep the supply of medical practitioners low, realizing that an oversupply might depress wages. The United States continues to have regional shortages of medical personnel, partly because of similar restrictive policies. Other professional groups have also reduced entry into their fields by requiring licensing and certification.[12]

In summary, if we are only looking at the financial benefit of the household, the lesson should be clear: "Seek an occupation with few practitioners in a market of high demand, and woe unto them who by accident or design find themselves in a market of low demand with a large supply of skilled applicants." What is your occupation or planned occupation? And how do you think supply and demand will affect the market for *you?*

The discussion of incomes resulting from the supply-demand situation in the resource markets leads us to our final, and perhaps most significant, observation about households in a capitalist society. Recall (from Chapter 1) the basic economic question, "How does the economic system distribute the available output?" We are now able to answer that question. Output goes to those individuals and families who have sufficient incomes from the resource market *to generate effective demand in the goods and services markets.* If you do not have the opportunity to earn a decent income, you will not have the "dollar votes" in the product markets. Supply is forthcoming only if there is effective demand, or purchasing power.

A major problem arises, of course, when economic needs and purchasing power are not even remotely in balance. For example, a family might have a critical need for nutritious food (they may even be starving), but if they cannot generate effective demand (because of lack of income), no supply will be forthcoming to these individuals. An exaggerated (but real) example of this occurred during the Great Depression in the 1930s, when people went hungry while farmers plowed under perfectly nutritious food; there was insufficient income to purchase food and, therefore, insufficient demand to make it profitable to produce food. Poor people in the United States and in the less-developed countries of the world face the same situation today.

On the other hand, we might find (even during a depression) a wealthy family feeding their dogs steak every day, because the income is there and the purchasing power is there—and the economic system responds to these factors. Thus, the "second tragic flaw of capitalism" is its tendency to be unresponsive in the absence of effective demand, *no matter what the basic need may be.*

What can be done about such critical flaws in our economic system? How does our basically capitalist economy resolve the conflicts posed by increasing industrial pollution and a lack of purchasing power for the poor?

We deal with them primarily through government action. Government, then, is the third major sector in our economy. In a sense, government takes over when private-enterprise capitalism fails to deal with fundamental economic problems. Government is a large sector and exerts tremendous influence in economic affairs. It's time we took a closer look at its function and operation.

Questions for Thought and Discussion

1. Do you believe that it might be possible to correct the "first tragic flaw of capitalism" without government intervention? Why or why not?

2. What would happen to the circular flow of our economic system if consumers began saving large percentages of their incomes?

3. How is the concentration of economic power over time in the United States related to the ideas of vertical expansion, horizontal expansion, and conglomeration?

4. What would the world be like if the law of diminishing returns did not apply when a variable input, such as labor, was applied to a fixed input, such as land or capital?

5. The parties involved in any economic flow or transaction can be viewed as two opposite sides of the same coin. Explain.

5

Government

Why do we have government? I once met a man who stated quite emphatically that society would be better off with no government whatsoever, except for police protection and national defense. "Government is basically evil," he said. "It's not only very costly, but every government action subtracts from individual freedom." He concluded that everything the government is doing now could be accomplished more efficiently by an unregulated free-enterprise market system. So once more: "Why do we have government? What's it doing for us?"

Tragic Flaws

Of course, we have already started to build a case for government activity, beginning with the circular flowchart in Figure 4-1 (page 51). For example, without government, who would provide for (and regulate) the money supply? We have seen that money is essential to the operation of our complex economy; the amount of money in circulation must be carefully adjusted to changing economic conditions. Also recall our discussion of the two tragic flaws of capitalism. Addressing the first flaw, how would our present private-enterprise system halt pollution without government intervention? How could we prevent businesses from using the air and water as "free garbage cans" to lower their production costs? Self-regulation has not worked very well, nor will it work as long as pollution-prone industries feel pressured to minimize costs and maximize profits. There seems to be only one realistic solution to this problem. The government must step in to force producers to pay the full costs of production, including pollution control.

In many cases, the pollution problem cannot be solved on the local level alone. There are two reasons for this. First, the neighborhood effects of polluted water (or air) often extend beyond the confines of a specific locality. A river does not recognize municipal or state boundaries. If some company pollutes the Mississippi River in Minneapolis, it will affect residents not only in Moline, Illinois, but also farther down river in St. Louis, Missouri, and New Orleans, Louisiana.

Second, national pollution laws are necessary to prevent polluters from shutting down their operations in a state that has strict controls and moving them to a state with more lenient "controls." State governments might hesitate to stop polluters if it meant throwing local residents out of work.

Carrying this point one step further, what about *international* pollution? Shouldn't there be worldwide laws (and provisions for their enforcement) to prevent the pollution of the global oceans and atmosphere? We have already seen some of the severe consequences of international pollution, including the incidence of radiation drift from a Soviet Union nuclear reactor accident in 1986. Also consider the continuing environmental problems of acid rain, the greenhouse effect, and the depletion of the upper ozone layer of our atmosphere. If we apply the logic of neighborhood effects on a global scale, we must conclude that, in certain cases, international laws are absolutely necessary.

According to some observers, the question we should be asking is not so much do we need controls but will we be able to control worldwide pollution in time? Indeed, there is growing evidence that the oceans are generally becoming less habitable for marine life. Industrial pollution, garbage, and invisible poisons have been detected in almost every major ocean zone. In addition, some scientists predict the eventual extinction of a wide variety of life forms if present pollution and tropical deforestation trends continue. There is a growing awareness that the problem of worldwide pollution cannot be solved by the market system on its own. Government action—supported by people attuned to the dictum "think globally, act locally"—may just become the critical component of our quality of life as we approach a new century.*

The second basic flaw of capitalism is its inability to meet fundamental human needs in the absence of effective demand. So many families and individuals in our society, for one reason or another, do not or cannot earn sufficient incomes to purchase the minimum necessities of life. Some are too old; others are disabled, and many are children. Some are unskilled and can't find work; the skills of many others are no longer in demand. We need to ask ourselves, "What obligations do we, as a comparatively wealthy society, have to these people?" Few would want to see them go hungry or be without shelter or minimum health care.

Consider, too, the question of social stability. In his critique of "Reaganomics" (which made large cuts in social programs but reduced tax rates for upper-income groups), historian Arthur Schlesinger, Jr., argued that our government's sensitivity to people in need has helped maintain capitalism's amazing continuity:

> Capitalism has survived because of a continuing and remarkably successful effort to humanize the industrial order, to cushion the operations of the economic system, to combine pecuniary opportunity with social cohesion. It has survived because of a long campaign, mounted by liberals, to reduce the suffering—and thereby the resentment and rebelliousness—of those to whom the accidents of birth deny an equal chance.[13]

Income redistribution comes in all kinds of packages: welfare and public health programs, Medicare, etc. Although there is general agreement that the government should play *some* role in income redistribution, there is much argument over *how much* public subsidy should be made available to the poor. Indeed, few subjects in economics generate such a heated and bitter debate. Some have suggested that income be redistributed in the form of government jobs or even a guaranteed minimum income. But should this subsidy be maintained at a bare survival level, or should enough money be distributed to provide needy families with a moderate standard of living? We will examine this subject further in Chapter 6.

---

*A more detailed discussion of atmospheric pollution and possible climate change appears in Chapter 20.

We also need government to help maintain *competition*. Even the most bitter opponent of government practices can appreciate the value of some type of antitrust legislation. Capitalism, left on its own, has often produced an increasing concentration of economic power, as large and powerful firms eliminated rivals by fair (or foul) means. As proof, we have only to look at the pre-antitrust days of the late nineteenth century. It was an age when gigantic trusts fixed prices and monopolized manufacturing and commerce, with little regard for overall economic efficiency or the interest of the consumer. It may seem ironic that we need strong *public* intervention to guarantee the survival of our *private* competitive capitalist system, but most economists feel that we do.

Public Goods

Without government, who would provide us with our **public goods?** Public goods are essential to the welfare of society, yet they are either too cumbersome or unprofitable to be supplied to consumers by private industries. A road is a good example. It's doubtful that you would ever consider building a highway. Even if you could afford it, why would you personally make such a large investment when a lot of other people would also be using the road—at your expense? Nor would we expect General Motors or Ford to build millions of miles of roads, or doctors to finance hospitals, or campers to totally subsidize national, state, and local parks.

What about libraries, police and fire protection, public radio and television, plus the thousands of local schools and universities in our country? These are all public goods, and if everyone is to enjoy them, we need to generate "demand" for these goods and services through a system of taxation and public expenditure. Without a social commitment to financing public goods, these necessities of a civilized society would be available only to the relatively wealthy.

Without government, who would be "the umpire" to enforce the so-called "rules of the game"? Who would make sure that everyone plays fairly? Someone must define the legal responsibilities of business operations; someone must enforce contracts, and spell out property rights. Someone must keep an eye out for misleading advertising, for foods and drugs that might impair the public health, and for unsafe products that could kill or maim thousands of consumers. We can be sure that this "someone" will probably not step forward from private industry. We know that some businesses, left unregulated, *will* engage in deceitful advertising or, for example, sell baby cribs in which hundreds of infants could strangle themselves or manufacture dangerous toys. In these and many other situations, we can't expect consumers to always know how to protect themselves.

But how far should government regulation of business go? Where is that line between government as "big brother" and government as legitimate protector? We know, for example, that some people slip and fracture their skulls in their bathtubs each year. Should we require all persons to wear safety helmets when they step into the tub? Of course not. But what about requiring children and adults to wear helmets when they ride bicycles or motorcycles? Just how much regulated safety is *too* much? To what degree should we pursue a philosophy of individual responsibility and "let the consumer beware"? Taking this issue one step further, when does excessive government protection tend to *destroy* consumers' initiatives to defend themselves?

We should also take a look at the *cost* of consumer protection. For example, would it be wise to require Detroit to build an automobile bumper designed to withstand a crash at 50 miles per hour? This is a good idea in theory, but how much more would this "super" bumper cost the consumer? Where do we draw the line?

Unfortunately, the study of economics does not always give us clear-cut answers to these questions. Economists, with their tools of analysis, can help to determine the economic costs and benefits of different actions and policies. In the end, however, such decisions are usually made by lawmakers and regulatory agencies that attempt to strike a political balance between the interests of businesses, consumers, and taxpayers.

The Business Cycle

Finally, in our quest to explore government's role, we might take a moment to consider Figure 5-1. First of all, note that the heavy line is an approximate indicator of what economists call the

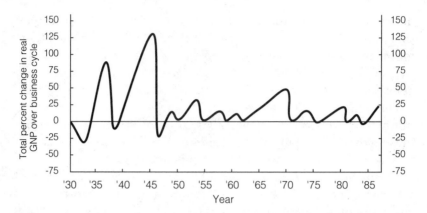

FIGURE 5-1 The severity of economic swings in the U.S. business cycles has been reduced since World War II, partly due to government intervention. A variety of stabilization policies are related to taxes, expenditures, and periodic adjustments in the money supply and interest rate. (Graph concept: R. J. Eggert).

business cycle,[*]—the large (and sometimes not so large) swings in business activity over time. Note especially the downward trends—from the cycle's peaks to its troughs, or low points.

These downward movements represent times of special economic hardship, including periods of higher than average unemployment, bankruptcies, and underutilization of resources. Indeed, we learned the hard lesson during the Great Depression of the 1930s that *unregulated capitalism does not have an automatic mechanism to pull the economy out of a severe slump.* Also, during periods of extremely high economic activity, we may be confronted with a problem on the other side of the business cycle—unacceptable inflation such as we experienced toward the end of the 1970s. It is the existence of these large swings in the economy's business cycle and the accompanying problems that we will now call "the third tragic flaw of capitalism."

In times of economic slumps and high inflation, the government is pressured to take initiatives to help smooth out the severe swings in the business cycle. Note in Figure 5-1 that although the cycle has not been eliminated, each of its exaggerated parts has, since World War II, been leveled out somewhat (and

---

[*]For a superb discussion on business cycles—how they start, how they are measured, how they end—see Alfred Malabre's *Understanding the New Economy* (Dow Jones—Irwin, 1989), particularly Chapter 5, "Ups and Downs."

its duration has been shortened)—primarily through government budgetary and monetary policies (more on these policies in Chapters 8 and 9).

In summary, then, the business cycle forces government to become an active defender of the economy. Like the white knight in the fairy tale, government intervention attempts to slay the "double-headed dragon" of depression and inflation and to generally smooth out the business cycle.

Yet as successfully as government solves problems in some areas of the economy, our "white knight" can also have an unpleasant side. We know that some government activity is badly planned, expensive, and (at times) downright harmful. We can cite numerous examples of overregulation and needless meddling in affairs that are none of the government's business.

We have also seen certain safety laws enacted that are good in theory but, when the fine print is read, turn out to be unrealistic impediments to the operation of legitimate small businesses. We have seen some bad effects from restrictive zoning and outmoded building codes, as well as unnecessary harassment from inspectors, all of which may stifle innovation and initiative. We have seen government-sponsored urban "renewal" programs disembowel neighborhoods and build poorly planned public-housing highrises in their place. And, finally, we have seen how chilling the effects of government intelligence systems can become—an insidious world of phone taps and computer-bank retrieval systems where a sense of privacy is all but destroyed. No, not all government action is good.

But certainly some government regulation is essential in a complex society. If government destroys some freedoms, it enhances others. Although it does so imperfectly at times, government subsidizes education for everyone, creates employment in times of recession, enforces equal-employment rights, and tries to evolve policies to deal with severe and pervasive national problems as drugs and public housing. Government also builds clinics and public parks, supports agricultural research, and looks after the environment. It finances countless programs that try to help people who need help. Without government intervention, our complex economy would have a difficult time surviving.

The ambivalence of big government—combining both the good and the bad (and often not being able to tell the difference)—sometimes creates an identity problem for this benevolent titan. Perhaps no one captured this sense of ambivalence better than Associated Press writer Saul Pett, when he likened our federal government to a

> ... big, bumbling, generous, naive, inquisitive, acquisitive, intrusive, meddlesome giant ... with a heart of gold and holes in his pockets, an incredible hulk, a "10-ton marshmallow" lumbering along an uncertain road of good intentions somewhere between capitalism and socialism, an implausible giant who fights wars, sends men to the moon, explores the ends of the universe, feeds the hungry, heals the sick, helps the helpless, a thumping complex of guilt trying mightily to make up for past sins to the satisfaction of nobody ... a malleable vulnerable colossus pulled every which way by everybody who wants a piece of him, which is everybody.[14]

We can thus recognize the tremendous pressure on government to intervene in the private economy: to regulate, to provide public goods and services, to subsidize, to redistribute income, and at times to stabilize the business cycle. Although it would be difficult to determine precisely, economists have estimated that roughly one-quarter to one-third of all U.S. economic activity is strongly influenced by public or government decisions. Indeed, the economic reality of our system is a far cry from the "pure capitalist" model, in which the means of production and control over resources would be strictly in private hands. We therefore say that our economic system is not pure capitalism but **mixed capitalism**—mixed with a large dose of government financed by taxes.

It is perhaps time to take a closer look at the details of these taxes—the resultant expenditures. Indeed, there are so many different sources of government revenue and areas of expenditure (federal, state, and local), it's no wonder the average voter-taxpayer is bewildered. So where do we start?

Taxes and Expenditures

Let's begin with the broad flows of government finance on the federal level. The largest single source of federal income is the **personal income tax** that many of us dread when the middle of April rolls around each year. In fact, almost one-half of all federal revenue comes from this tax. The second largest tax, contributing about one-third of all federal tax receipts, is the **payroll tax** *(Social Security)*. The **corporate income tax** is third in importance. **Excise taxes** (a tax on a specific item like cigarettes), *customs duties,* and *estate taxes* make up the remainder.

Where does the federal government spend our tax money? The largest single area of federal spending is *domestic social expenditures* (Social Security, health, education, and vocational training), which take up about 50 percent of all federal expenditures. The next largest area is *defense* and defense-related spending. But if we add the various defense-related categories (veterans' benefits, interest on the public debt derived from defense spending and American wars, international military aid, etc.) to regular national security costs, we find that expenditures on "past wars and future defense" account for slightly more than one-third of the federal budget.

At the state level, we find that, on average, the **sales tax** contributes roughly one-half of the revenue; the other half is derived from personal and corporate income taxes plus licenses, permits, and fees. The states spend over one-quarter of this revenue on education, with public welfare coming in a close second. Health, highways, and public safety follow in overall importance.

The local tax scene is dramatically different. Local governments derive almost all their revenues from the **property tax.** Education takes more than 40 percent of this money. Welfare, health, housing, and public safety (police and fire) follow in diminishing importance. The total amount of federal, state, and local taxes spent on publicly supported education is a very large sum indeed.

Tax Philosophies

What are the basic differences between the taxes we pay? We generally categorize a tax as either a *benefits-received tax* or an *ability-to-pay tax.* The philosophy of **benefits-received taxation** is that "The person who pays the tax ought to get the benefits from the expenditure of that tax." Perhaps the best illustration of this is gasoline tax revenue, which is specifically earmarked for highway construction and maintenance. Hunting-license fees, tuition for state universities, and airport tax (to pay for anti-hijacking security) are other examples. In each case, the money from the tax is earmarked and funneled back into a direct service for the taxpayer. To many people, the benefits-received approach seems to be the fairest possible taxation system. But if this is true, then why don't we base all our taxes on this principle?

If we applied *only* the benefits-received principle, there would be some major problems. For example, how would we pay for national defense? Would everyone—rich and poor alike—pay the same dollar amount? That would hardly be practical. How would we finance public schools on a benefits-received principle? Would we only tax families with children (the larger the family, the greater the tax)? How could we guarantee that everyone received an equal opportunity to pursue an education? We couldn't. For this reason, and others, we have some taxes based on the **ability-to-pay principle,** which do not penalize lower-income groups or deprive them of the various benefits of government expenditures.

More specifically, the ability-to-pay philosophy says, "Those people who have more financial resources (income and wealth) should pay more tax." Many economists feel that the best example of this kind of tax is the **progressive income tax.** A progressive tax means that *the greater your income, the greater the percentage of tax you pay.*

A simplified progressive income tax became law with the Tax Reform act of 1986—modified again in 1990. The elimination of many loopholes made it possible to lower the maximum bracket rate from 50 to 31 percent. Combined with the intermediate brackets of 15 and 28 percent, Congress continued the progressive philosophy but reduced the number of brackets compared to the pre-1986 system.

There are also **regressive taxes.** If a purely progressive tax is a good example of ability-to-pay, a regressive tax is a good example of the opposite situation. With a regressive tax, the poor *pay a higher percentage of their income* in taxes than the wealthy do. A good example is a $1 park-entrance fee. Obviously, $1 is a larger percentage of a poor person's income than of a rich person's income. Also, tuition can sometimes be considered regressive, as can the property tax. For example, a home-owning retired couple may easily find themselves paying a sizable percentage of their relatively small income as property tax.

The sales tax might also be considered an example of a regressive tax, since poor families usually pay tax on all their income (because all or nearly all of it is usually spent). The wealthy save or invest much of their income, so that a sizable portion of it is not exposed to the sales tax. Thus, looking at total incomes, the poor wind up paying a higher percentage as sales tax. A number of states have minimized the regressiveness of their sales tax by exempting some necessary items, such as food and prescription medicines.

Generally, most economists feel that a simplified progressive income tax is a fairer way to raise government revenue than sales or property taxes. Of course, any method of taxing away spending power from the public is going to be unpopular. Taxpayer hostility can often be traced to objections to specific public expenditures. The one expenditure that is perhaps the most controversial is welfare. Let's take a closer look at this issue, as well as at the broader problem of poverty in the United States.

Questions for Thought and Discussion

1. If "big brother" was not here in 1984 (as George Orwell's novel predicted), when will he be here? Is he already here? Explain.

2. Are the economic functions of government *really* needed? Could a society get along without them?

3. How important are property taxes to *your* local community? Are they collected at the state level, county level, or city level? What is the resulting tax revenue used to buy?

4. If there is a "business cycle," does that mean a business does well at the top peak of the cycle and does not do as well at the bottom of the cycle (during recessions)? Why or why not?

5. Public goods are consumed in equal amounts by everyone in the public. Comment.

6

Poverty

The following portion of a letter to the editor of a newspaper in St. Paul, Minnesota, describes the writer's feelings about people who receive public assistance:

> . . . according to a newspaper item, one AFDC [Aid to Families with Dependent Children] recipient said, "We are people too." Yes, they "are people too," people who are unwilling to go to work to support themselves and their children as long as they are able to steal from the rest of us who have worked hard and long for many years. . . . What about the rest of us who have worked all of our lives and now find ourselves "short of money" too, because we have to share with these people our hard-earned money? Where do they think we get our money?

It's certainly an honest letter—and an angry one, too. But it's also, it seems, a somewhat misleading letter, because the writer appears to be blaming all those who are poor for creating their own poverty. There are, in fact, more than 30 million men, women, and children (mostly children) who are unable to participate successfully in our economic system. For one reason or another, they simply do not earn adequate incomes to buy the necessities of life.

Still, research indicates that most adults want to work and will work, given the chance. For example, in 50 percent of all

poverty families, at least one member of the household holds a job; in 20 percent of all poverty families, both parents are working.[15] Working families often remain poor because wages are too low. If, for example, a person worked full time, 40 hours a week, 52 weeks a year at the federal minimum wage, that person's yearly income would still fall significantly below the income definition of poverty in the United States for an urban family of four!

The writer of the opening letter was apparently not aware of some other statistics related to our welfare programs. The federal government reports that, on national average, *most welfare recipients are children.* (Today, one out of every five American children under six years of age lives in poverty!) The second largest category includes the blind, aged, and disabled. Mothers of poverty children are third; able-bodied fathers, fourth.

The widespread belief "Once on welfare, always on welfare" is another of the many misconceptions about our welfare programs. Examining national averages, 50 percent of poverty families are considered "temporarily poor"; they have been on welfare only one or two years out of the ten years studied. One in six poverty families are "persistently poor"; they have been receiving welfare for more than eight years. In most cases, poverty families mix work and welfare with assistance when needed, particularly in times of family break-ups, unemployment, or serious illness.[16]

Another commonly stated belief is, "Welfare's getting most of our tax money." Out of all federal expenditures in the early 1990s, federal income payments to the poor were a distant fourth in overall importance—after (1) programs for the elderly (Social Security and Medicare), (2) defense, and (3) interest on the public debt. In many states, assistance payments to the poor are so low that they do not even meet the state's own definition of poverty.

Of course, there are the infuriating cases of people who, through welfare fraud, live "high off the hog," buying expensive electronic gadgets, new cars, or other items that average, hardworking, taxpaying families feel they cannot afford. These are the cases that make the headlines; critics jump on them, and they become the grist for resentful gossip. From a broad statistical point of view, such criticism is generally undeserved. Most poor families, given a choice, don't want handouts; they need income assistance to get through short- to medium-term family and financial crises. In short, our poor need a level of understanding from those of us who aren't doing so badly—not misconceptions based on prejudice or sentimentality, but a true understanding of the realities of poverty in the United States.

What are these realities? From a historical point of view, one of the classics on this subject is Michael Harrington's *The Other America.* Although Harrington's statistics are dated (the book was originally published in the early 1960s), many feel that his observations are still surprisingly true in the 1990s. What specifically does he say?

First of all, the poor are *invisible.* Except for the urban homeless, most poor people live off the beaten track. We do not normally encounter these pockets of poverty, whether they occur in deep southern rural areas, black or hispanic ghettos, or even the American suburbs.[17]

What is even more important, however, is that the poor are *politically invisible,* making them vulnerable to shifts in national sentiment and often powerless to initiate programs to defend themselves within the political arena:

> . . . the poor are politically invisible. . . . The people of the other America do not, by far and large, belong to unions, to fraternal organizations, or to political parties. They are without lobbies of their own; they put forward no legislative program. As a group, they are atomized. They have no face; they have no voice.[18]

Poverty Groups

The poor belong to different subgroups that share the common problem of low income but have their own special difficulties. There are, for example, the *aged.* Although their poverty percentage has come down over the years (due mainly to inflation-adjusted Social Security and Medicare), over 10 percent of this group still falls below the poverty line. Especially vulnerable are widowed women over 65 years of age; their poverty percentages are much higher than the national averages. A black retired woman living alone has, for example, nearly a 50-percent chance of living below the poverty line!

Another poverty group is the **structurally unemployed.** The people in this group, even though they have skills and even though the economy may be booming, still find themselves without work. This can happen, for example, when employment opportunities disappear due to a fundamental change in technology, global competition, or a major shift in consumer demand. Such structural changes in the economy often leave "pockets of poverty" that can continue for years and years. The structurally unemployed include the underground coal miners in Kentucky and West Virginia and the iron-ore workers in northern Michigan and Minnesota who watched their livelihoods dissolve as the mines closed down temporarily or, more often than not, permanently. This group also includes the New England textile workers whose jobs were "exported" to low-paid Italians, Mexicans, and Taiwanese, as well as the autoworkers and steelworkers whose factories have been closing down as large-scale manufacturing modernizes or trims down or as the nation itself slowly changes from durable-goods industries to services and high-technology production.

Other poverty groups include the migrant workers of the fruit- and vegetable-producing states, the marginal farmers and sharecroppers of the deep South, and the millions living in the black and Spanish-speaking slums of our northeastern cities. And since *The Other America* was published in 1962, we've witnessed a surprisingly large increase in the poverty of *single-parent households,* 90 percent of which are headed by the mother. The rise of unwed motherhood and divorce, combined with little or no financial commitment from the fathers (over 50 percent of these families, for example, receive no child-care support), has created the most significant change in poverty statistics in the past couple of decades—what is sometimes referred to as **the feminization of poverty.**

And, finally, another poverty group also on the increase is simply called "the underclass." The people of this group are essentially uprooted and frequently homeless. Although many are living on the streets of large American cities, their precise numbers are unknown because they exist outside of the regular social-services network. They include drug addicts, the rural unemployed, undocumented aliens, teenage runaways, and nonviolent mental patients who have been "deinstitutionalized" but given insufficient economic resources to purchase or rent shelter.[19] The American underclass provides us with vivid evidence of capitalism's second tragic flaw—its inability to meet the basic economic needs of its poorest and most vulnerable class of citizens.

The reality of poverty includes some individuals who were simply born with the "wrong" set of parents, with the "wrong" color skin, or in the "wrong" part of the country—born into a kind of *vicious circle.* The average beginning incomes of nonwhites, for example, are roughly 60 percent of those of whites. As for education, more than twice as many whites finish high school as nonwhites do. All the way down the list, whites enjoy clear-cut

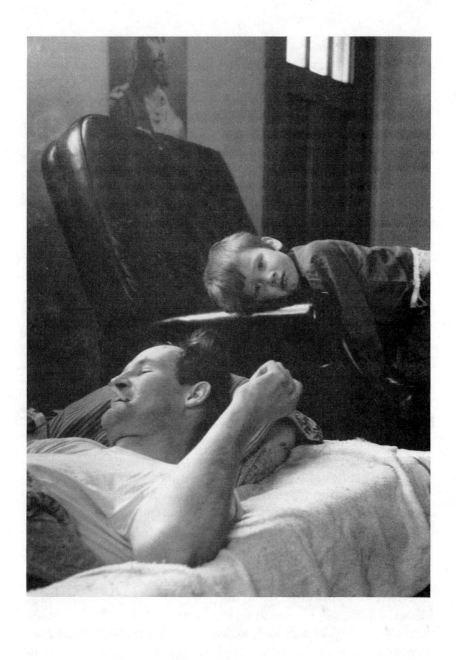

advantages in every economic category. One out of every two whites has a *white-collar* occupation, compared with one in three nonwhites. Unemployment is at least double for nonwhites in all age groups, and nonwhite unemployment among young college graduates is more than triple that of whites. When we examine the unemployment statistics for minority teenagers, we discover that between 25 and 30 percent of all nonwhite teenagers are actively searching for employment but can't find jobs! Indeed, this may be America's most profound economic tragedy—that a sizable group of young men and women are not given the opportunity to become integrated into the mainstream of society with an entry-level job.

This vicious economic circle can be viewed as a kind of sickness, with the cure often out of the patient's control. Communities with low incomes, for example, may very well have substandard schools, staffed either with young, inexperienced teachers (at the lowest end of the salary scale) or uninspired teachers who are not good enough to move on (even though they would like to). Lacking good models of middle-class mobility and economic success, young people receive little inspiration or encouragement and tend to drop out more frequently than middle-class students. Students coming out of a low-expectation environment with few, if any, marketable skills, wind up with the economy's

most menial, dead-end, lowest-paying jobs (or no jobs at all)—and
the economic circle of poverty begins all over again. You can start
anywhere in this circle and eventually wind up in the same place.

There are other factors to consider as well, such as racial
and sexual discrimination, mental and physical handicaps, chronic
drug dependence, poor health, crime, and defeatist attitudes.
Even in the purchase of necessities, such as food, transportation,
and shelter, poor families find it difficult to be "efficient consumers." For example, food is often bought in smaller quantities, but
at higher prices per unit weight. Lower-income housing is frequently not energy-efficient, making it more expensive to keep
warm in the winter or cool in the summer. Each additional factor
makes it more and more difficult to break out of the poverty circle.

Of course, there have been numerous successful breakaways
—individuals who have triumphed over the poverty environment
with intelligence, hard work, good luck, and, frequently, good
connections. They are now highly skilled tradespeople, wealthy
businessmen and women, bank presidents, college professors.
But like the welfare myths (the ten-children families living it up
with expensive food and driving Cadillacs), people who have
beaten poverty are the exceptions, the statistical aberrations.
The truth is that the vicious circle of poverty is just that—and
to make headway against its odds, you usually need help.

Government Assistance

But what kind of help? Henry David Thoreau once said, "If I knew
for a certainty that a man was coming to my house with the
conscious design of doing me good, I should run for my life—for fear
that I should get some of his good done to me."[20] Most poor people
would probably agree with Thoreau's distaste for the "do-gooder"
or meddler. The poor often resent the battalions of government
researchers and even the well-intentioned volunteer workers who
may irritate more than they help. This is not to say that certain
government and private programs have not done some good.

We have to keep in mind, though, that poverty is basically
an economic problem; it's solution, therefore, must also be economic. In short, the poor need one of two things:

1. Help to become economically productive, *or*
2. To have access to subsidized incomes

When we can guarantee everyone access to educational/ training programs and commensurate job opportunities or a guaranteed minimum income, we will have come a long way toward removing capitalism's basic flaw of "need versus demand." But how far have we moved in this direction?

First, let's consider the question of productivity and education. Although everyone has the legal right to a free public education, early schooling for many poor people is more often than not substandard. In many cases, even functional literacy is not guaranteed at the conclusion of 12 years of school. Schools and facilities in poor districts simply must be upgraded, particularly in the basic skills area. Fortunately, many states, prodded by alarming educational reports and growing public concern, are making headway in this area.

Yet to be productive in a modern, changing economy, it is also desirable (even necessary) to go beyond high school. Research shows that high-school graduates who continue their education become more productive and earn substantially more than their counterparts who do not.

Some observers point out that college students in the mid-1980s received approximately $12,000 of direct or indirect public subsidy and ask why noncollege-bound high-school graduates (and dropouts) cannot have access to a similar subsidy. Economists suggest offering these individuals "skill vouchers" worth an equivalent amount of subsidy that, in turn, could be used for vocational training.[21] This proposal, along with a high-growth, job-creating economy (see Chapter 8), could indeed help to upgrade the living standards of people who are currently nonproductive.

Other individuals or families will, either intermittently or (in some cases) permanently, need subsidized incomes. What then are our current programs in this area, and equally important, how effective are they? Let's take a look.

Currently, our government helps to subsidize poor people in two ways—with *transfer payments* and *goods and services.* Specific programs direct **transfer payments** to certain qualified families. These programs are aimed at the elderly, blind, and disabled (Supplemental Security Income Program) and at children and their mothers (Aid to Families with Dependent Children, or AFDC). Social Security, unemployment compensation, and veterans' benefits are also considered transfer payments, although they are paid to people in all income groups and not just to the poor.

Our government also distributes goods and services to the needy in lieu of cash. A prime example of this is the Food Stamp Program. Another example is Medical Assistance, or Medicaid, which provides families with medical care at the government's expense. Others are public housing and rent-supplement programs. In larger cities, free medical clinics are also made available to lower-income families. Whether these types of service programs should be "cashed out" and the money supplied directly to these families in place of free goods and services is a subject of debate. If this were done, the families could use the cash to compete for food, housing, and medical care in the free market.

Let's return to transfer payments and take an in-depth look at one of our largest income subsidy programs—welfare. We have already noted that intense resentment is frequently directed toward the beneficiaries of welfare; we have also examined some of the myths surrounding welfare and discovered that many of these opinions are simply not supported by fact. However, we have yet to analyze this program from the standpoint of its economic effectiveness. Is welfare good or bad? Does it help or hinder the poor? Evaluating the program as a whole, most economists feel that the present-day welfare system is less than a complete success. Some feel it is poorly designed, inefficient, and expensive—that it often does more harm than good in its attempts to solve the overall problem of poverty. Let's look at some of the problems.

First, the welfare program does not always satisfy the basic economic needs of the people it is designed to serve. Remember that in many states, the amount of welfare paid does not even meet the state's own definition of poverty. The states come up with a figure that reflects a poverty level of living, and then pay the welfare family anywhere from 50 to 100 percent of that amount.

Next, the welfare system (like many bureaucracies) is frequently inefficient. Study the welfare procedures in your city or county, or visit your local welfare office and talk to the employees. You will soon realize that a great deal of energy, money, and manpower are spent on red tape, paperwork, income or "means" tests, questionnaires, evaluations, and investigations. As a result, valuable resources are not available to help the poor.

Welfare can also be dehumanizing. Unsympathetic administrators can be suspicious, demeaning, and condescending to new applicants. Those already on welfare are subjected to inquiries and potential surveillance of their lives. Welfare agencies often reflect the prevailing attitude that to receive public assistance is shameful: "The poor have only themselves to blame." Thus, many deserving poor people are too proud to ask for financial help, even when they need it.

Finally, our present welfare system has the unintended effect of encouraging the breakup of families. In some states, for example, a woman with children is refused aid if her able-bodied husband is still a part of the family, even though he may be unemployed. Financial pressures frequently translate into personal tensions and animosities that often lead to the separation or divorce of parents.

Why have we retained such an inefficient income-subsidy system for so long? We tolerate it partly because welfare does have its advantages. Welfare does allow children to stay with their mothers, and it does add something to the meager incomes of the aged and disabled. In addition, it has paid for health services and nursing care when they were critically needed. Furthermore, billion-dollar bureaucracies, no matter how inefficient or potentially destructive they are, have an uncanny knack for survival within our political system. But surely there must be a better way to deliver financial assistance to millions of poor Americans without the drawbacks we have outlined here. Some economists feel that, in fact, there is a more efficient method; it's called the *negative income tax.*

The idea of a negative income tax originated with Milton Friedman, a conservative economist and an influential maverick of the economics profession. Friedman has long advocated policies that adhere to a fundamental criterion: the enhancement of personal economic freedom and choice. In general, he believes that a decentralized market system will best meet this objective, although it won't necessarily alleviate poverty. Friedman first outlined his alternative to our present welfare system in his book *Capitalism and Freedom*; since the early 1960s, the concept of a negative income tax has gained wide respect.

To understand Friedman's ideas, let's look at the income situations of the Smith, Jones, and Baker families. We will assume that Smith has the largest annual income of $14,000; next comes Jones with $12,000 and, finally, Baker with $9000:

SMITH	JONES	BAKER
$14,000	$12,000	$9000

What amount of federal income tax will each of these three families pay? Let's review the procedure for determining income tax, using the Smith family as an example.

Smith will not pay tax on his entire income of $14,000 because all taxpayers are allowed to subtract certain exemptions and deductions from their gross income. Let's say that the tax exemption for each dependent (including Smith, the head of the household) is $2,000. Thus, for a family of four, the total exemption (what Smith can subtract from his gross income) is $8000 ($2000 × 4).

Taxpayers are also allowed to take specific deductions. Although middle- and higher-income families often itemize, a standard deduction is usually taken by lower-income families. Smith has $8000 in exemptions. If we assume that he can also take a standard deduction of $4000, then the combined total exemptions and deductions for the Smith family will be $12,000:

Exemptions	$8,000
Standard deduction	4,000
Total	$12,000

Thus, instead of paying tax on his total $14,000 income, Smith is allowed to subtract exemptions and deductions of $12,000. His *taxable income* will therefore be only $2000. The lowest tax rate is 15 percent, so Smith will pay a net tax of $300 (15 percent of $2000).

For simplicity's sake, let's assume that each family in our example can take the same $4000 standard deduction: Jones and Baker are, therefore, allowed to deduct $4000 from their total incomes, too. It should be obvious that if Jones has four exemptions (worth $8000) and a $4000 standard deduction, then he will not have to pay any tax at all on his $12,000 income ($12,000 − $12,000 = $0). Baker's income of $9000 is the lowest of the three. Baker also has exemptions and deductions of $12,000 and will not have to pay any tax either.

The question of equity now arises. There is a large difference between Jones's and Baker's incomes; why does the government treat them the same? Baker has $3000 of *unused exemptions and deductions* for which he is getting no financial recognition. If we were to institute the negative income tax, Baker would receive some kind of financial credit for these unused exemptions and deductions; the government would give Baker a *negative tax* (a tax rebate) amounting to some percentage of the $3000. Friedman has suggested a rebate of 50 percent of any unused exemptions and deductions. Thus, the Baker family would receive a subsidy— a check from the government for $1500 (50 percent of $3000). This supplementary income, added to his regular income, would give Baker and his family $10,500 to spend.

Now let's look at Baker's situation if he were to lose his job. What would his subsidy be if he had no income at all? If Baker's exemptions and deductions are worth $12,000, then the family would receive a subsidy of 50 percent of that amount, or $6000. This figure represents an **income floor.** All families of four in the United States, if they earn no income, would be eligible for this amount. The negative income tax is, in essence, a guaranteed-income plan.

What about incentives? Let's suppose that after Baker lost his job he was offered part-time work at $3000 a year. Is it to his financial benefit to take the job? From his $3000 income, he would subtract the same $12,000 in exemptions and deductions ($3000 – $12,000 = – $9000) and wind up with a subsidy of $4500 (50 percent of $9000 is $4500). Baker's total income would be this $4500 plus his earned income of $3000, or $7500. Yes, he *is* better off with the job!

Some people might argue that a 50-percent rebate rate (keeping only $0.50 of each earned dollar) is not enough incentive to go to work. But there is nothing in the basic idea that says the percentage *must* be 50 percent. The percentage could be determined so that families would keep 90 percent (or 100 percent) of the first $5000 or $6000 they earned. After this "grace period," the percentage might go back to 50 percent. At any rate, the levels of the percentage rates, exemptions, and deduction could be experimentally worked out to provide lower-income families with enough supplementary income to maintain a respectable standard of living and still not destroy work incentives.

We can now begin to see some of the major advantages of a negative income tax. In Friedman's words

It is directed specifically at the problem of poverty. It gives help in the form most useful to the individual, namely cash. It is general and could be substituted for the host of special measures now in effect.

Let's review its specific advantages. Compared to the present-day welfare system, the negative income tax:

- would cover all in need.
- could be adjusted to guarantee a basic standard of living for every family.
- would help to eliminate the humiliating and dehumanizing aspects of the present system. (Income supplements would be an informal matter, just like receiving a tax refund or a Social Security check; lower-income families would fill out their federal tax forms like everyone else.)
- would be a relatively simple system. (Bureaucratic paperwork, questionnaires, forms, means tests, etc., would be replaced by an uncomplicated income-tax statement.)
- could direct social and rehabilitation workers' efforts toward helping families solve specific problems (jobs, housing, transportation, nutrition, etc.), so that their skills are not wasted on the red tape involved in money transfer.
- would provide no incentive (no extra financial advantage) to encourage the family to break up.
- could be designed not to discourage people from working.

There are some disadvantages to the negative income tax as well. The program would, in the short run, be more expensive than the present welfare system. More people would be covered, and minimal income levels would probably be higher. Where the money would come from is another matter to consider. When unmarried or divorced women head lower-income households, public opinion strongly supports even greater efforts to collect child-support payments from absentee fathers. "Workfare," in which able-bodied recipients must accept public-service or private employment, is another possible way to help pay for the program. Friedman does feel, however, that in the long run, the effect of providing a positive work incentive (if the jobs are available) and eliminating all other subsidy programs (welfare, food stamps, and perhaps even Social Security) would make the cost of a negative income tax lower than the cost of all our existing supplemental income programs combined.

Yet however we pay for it, we must first decide that we really do *want* to help the poor. We do have the resources, but we seem to lack the public will. A while back, I received an advertisement in the mail called "Shop the Other America." In it was a statement that strongly supported the need for a change in our country's attitude:

> Before we can decide how to accomplish the goal of eliminating poverty, or whether we can afford to do the job, we must first decide that we want to do it—that we will no longer expect children to fill hungry bellies with Kool-Aid and candy, to be the prey of rats, to be weakened with tuberculosis, to grow up amid filth and organized vice, to be taught in deteriorating classrooms by teachers who have lost hope, and that we will no longer allow old people to huddle in lonely, heatless rooms, living on pennies, unable to afford needed medicines and services.

We began this chapter with a strongly worded letter written to a St. Paul newspaper and ended with another statement—equally strong in emotion, but light years away in ideology and purpose. Reconciling these two honest, but opposite, views is the unfinished business of us all.

Questions for Thought and Discussion

1. Why are there so many myths concerning the poor in the United States?

2. Is "poverty" an absolute or a relative concept? Explain.

3. To what degree does the exploitation of workers in a capitalist system contribute to poverty?

4. What are the arguments for or against the contention that people are poor "only because they are lazy"? What is your opinion? Explain.

5. Check with your local or state welfare department to determine what "means tests" must be met in your city in order to receive welfare assistance.

7

The Macroeconomy: Gross National Product

In Chapters 4 and 5, we moved away from the "microscopic" approach of supply and demand and proceeded to examine the major economic sectors of businesses, households, and government. Now we are ready to take an even broader point-of-view. This chapter is an introduction to large (macro) economic concepts. It will be as if we were looking at the broad outlines of our economy from some point in outer space, using an "economic telescope" that allows us, in effect, to view the whole picture at once. Economists call this panoramic view of the economy **macroeconomics.**

You probably know quite a bit about macroeconomics already. In fact, you undoubtedly read about it in the newspapers, hear about it on the morning or evening news each day, and listen to arguments about it in every election year. Macroeconomics is the *study of inflation, unemployment, recession, the gross national product (GNP), economic growth, and other broad concepts of an economic system.*

Who uses macroeconomic concepts? Our economic "soothsayers" use them when they attempt to "divine" the future. Economic forecasters ponder charts and tables like veteran handicappers at the racetrack. They pore over income trends, savings and interest rates, consumer attitudes, housing starts, automobile sales, birth rates, and other economic indicators, and then they ask such questions as, "Will we have recession or inflation next year—or both?," "Will interest rates go up or down?," and "What will happen to productivity?"

Then there are the popular oracles (and sometimes the charlatans) of the various investment markets (stocks and bonds, commodities, and gold and silver) who use macroeconomic concepts to help them predict the ups and downs of their respective markets, where a change of a fraction of a percent can add or subtract thousands of dollars to or from a client's account.

There are also the economic philosophers who ask the larger human questions: "Where are we now, and where are we going?" "What is the impact of materialism and technology on the global environment today, ten years from now, or even 100 years from now?" "Futurists" also utilize macroeconomic ideas and indicators.

Finally, our public officials must know something about macroeconomics. They have immediate, urgent concerns. They are like harried physicians, constantly checking the pulse of the economy, anxious to learn about its strength or weakness, growth or stagnation. These men and women have directly or indirectly accepted the responsibility for maintaining the economic health of the country. They include not only the President of the United States and his staff but also Congress and the decision makers in the hierarchy of the Federal Reserve banking system.

Their economic power is derived from controlling the federal budget, the money supply, and interest rates in response to changing economic conditions. A good understanding of macroeconomics is their best tool for intelligent planning and decision making.

Wealth and Gross National Product

Perhaps the best place to start our exploration of this vast area of economic theory and reality is with the idea of **wealth**—a yardstick by which many countries judge each other. Indeed, the United States is the envy of the world because of its tremendous man-made and natural wealth. If we were to add up the value of all our buildings and structures, our equipment and inventories, our land and other natural resources, we would be

worth something over 20 trillion dollars (1 trillion is 1000 billion). This figure, however, does not tell us very much about our
current economic health. Why? There are two reasons.

First, wealth must be *utilized* before it can contribute to
present-day living standards. Black Africa, for example, has
tremendous natural wealth, but this wealth has generally not
been utilized and, consequently, most of its people remain economically poor.

Second, the value of a nation's resources in the form of
wealth does not necessarily tell us anything about that nation's
current production. Without a continuous flow of new goods
and services, nations eventually consume their available wealth
(like retired couples who use up their savings and are eventually forced to sell their personal belongings to purchase food).
Our economy, like a growing family, must have a *continuous*
flow of income and real output if it is to maintain present living
standards.

What we are looking for is a concept that goes beyond
wealth—a concept that will tell us something about the total
output that our land, machines, and labor produce year after
year. This concept is the **gross national product** (GNP).
Economists define GNP as a *measure of the final value of all
goods and services produced in the economy in a year's time.* Like
the amount of our national wealth, GNP is an enormous figure
almost too large to comprehend. By the turn of the decade
(1989–1990), for example, the total GNP was approximately
$5 trillion per year!

We should pause a moment to consider the difficulties in
computing a precise value for the GNP. Of course, much of our
total national output can easily be traced simply by adding up
total incomes (as shown on our personal income-tax returns, for
example). There are, however, many goods and services that do
not see the "light of day" and are never officially recorded. An
unrecorded "cash" transaction (designed to bypass the Internal
Revenue Service) is one example; billions of dollars in illegal
drug trade represent another.

Probably a much larger category of unrecorded production
takes place (perfectly legally) under the heading of *nonmarket
transactions.* We are all a part of this "underground" market in
one way or another. For example, each time we do something for
ourselves that we *could have paid someone else to do,* our

economic activity goes unrecorded in the official GNP statistics. Mary Smith, for example, tunes her car every six months, but Mary doesn't pay herself (and record it on her income-tax form). But if a garage had done the same work, the labor bill might have been $50 or $100. The garage, in turn, would report this amount to the government as "service performed," and Mary's tune-up *would* become part of our GNP.

Obviously, these do-it-yourself projects—from growing your own food to remodeling a basement—cannot be accurately accounted for in our national income statistics. The problem posed by nonmarket transactions is considerably amplified when we note the billions of dollars of unpaid household services that are performed mainly by women. Then add to this the billions of dollars of unpaid volunteer services. Although our government does attempt to estimate the value of some of these unrecorded transactions, it is impossible to do this with any precision.

Another problem associated with the GNP is our strong belief in the dictum that "happiness is a rising GNP." We often assume that when GNP is rising, we are all automatically better off. Many economists, however, are now beginning to voice some important concerns about this philosophy.

For example, before we can say we are better off when the GNP goes up, we should look at what is happening to the *population* during the same period of time. If output rises by 1 percent and population increases by 3 percent, the average family will suffer a *decline* of 2 percent in their standard of living. It's a simple principle that is often ignored, especially in less-developed countries, where population growth frequently outstrips the rise in GNP.

Another point to consider is the *distribution* of the GNP pie. A rising GNP, for example, may be translated into 25 percent more housing, but if the extra houses are second homes for wealthy families, then we can hardly say that the average citizen is benefiting from this increase in the GNP. Brazil provides us with a good example. This South American county has certainly been maintaining a "growth economy," but the fruits of its rising GNP have been concentrated mainly in the modern sector. The majority of poor Brazilians, who live in the nonindustrial economy, benefit very little, if at all, from their country's rising GNP. Our generalization that "happiness is a rising GNP" in this case turns out to be a painful mockery to the poor families who watch their country's income differentials widen as the years go by.

We should also consider the questions of *quality*. Does the quality of our GNP change over time? Indeed it does. Many people argue that the quality of our merchandise and services has declined over the years; they point to shoddy workmanship, inferior materials, and "planned obsolescence" as proof of deteriorating product and service quality. Industry might reply, however, that the quality of some products has actually improved. Radios and televisions, for example, are cheaper and more reliable now than they were 20 years ago; radial tires are not only safer but will outlast the tire made 30 years ago; and the computer of today is better, faster, and generally cheaper than the one manufactured a decade ago.

What is your own opinion about the quality of products and services? On balance, has it gone up or down? Either way, product and service quality is an important factor to consider when comparing GNP statistics from year to year.

Instead of looking at individual products, we might also examine the general *composition* of the overall GNP. It has been said, for example, that "if we all came down with cancer, it would boost the GNP." Hospital revenues and the incomes of doctors, nurses, radiologists, and drug companies would go up—at least temporarily. Yet clearly no one could say that we would be "better off" in such a situation.

Thus, there are economic "bads" as well as "goods." Many economists are beginning to look at GNP growth to try and analyze which expenditures are truly beneficial and which ones are not. For example, it is generally agreed that health-care costs associated with air and water pollution do not add to our net economic well-being, nor do excessive military expenditures.

British economist Leopold Kohr has identified a whole range of products and services that he labels *density commodities*. These goods are purchased by consumers, government agencies, and businesses simply to *offset the impact of living in a high-density environment* among large-scale social institutions (schools, businesses, cities, etc.[22]). *Density expenditures* include the cost of traffic accidents, many legal services, commuting expenses, escapist media, illegal opiates, prescribed relaxants and stimulants, and the ever-more powerful headache remedies ("Life got tougher, so we got stronger," says an Excedrin advertisement). Add to this list the expenditures associated with crime (squad cars, prisons, protective services, exotic burglar alarms and foolproof locks, personalized handguns, mace, etc.), and you begin to get an idea of how much our GNP is devoted to these goods. We are forced to purchase density goods, says Kohr, not because they offer us a net improvement in our standard of living, but because we have evolved into a society in which such goods are necessary to offset the negative side effects of modern urban life. Again, the billions of dollars spent on these types of goods may not add much to the net welfare of the population, but they are all counted as part of our official GNP statistics.

Progrowth versus Antigrowth

Kohr and other maverick economists have actually questioned the prevailing economic ethic that continuous growth is desirable, particularly for the United States and other highly industrialized countries ("the overdeveloped nations," as Kohr calls them). Kohr and those who share his way of thinking are considered advocates of an "antigrowth" or "steady-state" policy that some label "sustainable economics." In this camp, we would also include Herman E. Daley, Paul Ehrlich, and Lester Brown, head of the World Watch Institute and author of *Building a Sustainable Society* (W. W. Norton, 1981). All of these economists are concerned with what they see as the results of economic growth: the steady erosion of the quality of the global environment and the decline of the world's nonrenewable resources. Perhaps the extreme point of view comes from Professor Ezra Mishan of The London School of Economics:

> You could very well have stopped growing after the First World War. There was enough technology to make life quite pleasant. Cities weren't overgrown. People weren't too avaricious. You hadn't really ruined the environment as you have now.[23]

Most economists, however, continue to be defenders of growth, agreeing with Adam Smith's historic contention that "the progressive state is in reality the cheerful and the hearty state to all order of society. The stationary is dull; the declining, melancholy."

There is the view among progrowth advocates that humans are surprisingly *adaptable* and that our species has proven over thousands of years that it is capable of making appropriate change when change is warranted. If we run low on certain resources, our market economy (through higher prices) will signal that it's time to find (or create) new substitutes: fiber optics instead of copper, strong (and inexpensive) plastics in place of steel or aluminum; or perhaps a trend toward miniaturization to conserve a myriad of scarce resources. If fossil-fuel supplies become depleted, we will (progrowth economists say) find substitutes or evolve more highly efficient systems with our technological know-how. In this sense, the progrowth position seems to go hand-in-hand with what we might call "technological optimism."

And we should pause to consider Irving Kristol's argument that growth is, in fact, *a necessary precondition* to a modern democracy in which "the expectations of tomorrow's bigger pie, from which everyone will receive a larger slice, . . . prevent people from fighting to the bitter end over the division of today's pie."[24] Defenders of economic growth also point out that very few families can say that they are satisfied with their current economic status. In addition, they remind us that we still have many lower-income people in the United States who are likely to be permanently poor in a zero-growth economy. A final point from progrowth economists is that it is much easier to deal with pollution in a growing economy; cleaning up the environment will be expensive, and the additional resources must come from somewhere.

Defenders of economic growth are greatly disturbed that an increasing number of people want to go back to the "good old days"—days that progrowth people believe were not so good. They ask, "Why can't environmentalists and other antigrowth advocates understand that technology and economic growth are conquering nature for the benefit of mankind?"

Author Mel Ellis, a naturalist who has demonstrated unique sensitivity for both economic and environmental problems, writes

> Man almost literally made the cow, the fat corn kernel, the plump turkey, the beautiful rose. And if he erred in his enthusiasm and polluted his raw materials, his resources, he still made the world enormously better.[25]

Most environmental advocates probably do understand the benefits of technology, progress, and economic growth, but their attention is directed to different concerns. They are listening to different sounds. Essayist E. B. White once summed up this attitude with the comment, "I would feel more optimistic about a bright future for man if he spent less time proving that he can outwit Nature and more time tasting her sweetness and respecting her seniority."[26]

The immediate concerns of environmentalists are not the eradication of poverty or the benefits of high-speed air travel or the advantages of the computer over the abacus. They do not see a thousand acres of timber as so many completed homes. They see the grandeur of the forest and its enduring value as a generator of oxygen, a climatic stabilizer, and a habitat for plants and wildlife—and they work for its preservation. Instead of seeing the Appalachian hills as a source of strip-mined coal for heating homes, they ask, "What are the adverse consequences of strip mining for the land and its inhabitants?"

> The D-9 bulldozer is the largest built by the Caterpillar Tractor Corporation. It weighs some 48 tons and is priced at $108,000. With a blade that weighs 5000 pounds, rising five feet and curved like some monstrous scimitar, it shears away not only soil and trees but a thousand other things—grapevines, briars, ferns, toadstools, wild garlic, plantain, dandelions, moss, a colony of pink lady-slippers, fragmented slate, an ancient plow point, a nest of squeaking field mice—and sends them hurtling down the slope, an avalanche of the organic and the inorganic, the living and the dead. The larger trees that stand in the path of the bull-dozer—persimmons, walnuts, mulberries, oaks, and butternuts—meet the same fate. Toppled, they are crushed and buried in the tide of rubble.[27]

Along the same line, who could not empathize with novelist James Michener's feelings of sadness and guilt after he returned to the site of his boyhood stream?

> This marvelous stream in which I used to fish and where as a boy I had gone swimming, this ribbon of cool water which has been a delight to generations of farmers, was now a fetid body of yel-lowish water with not a living thing in it. Frogs, fish, waterlilies, bullrushes, and ducks' nests had all vanished. . . . The loss of my stream had occurred under my nose, as it were, and with me making no protest. When I finally saw what had happened, I was ashamed of my inattention. What in those years had I been doing that was

more important than saving a stream? If we continue to abuse and destroy our resources, many of us will be asking that question thirty years from now, but by then it will be too late, and some of the precious things we have lost will not be recoverable.[28]

Environmentalists, in short, are distressed by the ugliness of overdevelopment. They are angered by worldwide pollution in such forms as oil spills and acid rain and also by the growing lists of extinct or endangered species of wildlife. They feel that these are the unnecessary consequences of human selfishness. They are saddened by our blindness—a blindness to the possibility that much of what we value today may be lost forever. Of those who favor "development at any cost," they ask, "Why can't you see what uninhibited growth is doing to those things we must preserve for future generations?" The great debate over growth is based on simple but profound differences in values. It will, undoubtedly, remain a public issue of great magnitude for years to come.

GNP and Inflation

We will consider one more major challenge to the attitude that "happiness is a rising GNP." Imagine the following scene. George and Mary Franklin were overjoyed when their joint income increased to $45,000 a year; they had never dreamed they would make that much money. Yet by the end of the year, the Franklin family felt poorer than ever. Not only had they failed to save any money, but Mary Franklin claimed that their standard of living was worse now than it was five years ago. What went wrong?

The answer to this question should be obvious, since we are all adversely affected by the same economic malady. The problem was *the rise in the general price level*—what economists commonly call **inflation.** Not only does inflation distort and diminish your income, my income, and the Franklins' income, but inflation also distorts the GNP statistics.

A simple example can illustrate this point. Let's assume, for the sake of simplicity, that the U.S. economy produces only one product, wheat. Over a time period of three years, watch what happens to GNP when the price of wheat is inflated from $1 to $5 per bushel:

YEAR	OUTPUT (in bushels)	PRICE (per bushel)	GNP (price × output)
1	3	$1	$3
2	5	4	20
3	9	5	45

Take a look at the GNP column. If someone gave you only the GNP figures $3, $20, and $45, would you say that these figures were a good representation of output? Of course not, because they do not give you the whole story. These GNP figures are, in fact, greatly inflated when you compare them with the increase in actual output of wheat: the GNP has increased to 15 times its original value (from $3 to $45), while output has increased to only three times its original value (from 3 to 9 bushels). In short, if all you saw were these GNP statistics, you would have a very distorted picture of the economic situation. Economists have a name for this "distorted" or inflated GNP; they call it **money GNP.** Using the same idea, we can now see why Mary and George Franklin felt a little bewildered when they discovered that their *money income* did not seem to give them any additional purchasing power. Money income and money GNP are, by themselves, inaccurate indicators of the real economic situation.

Unfortunately, money GNP *is* the figure that is commonly quoted by newspapers, public officials, writers, and teachers. The 1989–1990 total GNP figure of $5 trillion mentioned earlier is, in fact, money GNP. Is there any way of getting a more accurate picture of our GNP? What we need is a more realistic value for the GNP—a GNP figure that does not include inflated prices.

To adjust for inflation in our example, we must compare each year's output with the wheat price of a single *base year.* We could choose any of the three years for our base, and then apply this base-year price to the outputs of the other two years. Let's make year 1 our base. We then multiply the base-year price ($1 per bushel) by the actual output *of all three years:*

YEAR	OUTPUT (in bushels)	REAL GNP (Year 1 = base year)
1	3	$ 3
2	5	5
3	9	9

The result is **real GNP,** which, as you can see in the table, gives us a far more accurate picture of each year's production than money GNP did.

Of course, the United States does not make one product; it produces millions and millions of goods and services. How can the GNP be adjusted for inflation when there are so many different prices to consider? The same principle applies; economists compare the outputs of all other years to a base-year price. The big difference is that now the price changes of many goods and services (not just one) must be averaged. This average price level can easily be summarized in one statistic, called the **price index,** or the **GNP price deflator.** The price index for the base year is always equal to 100, no matter which year we choose. Any change in overall prices is reflected by a change in the price index.

For example, if we use 1982 as the base year (price index = 100) and we find that prices between 1982 and 1985, on average, went up 10.9 percent, then the price index for 1985 would be 110.9. Once we knew that the 1985 index was 110.9, then we would be able to convert 1985 output "into 1982 dollars." So suppose you hear someone report that the GNP in 1985 was $4015 billion. You now know that this person is giving you the inflated money GNP figure. How then do you calculate real GNP for 1985? You simply divide the price index for 1985 (110.9) into the money GNP ($4015 bil.) and then multiply your answer by 100:

$$\text{Real GNP (1985)} = \frac{4015}{110.9} \times 100 = \$3620 \text{ billion}$$

Now you know the value of real GNP (in 1982 dollars) for 1985. The $3620 billion figure is somewhat less than the inflated $4015 billion figure originally quoted. Unfortunately, the distinction between real and money GNP is rarely made, and the public is often misled by published figures.

We are now prepared for what might be called "The Shortest Economic History Course Ever," as we sum up 60 years of U.S. economic history in less than a page! Look carefully at the chart below. Do you notice any interesting trends in the following figures? (If you read them carefully, you will notice four major economic events in this 60-year history.)

The first significant event is the *deflation* (a drop in price) and the Great Depression of the 1930s. In this insecure decade, Americans were faced with high unemployment, a severe drought, and widespread poverty.

The second period of interest is the great upsurge of real economic growth from the early 1940s to the late 1960s. In an accounting sense, this 30-year period was a phenomenal age of American prosperity. In the decade of the 1960s alone, *real* growth per year averaged nearly 4-1/2 percent! By the middle of this decade, political writer Theodore White would write in his book, *The Making of the President, 1964*:

YEAR	MONEY GNP (in billions)	PRICE INDEX (1982 = 100)	REAL GNP (in billions)
1930	$91.2	14.2	$ 642
1935	72.8	12.5	582
1940	100.4	13.0	772
1945	213.4	15.7	1359
1950	288.3	23.9	1206
1955	405.9	27.2	1492
1960	515.3	30.9	1668
1965	705.1	33.8	2086
1970	1015.5	42.0	2418
1975	1598.4	59.3	2695
1980	2732.0	85.7	3188
1985	4014.9	110.9	3620
1990*	5463.0	131.5	4154

*preliminary

1982= base year

Source: Economic Report of the President, February, 1991. BEA (U.S. Department of Commerce). 1990 estimate from *Blue Chip Economic Indicators*, Sedona, AZ, Aug. 10, 1990; p. 5.

There was no doubt that John F. Kennedy and his economists had brought about the first fundamental change in American economic policy since Franklin D. Roosevelt—and the nation glowed with a boom that was one of the world's wonders. The boom terrified Europeans, angered the underdeveloped in the world, baffled the Russians.[29]

Yet only five years later, after our long Vietnam war, the glow of economic boom and prosperity turned into a bonfire of inflation, the third major event of this 60-year period. During the 1970s, overall prices in the United States rose some 104 percent—a greater increase than in any other comparable period!

And finally, we come to the fourth and most recent period. If the 1970s were characterized by unprecedented inflation, the 1980s was an era of **disinflation,** or a rapid decline in the inflation rate. It began with the initiation of a tight monetary policy in the fall of 1979 and was fortified by two recessions (in 1980 and in 1982), greater international competition in manufacturing, and the collapse of OPEC (the international oil cartel). Few, if any, of America's best economic forecasters predicted the magnitude of this reduction in the inflation rate:[30] from 9 to 10 percent in 1979, 1980, and 1981 down to 3 or 4 percent by the middle of the 1980s. Although it set the stage for a more stable, moderate-growth economy during the rest of the decade, the sudden drop in inflation was initially accompanied by high unemployment and an alarming number of bankruptcies, especially in farm, oil, mining, and related industries.

Thus, unemployment and, at times, inflation mar much of our economic history and continue to plague us as we approach a new century. We will now examine these two extreme economic maladies in more detail in our continuing exploration of macroeconomics.

Questions for Thought and Discussion

1. How difficult would it be to compare the GNP of an industrialized country with the GNP of a Third World country?

2. How is GNP data actually collected in the United States?

3. How would the viewpoints of members of a local chamber of commerce compare with the idea that "happiness is a rising GNP"?

4. What do you think the major economic characteristics of the
   1990s will be? Why?

5. *True or false?* All nonmarket transactions are illegal. Explain.

8

Unemployment and Inflation

What do you think would happen if everyone in the United States woke up one morning and decided to start spending only half of the amount of money that they had been spending? This is a very unlikely situation, but let's suppose it really happens. What economic effect would this collective decision produce?

The total impact on the economy would be very large indeed. Let's pull out our economic microscope once again and focus on one small retail store—Joe's Super Sportshop in Plum City, Washington. Joe's business will, in effect, become a microcosm of how businesses will react all across the United States.

First, Joe immediately begins to notice that fewer customers are coming into his store. Before long, he has to let his part-time clerk go. But for Joe himself: so far, so good; he is not yet facing any major problems. As time goes on, however, Joe observes something very disturbing: *inventory is piling up*. Walking into the storage room, he stumbles over a large box of unsold baseball mitts that he ordered two months ago when business was better. Things are a little more serious now.

Joe decides to try to get rid of his excess mitts by putting them on sale. More importantly (to the economy), he sends a message to the baseball-mitt distributor in Seattle, asking him not to ship any more mitts to the shop.

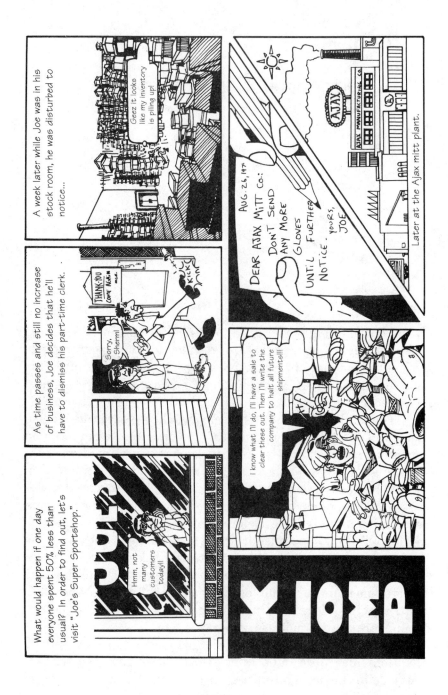

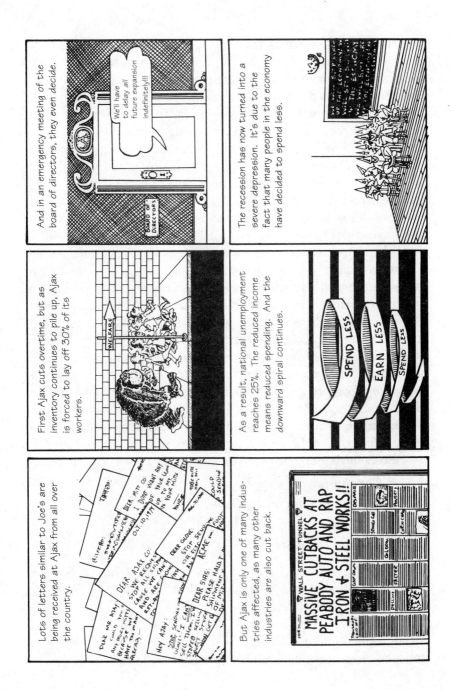

And in an emergency meeting of the board of directors, they even decide.

We'll have to delay all future expansion indefinitely!!!

First Ajax cuts overtime, but as inventory continues to pile up, Ajax is forced to lay off 30% of its workers.

Lots of letters similar to Joe's are being received at Ajax from all over the country.

The recession has now turned into a severe depression. It's due to the fact that many people in the economy have decided to spend less.

As a result, national unemployment reaches 25%. The reduced income means reduced spending. And the downward spiral continues.

SPEND LESS — EARN LESS — SPEND LESS

But Ajax is only one of many industries affected, as many other industries are also cut back.

WALL STREET FUNNEL — MASSIVE CUTBACKS AT PEABODY AUTO AND RAP IRON & STEEL WORKS!!

The bad news is channeled up to Ajax Mitt Company in Blackstone, Maine. Ajax, in fact, is getting the same bad news from all of its distributors around the country. At first, Ajax cuts overtime, but its directors soon realize that they must lay off 30 percent of their workers to keep inventory from piling up at Ajax. The directors meet in an emergency session to discuss the new plant that is scheduled for ground-breaking ceremonies next week. They decide to halt all expansion plans indefinitely.

Of course, similar actions are being taken by other industries throughout the nation. Major layoffs are made in the automobile, steel, and housing industries, and orders for new plants and equipment are reduced to a fraction of last year's level. National unemployment soon rises to 25 percent.

With many people on reduced incomes (or no incomes at all), spending falls to lower levels; this downward spiral continues to drag the economy down even further. What is the eventual result of this seemingly simple decision to curtail spending? It has brought on a devastating *depression!* Thus, recession, depression, high unemployment, and other extreme negative economic swings occur primarily because *enough individuals or groups of people somewhere in the economy decide* (for any number of reasons) *to spend less.* These people do not necessarily have to be consumers; they can be other major spenders, such as businesses, federal, state, or local governments, or foreign buyers.

Economists summarize the four major categories of spending as:

- Consumption expenditures C
- Investment spending I
- Government expenditures G
- Net foreign exports X_n

Thus, we can now say that any large reduction in C, I, G, or X_n spending will set forces into motion that can lead to a recession or, possibly, to a depression.

Returning to our example, let's assume we are now going through the economic stage called recession. What is a recession, and how does it differ from a depression?

Recession versus Depression

Economists say we are in a **recession** when the economy experiences at least *a one-half-year period of declining real GNP.* By this definition, our economy has experienced nine recessions since World War II: 1949, 1954, 1958, 1960, 1970, 1974, 1980, 1982, and 1990. In terms of unemployment, our most severe recent recession was in 1982 when, for a number of months, over 10 percent of the labor force was out of work. The mildest recession was in 1970, with only 5 percent unemployment.

If a recession is a bad cold, a depression is pneumonia. In effect, a **depression** *is a severe and prolonged recession.* During the Great Depression of the 1930s, which lasted approximately a decade, unemployment rates ranged from 12 to 25 percent (1933). In no year during the 1931–1941 decade did the national jobless rate drop below the 10 percent figure!

Depressions have a touch of economic insanity. In the 1930s, idle machines and idle men and women *could* have been producing goods and services that the nation desperately needed. But the people did no work and the machines rusted—and nobody knew what to do about it.

A comparable tragedy occurred in rural areas. In one part of the nation, fruit and grain ripened and livestock fattened in our great plains and fertile valleys. But some farmers actually destroyed their livestock or burned their grain or let the ripened fruit rot while other people went hungry because they had little or no income and therefore no purchasing power. In her book *The Invisible Scar* (New York: David McKay, 1966), Caroline Bird retells a number of stories that illustrate some of the sadness and suffering during those years:

> Miners tried to plant vegetables, but they were often so hungry that they ate them before they were ripe. On her first trip to the mountains, Eleanor Roosevelt saw a little boy trying to hide his pet rabbit. "He thinks we are not going to eat it," his sister told her, "but we are." [pp. 26–27]
>
> A year after his defeat by Roosevelt, Hoover—who had repeated so many times that no one was starving—went on a fishing trip with cartoonist "Ding" Darling in the Rocky Mountains. One morning, a local man came into their camp, found Hoover awake, and led him to a shack where one child lay dead and seven others were in the last stages of starvation. Hoover took the children to a hospital, made a few phone calls, and raised a fund of $3030 for them. [p. 39]

In addition, disastrous weather conditions in some parts of the country added to the general economic suffering. In the midwestern wheat and corn belt, desperate, bankrupt farmers choked on dust from the worst drought that anyone could remember.

Some malicious and sinister force in the air seemed to paralyze all economic activity and turned topsy turvy the economic laws that had always worked for our benefit. This force almost broke our spirit, as John Steinbeck captures in *The Grapes of Wrath* (1939):

> The women studied the men's faces secretly, for the corn could go, as long as something else remained. The children stood nearby, drawing figures in the dust with bare toes, and the children sent exploring senses out to see whether men and women would break. The children peeked at the faces of the men and women, then drew careful lines in the dust with their toes. Horses came to the watering troughs and nuzzled the water to clear the surface dust. After a while the faces of the watching men lost their bemused perplexity and became hard and angry and resistant . . . . Then the women knew that they were safe and that there was no break. They asked, What'll we do? And the men replied, I don't know. . . . But it was all right.

We now know something about that "sinister force." It was caused by a large reduction in spending in all major sectors of the economy, set off by the great stock-market crash of 1929.[31] This inability of pure capitalism to regulate itself—to avoid the ups and downs of the business cycle—is, as we noted earlier, capitalism's third tragic flaw. We will soon see how this problem is dealt with in a modern economy. First, however, let's return to our example at the beginning of the chapter.

Remember, we first decided to spend less, then quickly found ourselves in a recession, and later dropped into a deep depression. Now let's assume that after this unhappy time, people, businesses, and government decide to begin spending again. What will it be like at Joe's Super Sportshop?

Joe's business immediately picks up, forcing him to rehire his part-time clerk. He is no longer tripping over surplus boxes of baseball mitts. In fact, when Margie Miller comes in to buy her autographed Lou Gehrig Little League baseball mitt, Joe discovers that he is all sold out. He quickly dials his distributor in Seattle, who quickly writes a purchase order to the Ajax Mitt Company. Ajax receives similar letters from distributors throughout the country. The plant immediately rehires its laid-off workers and gears up for full-capacity production. Finally, the directors of Ajax meet and approve the ground breaking for not one but two new midwestern plants.

Happy times have returned. Things are humming along in all of the economy's major industries. Everyone appears satisfied; more and more expenditures are flowing through the system, buying up greater and greater amounts of goods and services. Notice, too, that once there is upward motion in the economy, everything tends to reinforce this trend. Greater spending generates more employment, more income, and more investment spending. Each of these new spending dollars, in turn, generates another round of spending and enlarged incomes. The pace accelerates—perhaps too fast. At the point that resources become fully employed, the total demand begins to strain the available supply. The result is *the beginning of inflation, as more and more dollars "chase" after a limited supply of output.*

At first, of course, there is not much to worry about. A few prices increase here and there as inventories become depleted; product shortages are a little more frequent than before. But when demand begins to expand too fast, the existing plant capacity soon becomes overloaded as our labor force and industrial output become fully utilized. Businesses are under pressure to expand to meet the growing demands for their goods and services, but simply do not have enough resources to produce these products! As they attempt to buy existing raw materials and to attract skilled labor, businesses find they have to pay more and more. Labor unions are quick to take advantage of the "seller's market" for labor, and wages are pushed up before long. Businesses don't mind too much; they try to pass their increased costs on to consumers in the form of higher prices. Inflation that results from higher costs is often referred to as **cost-push inflation.** Higher labor costs, however, mean fatter paychecks. This extra demand pulls prices up again (too many dollars chasing after too few goods), and we experience another round of **demand-pull inflation.**

These two factors (excess demand and higher costs) pull and push the economy again and again, as if bending a wire back and forth. The heated-up economy soon reaches a breaking point. This **hyperinflation** can be as devastating to an economy as a depression; both are extreme economic conditions that can and must be avoided. We will look at these two problems in more detail in a moment, but first let's look at a diagram that shows what we have learned thus far.

Figure 8-1 looks something like the supply and demand graph we examined in Chapter 3. Here, however, the vertical axis represents the overall price level. Any upward movement on the price scale can be directly translated into inflation. The horizontal axis represents output and employment. Both of these

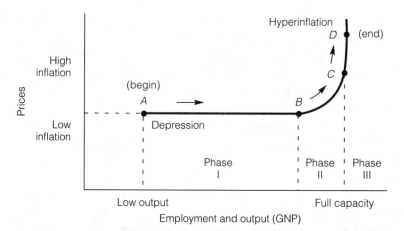

FIGURE 8-1 If we begin at depression point *A* and increase national spending, then GNP increases without any inflationary penalty through-out Phase I. If extra spending increases GNP with some inflationary penalty, then we are in Phase II, or the *trade-off area*. Finally, if extra spending results in only higher prices, then we are operating in Phase III.

values are directly related. If output is high, we know employ-ment will also be high; if output is low, employment will be low.

Let's begin at point *A* (in the midst of the Great Depres-sion). Note the relatively low price level combined with a small GNP and high unemployment. As we begin to spend more, we move along the solid line to the right. Each additional dollar spent increases employment and output *without* any inflation penalty. This remains true all the way through Phase I. Once we reach point *B*, any additional spending not only increases output but also creates some degree of inflation. We call this Phase II, or the *trade-off area.* If we want higher levels of output and employment, we must accept a trade-off in the form of higher prices. Once we reach point *C*, however, if we spend beyond it, we gain nothing in output and employment (because the economy is already operating at full-capacity output), but we completely lose out to hyperinflation.

We might generalize and say that to operate in either Phase I or III is a serious mistake, since we can still gain employment (without any inflation penalty) beyond Phase I and Phase III represents nothing more than sustained inflation (with no employment advantage). The logical place to operate (if we are in control of things) is in Phase II, or the trade-off area. Let's magnify this section of our graph (see Figure 8-2) to see precisely how the trade-off area operates.

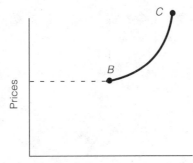

FIGURE 8-2 *Trade-off area* (magnified): note that prices tend to increase (inflation) when employment increases. On the other hand, if the economy is operating at a low price level, full employment will probably not be maintained.

Trade Off

In reality, a trade-off is actually a variation of the old saying, "You can't have your cake and eat it too." We can't have full employment and zero inflation at the same time. **Trade off** forces us to choose the objective that we value most: high employment or low inflation. For example, if we operate at point *B* in the trade-off area in Figure 8-2, we are choosing a low inflation and high unemployment. On the other hand, if we choose an area near point *C*, we are opting for full employment with relatively high inflation.

Sometimes economists prefer to portray this same trade-off problem in a slightly different format, popularly called the **Phillips curve** after A. W. Phillips, who studied historical trade-off data in Great Britain in the 1950s. Instead of plotting employment on the horizontal axis, the Phillips curve plots *unemployment,* which reverses the curve but shows essentially the same trade-off concept. In Figure 8-3, a Phillips curve indicates unemployment and inflation from 1964 to 1969. Take a careful look at the general shape of the Phillips curve, and note how it portrays the trade-off concept.

Over some time periods, as in Figure 8-3, a Phillips curve will show a fairly good trade-off relationship; over other time periods, the relationship will not be so neat and tidy. Still, government policymakers must often contend with the trade-off dilemma and make some tough choices. The comment "If we are

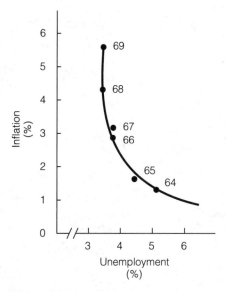

FIGURE 8-3 The *Phillip's curve* indicates a fairly clear trade-off between the inflation rate and the unemployment rate for 1964–1969.

ever going to solve our terrible inflation problem, we may have to have a recession" is an example of the sort of painful choice that sometimes must be made when dealing with a severe economic problem. How is such a choice made? For example, which problem—inflation or unemployment—is going to give the economy more trouble? Economists can't say for sure because each problem affects us differently. So, let's take a closer look at the specific economic impacts of both of these economic maladies.

Inflation

Exactly why is inflation bad? Most people have jobs during high inflationary periods, and inflation alone normally does not reduce output. The problem is that **inflation** *distorts the economy;* it redistributes large portions of the economic pie away from some people and places that income into the hands of others—often unfairly or free of charge.

Indeed, some groups fare well during inflationary times. Anyone on a *flexible income,* for example, will usually do all right. Workers represented by labor unions with bargaining clout (and inflation-based escalator clauses in their contracts) tend to benefit. Large corporations may also profit. Since demand is usually high, during an inflationary period, businesses are often able to raise their prices in response to higher labor and raw-materials costs. *Speculators* who purchase property, gold, rare coins, paintings, or other "inflation hedges" at bargain prices and then sit back to "let inflation do its work" also reap financial rewards from inflation. Finally, *borrowers* of large amounts of money often find themselves in good shape during an inflationary period because they can pay back their loans in inflated dollars, which are easy to come by.

It shouldn't be difficult to see which groups are the hardest hit by inflation. *Fixed-income families* suffer the most. These include, among others, the millions of marginal workers in low-paying, nonunion industries, retail clerks, hotel and restaurant workers, and others who work at or below the minimum wage.

Since borrowers gain as a result of inflation, *lenders* often lose out; so do *savers,* who watch (with great frustration and bitterness) their saved-up purchasing power evaporate under the heat of rising prices. The so-called "virtues" of a nation—hard work and thriftiness—become cruel hoaxes, and the "vices" of speculation and excessive borrowing are rewarded. Inflation becomes a silent economic disease that saps incentives—a disease that renders people unsure of the present economic reality and fearful of what the economic future will bring.

Unemployment

Now let's look at the other side of the trade-off dilemma—**unemployment.** To be unemployed means more than "just not having a job." By definition, a person is unemployed if they are actively seeking employment but cannot find work. To find out who is unemployed, the U.S. Census Bureau samples numerous households each month, asking the key question, "Have you been actively looking for work in the past four weeks?" If the person answers "yes" but has not been able to secure either part- or full-time employment, then they are considered officially "unemployed" by the federal government.

Surprisingly, not all unemployment is undesirable or harmful to the economy. Economists say that **frictional unemployment** affects about 4 percent of the labor force; people in this category are looking for work for the first time or are voluntarily changing jobs. They are actively seeking work, but their situation is not terribly serious. In fact, without some frictional unemployment, our economy would lose the measure of efficiency that is brought about by **labor mobility.** Since there is no way to reduce this kind of unemployment (and we would not necessarily want to), we can say that our economy is "fully employed" when we are at or near this 4-percent level. Putting it slightly differently, when 96 percent of all potential working people are employed, we can say that the labor force is operating at or near full capacity.

However, other categories or types of unemployment are more serious and often more intractable. For example, at any given time, there is a group of unemployed people that economists call **discouraged workers** who have simply given up hope of finding work. Although we don't know who all of these discouraged workers are, they include married, college-educated women who would like a good job but can find nothing available where they live and lack the mobility to move to where the jobs are. And there are middle-aged men and women who are fired, phased out, or indefinitely laid off; these individuals may have worked for years but now find that no one wants to hire them. There are also many Americans from minority groups who have simply given up trying to find jobs because of racial discrimination. These are just a few examples of the disappointed dropout workers who exist in an economic limbo.

Then there are the **structurally unemployed.** We already learned something about this group in Chapter 6. They are workers whose skills became obsolete or whose jobs disappeared when local businesses shut down or moved away. The problems of the structurally unemployed cannot be readily solved by more spending and greater economic expansion. These workers need to be retrained in new skills and often need assistance to relocate to areas where jobs are available.

Finally, we come to **Keynesian unemployment,** named after British economist John Maynard Keynes (1883–1946). This kind of unemployment results from a *lack of spending* and the resulting downturn of the business cycle (described at the beginning of the chapter). Keynes first devised the theory that this type of unemployment can be significantly reduced by *instituting government programs designed to stimulate additional* *spending.* This was indeed a revolutionary idea, as few economists before Keynes had ever dreamed of manipulating an economic system.

Of course, western economies had always experienced the business cycle (wide swings from unemployment to inflation and back to unemployment), but nineteenth- and early twentieth-century economists (often called **classical economists**) felt that an economy would automatically correct itself. It had to (they thought), because when output is produced by businesses, an equivalent amount of income must be generated by that production. As French economist Jean Baptiste Say (1767–1832) states in his famous **Say's Law,** "Supply creates its own demand."

So what did classical economists say would happen if we suddenly experienced a significant downturn in the business cycle, resulting in high unemployment? They reasoned that the unsold output would eventually force prices down. Low prices would, in turn, stimulate demand, and businesses would soon be rehiring their laid-off workers.

But what would happen if some people didn't get their jobs back? The classical economists had a logical answer for this, too. The lower wage would create an incentive for cost-conscious businesspeople to hire workers. The wage rate might drop considerably, but eventually everyone would be back at work, or so the reasoning went. The classical economist thought the worst thing that could happen to this neat, self-correcting system was to allow government to interfere. In short, the bywords of the classical age might have been "Stay cool and everything will take care of itself."

But then the Great Depression arrived. Something was terribly wrong. Unemployment went from bad to worse—and *stayed* that way year after year. Prices dropped; so did wages and interest rates. But there were no consumer spending sprees, and businesses did not invest or rehire the unemployed, even at the lower wage rates. Farmers found prices so low that at times they didn't bother to haul their crops to market. Incomes were so depressed that few consumers had sufficient purchasing power to buy up what was available. The nation was running out of patience. You don't "stay cool" for five years or more when you are out of work. What we needed was a new theory that worked. The time was ripe for the genius of John Maynard Keynes. Let's examine his theory in greater detail.

Keynes and the Great Depression

To understand Keynes's ideas fully, we must develop a new model of the economy. It will be something like our old market model, except that now we must consider the markets for *all* goods and services. When we talk about "total supply", we mean real GNP. When we speak of "total demand," we mean the sum of all types of spending: consumption, business investment, government, and net foreign spending.

What would the **total supply curve** look like in our new model? Recall that the single market supply curve (Chapter 3) describes how much of one product suppliers want to provide at different prices. We now want that same information with respect to total supply, but this time we are dealing with the variables of **spending** and **output,** not price and quantity.

Thus, we ask the suppliers (all businesses), "If total spending were $4 trillion, how much output (GNP) would you want to supply?" It should be obvious that if total spending ($C + I + G + X_n$) were at a level of $4 trillion, businesses would theoretically want to supply the *same* amount ($4 trillion) of GNP (see Figure 8-4a). Stated another way, suppliers would only produce $4 trillion of GNP if they thought consumers would buy it up.

All the other points on our total supply curve (see Figure 8-4b) are quite easy to locate. For example, if there were $8 trillion worth of spending ($C + I + G + X_n$), then businesses would want to supply $8 trillion worth of GNP output. In general, businesses would want to match any amount of spending with an equivalent amount of GNP supply. Each point dot on the total supply curve therefore falls on a straight line equally distant from both the output and spending axes. Our total supply curve (which doesn't really curve) therefore begins in the lower-left corner and shoots straight up to the right at an angle of 45°.

Now let's look at total demand. To construct our **total demand curve,** we must ask ourselves, "How do spenders react to changes in their incomes?" Let's look at an example. Suppose your individual income last year was $9000, but your income this year was reduced to $4000. What would happen to your spending pattern for this year? Most people faced with this situation would probably spend *more* than the $4000 income (in the short run at least). Let's say that you spend $8000, even though your income is only $4000. (For a while, therefore, you

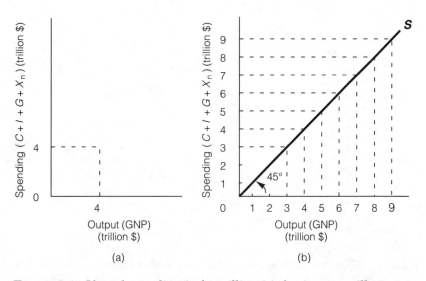

FIGURE 8-4 If total spending is $4 trillion (a), businesses will want to supply $4 trillion in GNP. At other levels of spending (b), businesses will also want to match each dollar amount spent with an equivalent amount of GNP output. The resulting *aggregate* (total) *supply curve* rises at a 45° angle.

will be borrowing money.) This point, which lies in the lower-left corner of the individual demand curve in Figure 8-5, represents something over $8000 in spending but only $4000 in income. Now suppose that you move up the income scale; your income is now $16,000, and you find that you are spending all of it. We will label this point on our demand curve "no savings." Finally, at a $32,000 income, you are able to save some money because you are spending only $24,000.

But what about the overall economy? Will the shape of the total demand curve, which comprises $C + I + G + X_n$, be similar to the demand curve in Figure 8-5? Yes. It is reasonable to assume that when our incomes are suddenly reduced, we tend to spend more (at least in the short run); if our incomes suddenly go up, we are more likely to save. Community spending patterns are therefore similar to the spending patterns of individual families.

Now let's see what the total supply curve and the total demand curve look like together. In Figure 8-6, note that we have added GNP (total output) to total income on the horizontal axis. You may wonder how we can equate both concepts. Are they the same?

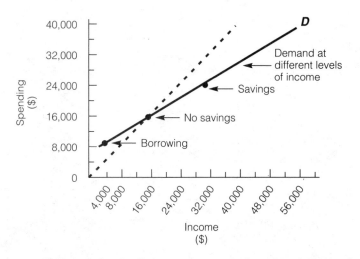

FIGURE 8-5   If an individual's income is severely reduced, he or she will tend to borrow money in the short run (note the point in the lower-left corner of the individual demand curve). A short-term rise in individual income makes savings more likely. At the "no savings" point somewhere in between these two income levels, a person's income is exactly equal to his or her spending.

Yes; for every dollar's worth of output, a dollar's worth of income is generated. Thus, if we added up the incomes from all economic activity (wages, rents, profits, and interest), the total would be equivalent to the final value of our goods and services (GNP). Take, for example, the chair you are presently sitting in. Isn't its final price a "summary" of all the different incomes that went into producing and distributing the chair? We therefore say that total income equals GNP.

Returning to Figure 8-6, we can see that there is an equilibrium level of income (point *B*) at which aggregate (total) supply crosses aggregate demand (just as in Chapter 3 we had an equilibrium for the supply of, and demand for, corn). To prove that point *B* must be the equilibrium level, let's see what happens when we are *not* at this point?

At point *A*, we find that the spending level ($C + I + G + X_n$) is *greater* than the amount of output produced. No equilibrium level of income can be achieved under these conditions, because if spending is greater than output, businesses must crank up production to meet the surplus demand. (Remember that businesses want to supply whatever is demanded.) Thus, at point *A*,

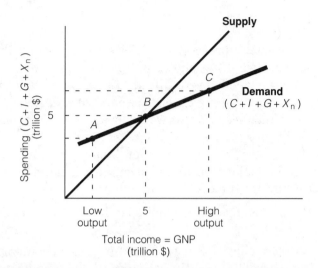

FIGURE 8-6 *Aggregate supply and demand:* at an equilibrium level (point *B*), the dollar value of GNP supplied ($5 trillion) is equal to the dollar value of total spending. If the economy temporarily functions at point *A* or point *C*, then market forces tend to move the economy back to equilibrium point *B*.

forces are set in motion that push output to higher levels (that is, toward point *B*).

The economy can't remain at point *C* for very long either. Here, the spending level is *less* than the amount of output. This situation forces producers to cut back on output, reducing GNP, and we soon return to the equilibrium level of income. *B* is the only point on our graph at which output exactly matches the level of spending; it is therefore the only point we might characterize as a **stable equilibrium.**

We are now ready to appreciate and understand Keynes's great discovery. Keynes saw that an economic system might be in a stable equilibrium at a *depression level of GNP.* Graphically, this means that if the supply curve crosses through the demand curve at a low level of national income, the country could economically sit there for years and years. Classical economists talked endlessly about declining wages and prices in the 1930s, but these same self-regulating mechanisms never pulled us out of the worst depression in U.S. history. What we needed was a new theory and, even more important, new policies to deal with the punishing economic realities.

Fiscal Policy

What was Keynes's prescription? If we closely study the total supply-demand graph, we should be able to see what Keynes had in mind. What is needed is to "lift up" the total demand curve to the point at which supply crosses demand at a *full-employment level of GNP*. Let's see how this would look on our supply-demand graph (see Figure 8-7).

Keynes's basic prescription for lifting the total demand curve was to have the government stimulate demand by *injecting new spending* into the economy in one of two ways:

1. By increasing government spending G (without altering taxes).

2. By decreasing taxes (without altering government spending, thereby increasing consumption expenditures C).

Either or both of these **fiscal** (budgetary) **policies** will shift the total demand curve upward, as we can see in Figure 8-7.

Now look closely again at this figure. Do you notice anything unusual? A careful examination of the upward shift in demand shows that a relatively *small* increase in spending results in a *large* increase in income and output. For example, a $10 billion increase in government spending might result in a $20 billion (or greater) increase in GNP. In short, any extra dollars spent are supercharged dollars! Economists call this the **multiplier effect.**

Why are these new spending dollars multiplied? Let's consider an example. If the government cuts my taxes by $5, my personal income will increase by $5. I may spend all or part of that $5. Let's say I save $1 and spend the rest. My $4 expenditure suddenly becomes *extra income* for someone else (perhaps the plumber who fixed my leaky kitchen sink). The plumber, in turn, may save a little of this extra income and spend the remainder, as will the next person, and the next. Now if $4 of extra spending has a supercharged effect, so will an extra $5 billion, or $50 billion. Of course, this effect can work in reverse, too; a $5 billion reduction in spending will obviously reduce GNP by much more than the original $5 billion.

Although the strategy to cure a recession can be rather simply stated—increase government spending and reduce taxes—the administration of these policies is another story. Any time you adjust expenditures and taxes you are tampering with the

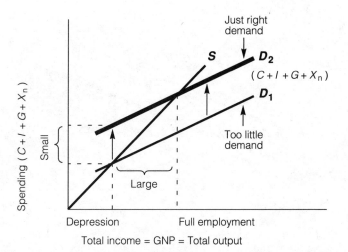

Figure 8-7 *The Keynesian solution:* if there is insufficient total demand in the economy (D_1), a depression may be avoided if the government institutes policies to increase total spending to D_2. Note that a relatively *small* increase in demand can create a relatively *large* increase in GNP. This is called the *multiplier effect*.

federal budget. What would the impact on our federal budget be if we lowered taxes and simultaneously increased government expenditures? We would obviously have a **deficit,** and budgetary deficits are usually considered "bad economics." Indeed, in the 1930s, "spending your way into prosperity" seemed rather odd to some and even dangerous to others. The federal budget simply *had* to be balanced.

The Great Depression of the 1930s might therefore have been avoided by federal budgetary manipulation. Even as recently as the Kennedy administration, members of Congress were not totally receptive to the idea of stimulating the economy with a tax cut. However, when the Kennedy tax bill was passed in 1964, the sluggish economy steamed ahead with such speed that the taxes collected on higher incomes eventually paid back the deficit incurred by the original tax cut!

It was, in fact, the spending for the Vietnam War *and* expensive social programs (in the late 1960s) plus the huge upsurge in OPEC oil prices (during the mid-1970s) that spoiled what might have been an age of real economic growth with only moderate inflation. Instead, the decade of the 1970s brought Americans a new and painful period of high inflation.

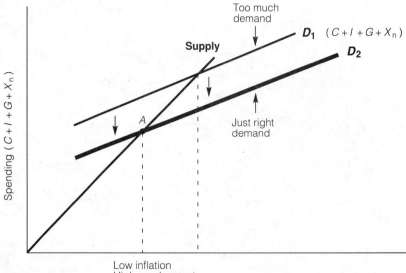

Figure 8-8 If there is too much total demand (D_1), inflation may be avoided if the government sets up policies to reduce total demand to a *noninflationary level* of GNP (D_2).

What would Keynes have said about inflation? What fiscal policies would be in order now? To answer this, let's take a look at how the problem of inflation affects the graph of total supply and total demand (see Figure 8-8).

Obviously, the problem is now *too much demand*. The economy is producing at full capacity (maximum output), but the spending level is even greater than the available GNP. It's a classic example of demand-pull inflation, when "too many dollars are chasing after too few goods."

Looking at Figure 8-8, we see that demand curve D_1 intersects the supply curve S far above the point of full-employment GNP and should be brought down to a *noninflationary* point. Although we may not be able to achieve the ideal of zero inflation and full employment at the same time (recall the trade-off problem), there is no reason why we cannot aim for minimal inflation with relatively high employment (point A).

The correct anti-inflationary prescription to pull demand down is to raise taxes, lower government spending, and generally work toward a budgetary **surplus**. Indeed, this solution seems relatively simple. So why is it so difficult to administer an anti-inflationary economic policy?

To come to grips with the problem of inflation, we must understand the mysteries of the political process, since fiscal policy is ultimately decided by the President and the Congress. Let's return for a moment to Keynes's prescription for combating unemployment. Although there were some qualms about budgetary deficits at one time, the remedies themselves (cutting taxes and increasing spending) can be almost "enjoyable" for a politician. Everyone likes a hefty tax cut, and special-interest groups—from the Army to the Peace Corps, from the poverty worker to the peanut farmer—thrive on additional spending programs. So the cure for a recession is kind of a "welcome problem," because every politician from the President on down stands to gain in popularity with each new tax cut, each new subsidized program, and each additional worker put back on the job.

Inflation is something else, however. Following up on the economists' recommendations to increase taxes and cut back vested interest programs can be political suicide. In fact, a number of economists have concluded that the Keynesian remedies for inflation are simply inoperable because of these political realities.

Thus, until the 1970s, we could say that the Keynesian revolution in economic policy gave us a good measure of economic security. Indeed, the United States has been pretty good at avoiding serious economic downturns since the 1930s. Most economists felt then that unless new and unknown factors (war, global drought, a world debt crisis, etc.), occurred in the near future, the United States would probably never live through another Great Depression—thanks, in a large part, to Keynes!

But then the 1970s arrived, with an energy crunch and unacceptable rates of inflation. Suddenly Keynesian policies did not seem to be working. Not only was there political paralysis in dealing with inflation (including the failure of price-wage controls), but the country was also moving toward a new era of inflation *and* recession combined. By the mid-1970s, we were hearing the ominous word **stagflation** (stagnation + inflation) more and more. By 1975, it was apparent that for the first time in our history, we would have inflation rates of greater than 8 percent, combined with a bonafide recession! Some economists were advocating contractive fiscal policies to combat inflation; others wanted just the opposite—large tax cuts to help put people back to work. In short, there were no longer any simple Keynesian remedies.

Supply-Side Economics

Thus, the stage was set in the early 1980s for a new approach—**supply-side economics**—to emerge. Supply-side theory revolves around two key ideas that are intimately intertwined: economic incentives and economic growth. More specifically, it assumes that what our stagflated economy needs is not an additional spending stimulus but *greater incentives to improve the supply of goods and services.*

The government (under the Reagan administration) chose to encourage these incentives by *reducing overall tax rates.* The centerpiece supply-side legislation, initiated in 1981 and reinforced in 1986, included large, across-the-board, individual tax-rate cuts designed to *stimulate work efforts and generate greater savings.* It was hoped that these reforms would (in the long run) translate into more investment spending and that this additional investment plus the work incentive would, in turn, *enhance the nation's productivity* (output per worker). Improved productivity might then moderate inflation and promote growth. Finally, the resulting growth (according to supply-side theory) would generate such a large increase in the nation's income that the additional tax revenues would eventually pay back the short-term loss of revenue caused by the lower tax rates. If everything worked as intended, a balanced budget and higher growth and productivity would be achieved without any inflationary penalty.

Supply-side recommendations also included offering greater incentives for business investment and for research and development and reducing the web of government regulation that often frustrates business activity and adds to production costs. Supply-side theorists claimed that far too much attention was being paid to stimulating the demand side of the economy, to enforcing cumbersome regulations, and to evolving a tax system that discouraged saving, risk-taking, and work effort, thereby diminishing the supply side of the equation.

Actually, supply-side economics is not an entirely new idea. Say emphasized supply, which he was certain would "create its own demand" sooner or later. Economic philosophers David Hume (1711–1776) and Charles Montesquieu (1689–1775) warned their eighteenth-century readers that excessive tax rates would result in a diminishing work effort. In fact, perhaps no one described the central thesis of supply-side economics better than Montesquieu, when he wrote

Nature is just to all mankind; she repays them for their labors; she renders them industrious because she attaches the greatest recompense to the greatest works. But if an arbitrary power snatches away the rewards of nature, one will learn distaste for work, and inactivity will appear to be the only good.[32]

Montesquieu's sentiments undoubtedly hit a responsive chord among Reagan's economic theorists, who were eagerly looking forward to the predicted benefits of the supply-side tax legislation and other initiatives.

Unfortunately, however, these supply-side policies did not achieve many hoped-for goals. For one thing, annual federal deficits had ballooned to unheard of heights by the end of the Reagan era. The **public debt** (the summation of all yearly federal deficits) nearly tripled from $909 billion in 1980 to $2.6 *trillion* in 1988. (A trillion, keep in mind, is equivalent to a thousand billion.) Nor did the U.S. savings rate improve. In fact, for a number of years, it actually declined. And productivity—a key to long-run inflation control and ultimately to our overall standard of living—continued at a low and worrisome rate. From 1980 to 1988, productivity increases averaged only 1.3 percent per year (about the same rate as in the 1970s and only one-half the rate of the 1960s). These were all, most experts agree, serious and continuing problems.

On the positive side of the performance ledger, the Reagan administration (with decisive help from the Federal Reserve System) had reduced the inflation rate significantly by 1983; thereafter, Americans enjoyed not dramatic growth, but steady improvements in the real GNP and relatively low joblessness. The economy kept plugging away, showing positive growth rates, and had achieved the longest peace-time expansion (with no recession) in U.S. history by the turn of the decade. Economists disagree as to whether supply-side policies should be credited for this economic growth or whether the credit should go to "old-fashioned" Keynesian deficit spending, combined with a concurrent expansion of consumer and business debt. Indeed, such interpretations are part of a continuing and healthy debate among economists and others who are concerned about the direction and performance of our economy.

Recall, too, that another group of economists see the future as a period of dwindling global resources and are skeptical about the possibility of continued economic expansion. Their ideas, in contrast to those of Reagan supply-siders and Keynesian demand-siders, revolve around how to rearrange the economic system so that we can be reasonably well off without continual exponential economic growth.

At any rate, new theories eventually supersede the old. Creative and innovative ideas, combined with specific policies to deal with changing economic conditions, are continually needed. Hence, we will always be looking for economic philosophers like Adam Smith or John Maynard Keynes—this time, however, for one who can match wits with our own troubled times.

Questions for Thought and Discussion

1. What are some solutions for "stagflation"?

2. What is a "peace dividend"? If the nation had a peace dividend of $100 billion dollars, how, in your opinion, should we use it? List priorities and defend your list.

3. Why did the classical economists cling so defiantly to their theory?

4. How can we say that output equals employment when they are not expressed in the same units of measure?

5. In the 1960s it was not uncommon to hear the opinion: "We need a war to maintain our prosperity." Evaluate this statement in terms of your knowledge of fiscal policy and recent economic history.

9

Money

Imagine that you and 50 friends, acquaintances, and relatives are all shipwrecked on a large, lovely island in the middle of the South Pacific. At first, it is an idyllic life as everyone lounges on the sunny beach waiting for the rescue ship to sail into view, but after a few days you begin to realize the seriousness of your predicament. With grim faces, everyone gathers on the beach to map out some kind of survival plan.

A governing body is elected, and soon the necessary tasks are taken up by different individuals. Since Joe Jones is a carpenter, he volunteers to build thatched huts for everyone. Smith and Baker are assigned to make fishing boats and nets. Chester Olson will gather wild foods for the community larder.

Time passes. The island economy becomes more specialized and complex. Before too long, major problems arise as people experience bottlenecks in their transactions. They become frustrated when they attempt to get their thatched roofs mended or to obtain food for the evening meal. What's wrong?

The problem is that our little economy has become so complex that some kind of monetary system is needed. The islanders are currently using the **barter system,** freely exchanging goods and services when they are needed. This works fine on a limited scale, but when a few more jobs are assigned to

1st day

Dear Journal:
There are 50 of us now stranded on this island due to our shipwreck. Weather's sunny and rescue boat is due soon. Found a polaroid camera.

2nd day

We elected a governing body today and assigned tasks to everyone. Joe will be building huts, Smith & Baker will be making fishing boats & nets, and Chester will be hunting for wild foods.

a few more people, the community begins to encounter some major problems.

As an example, suppose that your specific skill is mending clothing. One day you decide you would like some of Chester's wild foods, and you propose to trade your services for part of Chester's stores. Unfortunately, Chester tells you he doesn't need any of his clothing mended, so what do you do? In a moneyless economy, you must find a third party who not only needs clothing mended but also has a service that Chester wants. If you can't find that third person, you will be temporarily out of luck. Trying to track down all the people that you need to make all the exchanges you require would be time-consuming and exhausting. And, in the long run, you still might not locate the necessary people to make your final exchange.

Everyone on the island is becoming more and more convinced of the need to develop some kind of monetary system to make it easier to exchange goods and services. When **money** is effectively doing its job, it functions as a universally accepted *medium of exchange*. It also acts as a *standard of value*. As such, a **money supply** has a single monetary unit (for example, a dollar) that is a common denominator for all economic goods and services. (It's really amazing, for example, that we can use the same unit of currency to compare a dollar's worth of hamburger with a billion-dollar space telescope.) Finally, money can be used as a *store of value*. It can be saved or spent, hoarded or invested. It's a marvelous tool, and, without a doubt, one of our most useful inventions.

The islanders elect a banker (John Jacob Harrison III) and give him the responsibility of devising a monetary system for the island. Since John has never thought much about the characteristics of money, he forms a banking committee to discuss the issue. "First, let's list the different attributes that our new money system should have," John says, as the committee sits down for a meeting. Baker makes the first point: "Whatever we use for money must be fairly *durable* and something that can be *easily transferred* from person to person." Everyone nods in agreement.

After a moment's silence, Joe Jones suddenly says, "There must be a basic unit (like the dollar) that can be *divided* into smaller units as well as *multiplied* into larger units, right?" The group feels that although this is a sound point in theory, it is

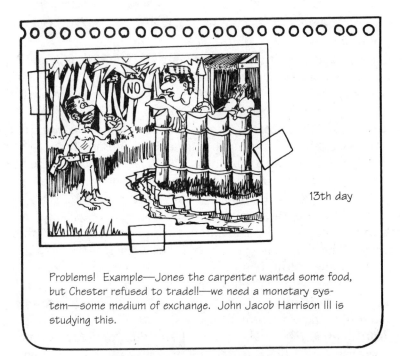

13th day

Problems! Example—Jones the carpenter wanted some food, but Chester refused to trade!!—we need a monetary system—some medium of exchange. John Jacob Harrison III is studying this.

15th day

John Jacob Harrison III's report: Money must be durable, easily transferred, divisible, have limited supply, and be easily duplicated only by the island bank.

16th day

Still money problems—what to use! The suggestions so far are buttons, braided hair, shoelaces, and notes from the banking committee.

Lots of argument

17th day

Today we've finally agreed on issuing bank committee notes!! They will be our official monetary units—each one will contain the signatures of each member of our banking committee.

impractical on the island, where supplies of suitable materials for money are limited.

Chester, sitting off by himself, is thinking very hard about something. He suddenly stands up and says, "Hold on, hold on. The most important thing about money is its *limited supply*—too much of the stuff will make it worthless." Everyone is impressed by Chester's insight. John (the banker) says, "You're absolutely right, Chester, but you haven't gone far enough." There is a hushed silence as John formulates his thoughts and then continues: "Yes, our money supply must be limited, but we must also be able to *expand the amount of money in the economy as the economy itself expands.* We have a problem here," the island banker continues, "because whatever we use for money must be easy for us (the authorized bankers) to duplicate but very difficult or impossible for any unauthorized person to counterfeit. Therefore, we need to be very careful in our choice of what to use as money."

Baker thinks that we could use buttons as monetary units. "The banking committee would need authorization to remove all the buttons from the islanders' clothing . . ."—but before Baker can say another word, he is told to sit down and think of something else. Someone else suggests shoelaces, pointing out that the laces could be cut up into different denominations. Other suggestions include everything from braided hair to pieces of paper signed by the banking committee. It might be worth our while to pause here, leave the island for a moment, and delve a little deeper into the actual history of money. Where did it get its first foothold? And how did it evolve into the monetary systems of today? Let's take a closer look.

The Origins of Money

No one knows for sure, but it's quite likely that the earliest medium of exchange was what economists call **commodity money**—money that has intrinsic worth in the form of some kind of valuable commodity. Some archaeologists suggest that the first commodity money may have been grain, which humans began to cultivate in small farming communities approximately 10,000 years ago. Such a scenario implies that some sort of standardized "measure of grain" became the commonly accepted "standard of value." We do know that roughly 4000 years ago, the Babylonian Code of Hammurabi specified that unskilled workers were to be paid in grain, and archaeological research has revealed that grain banking was prevalent in ancient Egypt. Commodity money is also implied in our common financial term "pecuniary" (meaning "of or involving money"), which was derived from the Latin word *pecus* and originally referred to a "head of cattle."

The first coins came into use in Greece somewhere between 700 and 1000 B.C. The advantage of using coins was that their weight or volume did not have to constantly be measured out, as grain did; a coin could therefore be accepted "on sight." This characteristic undoubtedly added to the efficiency of doing business in a money economy, and thus coins became the currency of choice in the early Greek and Roman worlds. These coins were made of metal, but other cultures and communities used different forms of standardized monetary objects made out of bone, shells, baked clay, and similar materials.

Henry Lindgren, whose interest lies in the psychology of money, informs us that the Greeks first stamped their coins with the faces of their gods. It didn't take too long, however, for Greek political leaders to spread a little propaganda by changing the faces of the gods to appear more and more like their own:

> Once Alexander was dead, all doubt about his divinity vanished. Coins bearing the head of Hercules continued to be issued in Alexander's name by local mints, but Hercules now distinctly resembled Alexander. As far as the man in the street was concerned, the face *was* that of the deified Alexander. These coins, which circulated throughout the ancient world for hundreds of years, gave visible support to the Alexander legend.[33]

Thus, not only did money help to expand trade and commerce, but it also helped to bind large and disparate communities together and to legitimize political leadership. In addition, historians have suggested that the sciences and arts of this highly civilized Greek and Roman period were, in part, byproducts of expanded money and trade and the concurrent improvement in the standard of living.

The first coins were probably commodity money consisting of gold or silver (or, in the case of the early Greek "Dumps,"— bean-shaped lumps—that were amalgams of precious metals). With the expansion of trade and the inherent limitations of mining sufficient quantities of gold and silver, the Greeks and others eventually turned to what we call **fiat money**—money that is *declared by the government to have value*. Such coinage becomes mere **token money,** since its metal content (usually bronze and copper) is decidedly less than the face value of the coin. Paper currency (such as our own dollars) would also be, by definition, fiat money. The Chinese are believed to have used the first paper money, which (as reported by Marco Polo) was made out of the bark of the mulberry tree.*

Returning once more to our desert island example, the banking committee now must consider whether to go with commodity money (shoelaces, buttons, etc.) or fiat money made up and issued by the committee itself. They finally decide, with great solemnity, to issue signed pieces of paper as their official money supply.

The last problem the islanders must face is how they are going to make the new currency valuable. What, in fact, makes *any* currency valuable? Shifting from our desert island to the U.S. economy, we might ask, "What makes our own dollar valuable?"

The U.S. Dollar

Many people are under the misconception that the government "backs up" the value of every dollar with a precious commodity metal, such as gold or silver. They may be surprised to discover that the last vestige of gold backing (25 cents the dollar) was removed by Congress in 1967. Thus, the $1 or $5 bill in your pocket or wallet is unbacked fiat money.

If you check the front of a $1 bill (or any U.S. paper currency), you will see to the upper left the declaration "THIS NOTE IS LEGAL TENDER FOR ALL DEBTS, PUBLIC AND PRIVATE." This printed statement does not, however, guarantee the inherent value and spending potential of the bill. Other currencies with similar declarations have hyperinflated to the point of uselessness, grossly eroding the public's faith and purchasing power. No,

*I am indebted to Professor Henry Lindgren for the details in this discussion of monetary history. [See Lindgren's *Great Expectations* (Los Altos, CA: William Kaufmann, 1980).]

what makes our dollars valuable is really a matter of *social trust*. Money is valuable because we have faith that *each one of us will accept it as a legitimate medium of exchange*. If all of a sudden everyone thought that money had no value, then indeed it would have no value.

Fortunately, there is no reason for people to abandon faith in their dollars—unless, of course, the government doesn't do its job. If, for example, the government issued *too much* money, then money would become too plentiful, and there would be a relative shortage of things to buy. We would then experience inflation. Under extreme conditions of hyperinflation, the public could lose faith in government currency and return to bartering or develop black-market currencies.

On the other hand, if there is *not enough* money to go around, normal economic transactions would be stifled, which can also be dangerous for the economy. Just the right balance between output and money must be achieved for our dollars to remain valuable.

There was a time, however, when our citizens did not accept the legitimacy of the federal currency. The man who became our first President spoke with great fervor on this subject:

> George Washington . . . denounced those who refused to accept at full value the bills of the Continental Congress as "pests to society and the greatest enemies we have to the happiness of America. I would to God that some one of the more atrocious in each state was hung in gibbets upon a gallows five times as high as the one prepared by Haman.[34]

People do not put their faith and trust in a monetary system automatically; the public's faith and trust must be earned by careful monetary regulation and controls. How then is the U.S. money supply controlled? This is a good question, but one that most Americans probably would not answer correctly.

It is generally thought that our money supply is controlled simply by turning the printing presses on and off. If we want more money, the government just prints it up. This notion is only partly true, since our money supply (our assets that can be *spent immediately*) is more than just *currency* (bills and coins); it is also in the form of **demand deposits,** or checking accounts. Today, in fact, there is considerably more money in demand deposits than in total currency. Thus, to control the money supply, we must be able to regulate these demand-deposit dollars as well as the paper currency. How is this done?

Think of the billions of dollars in checking accounts throughout the United States. Much of this money must be derived from a variety of credit forms, such as mortgages, installment credit, and business credit. Thus, it is reasonable to assume that if the government could *manipulate credit conditions* in some way, it would have some control over the money supply. Easy credit conditions usually mean more loans; more loans, in turn, mean more dollars flowing through the economy.

Thus, if the government can control credit conditions, not only can it affect the money supply but also, perhaps more importantly, it can influence the total amount of spending. This means that whoever is in charge of the money supply (through credit manipulation) can have as much power over the economic system as those who control the federal budget. We already know that the President and Congress regulate the budget, but who is responsible for regulating credit conditions and the money supply?

The Federal Reserve System

The money supply is determined and regulated in large part by our central banking system, the **Federal Reserve System** (often simply called "the Fed"). In fact, if we were to pinpoint where major decisions are made on money matters, we would zero in on the seven-person Board of Governors of the Federal Reserve System in Washington, D.C. From there, we would move down to the 12 regional Federal Reserve Banks situated in major cities around the country. Take a moment to look at a $1 bill and see from which Federal Reserve Bank it was issued. (The source is written around the large letter to the left of Washington's face.) Your dollar was probably issued by a Federal Reserve Bank nearby. Three bills randomly selected from my wallet came from Minneapolis (I), St. Louis (H), and Chicago (G).

Monetary control then flows from the 12 regional Federal Reserve Banks down to the commercial banks that "belong" to the Federal Reserve System. These commercial banks, often called **member banks,** hold stock in the Federal Reserve System and are required to follow certain policies established by the Fed. Perhaps you know of a "First National" bank in your area; you can be sure that it is one of these member banks.

Not all banks belong to the Fed, however. Only about one-third of all commercial banks are members of the system. Before 1980, this distinction was fairly important because member banks had to meet stiffer requirements that tied up money that could otherwise be earning interest. Thus, it was not surprising to see a sizable number of national banks defect from Fed membership and become state banks, so that they could, in effect, utilize more of their funds.

In this pre-1980 period, even greater distinctions were made between regular banks and other so-called "thrift" institutions, such as savings and loans (S&Ls) and credit unions. For example, an S&L was allowed to offer savers slightly higher interest returns, with the expectation that they would specialize in meeting their community's housing loan needs. They were not, however, allowed to compete with banks on several fronts, including the issuing of checking accounts. Rigid compartmentalization was the rule of the day.

All this changed during the deregulation of the Carter and Reagan administrations. Specifically, the Depository Institutions Deregulation and Monetary Control Act of 1980 phased in new policies that effectively blurred many previous distinctions. Today, as you probably know, all depository institutions can offer their customers some type of checking (demand-deposit) account. In return for this privilege, these institutions adhere to many of the same rules that member banks follow, including the same reserve requirements; this, in turn, helps the Federal Reserve to maintain its broad-based control of the credit system. Putting it another way, the Deregulation Act of 1980 created a competitive "free-for-all" that essentially made all financial institutions rivals for the same business. How then do these banks and thrift institutions make their profits?

The profit philosophy is actually quite simple: "Borrow money cheap; lend it dear." The difference between the rate of interest paid out for saving, checking, and other depositor accounts and the rate of interest charged for mortgage, installment, and business loans is the primary source of industry profits. Thus, the major responsibility of commercial banks and thrift institutions is to take in the deposits from those who want to save and to lend out that money to those who want to borrow. These institutions are what economists call **financial intermediaries**—the middle operators (and profiteers) between savers and investors.

If commercial banks and thrift institutions hold deposits and make loans, then what do regional Federal Reserve Banks do? Each regional bank is a kind of "banker's bank"; it also holds deposits and makes loans. The deposits are called **reserves** (hence, "Federal Reserve"), and the loans are called **discounts.** The regional reserve banks also function as clearinghouses for the millions and millions of checks sent around the country, and they supervise the member banks in their region. Finally, the 12 regional Federal Reserve Banks supply their districts with Federal Reserve Notes (the commonly used paper currency in our wallets).

However, the real power within the Federal Reserve System—the power to influence credit and spending and, ultimately, unemployment and inflation—rests with the Board of Governors and its various committees. How does the Board influence the money supply, and what mysterious tools does this small band of government bankers have at its command?

We learned earlier in this chapter that *the key to influencing the money supply is the control of credit.* Therefore, when the Fed makes it difficult for the commercial banking system to give out loans, the growth of the money supply should slow down. When loans are easy to obtain, the money supply should grow at a faster rate. But how can the loan decisions of individual financial officers throughout the country be regulated? To see how this is done, we must return to the concept of reserves.

Every bank and every other depository institution must set aside a certain percentage of its deposits in the form of reserves. For example, Federal Reserve guidelines might say that your local bank must set aside at least 12 percent of its total demand deposits (assets in checking accounts). We call this percentage the **reserve ratio.** Let's look at an example to see how this works.

Suppose that you live in Central City, New York, and that your newly established commercial bank has an initial deposit of $1000 in demand deposits. If the reserve ratio for checking accounts is 12 percent, then your bank must set aside a reserve of $120. However, the directors of the Central City First National Bank might decide that if they want to make any loans, they should maintain some *excess reserves* above and beyond the required $120. Do you see why?

If any customers borrow money from the Central City bank and then cash their loan checks at another bank, Central City would lose those reserves and the other bank would gain them. Assume that our bank (with only $120 in reserves) just loans Sarah Smith $500, which she immediately deposits in her checking account. If Sarah later decides to take the full $500 and spend it all out of state while vacationing in Florida, then the Central City bank won't have sufficient funds to transfer to the Florida bank. (Remember that all payments between banks involve a transfer of reserves.) Therefore, to *safely* loan Sarah the $500, Central City bank would be wise to have at least $500 in excess reserves to cover the loan.

In summary, a bank's capacity to lend out money depends primarily on the size of its excess reserves. When large amounts of excess reserves are generally distributed throughout the country, we usually find *easy* money conditions; if commercial banks around the country are holding few excess reserves, we can expect *tight* money conditions. We should also note that when "new" dollars are loaned out (and "new" money is created), other banks receive this additional money. These banks can, in turn, use this money (after holding the required fraction of reserves) to further expand the money supply—in a way similar to the multiplier effect we examined in Chapter 8. Naturally, this monetary multiplier works in reverse if there is a net reduction in commercial loans.

Monetary Policy

The obvious question we must now ask is, "Since the key to controlling credit conditions and the money supply lies in controlling excess reserves, exactly how does the Federal Reserve influence the amount of excess reserves in the banking system?"

One way is simply *by raising or lowering the reserve ratio.* To use an exaggerated example, what would happen if the Fed increased the reserve ratio from 12 to 20 percent? The excess reserves of all U.S. commercial lending institutions would suddenly be diminished by billions and billions of dollars, and credit would become tight. On the other hand, if the Fed lowered the reserve ratio requirement, then the excess reserves of all depository institutions would automatically expand and credit conditions would ease up. Power over the reserve ratio therefore translates into power over the money supply.

Another monetary tool the Fed uses to manipulate excess reserves is the buying and selling of government securities, called **open-market operations.** U.S. commercial banks presently hold billions of dollars worth of government obligations in the form of bonds, notes, and other securities. Banks purchase these securities because the government frequently offers them at attractive interest rates. To *reduce* excess reserves, all the Fed has to do is *sell* more securities to the member banks. This reduction comes about because banks pay for the securities by *taking the money out of their reserve accounts.* The immediate lowering of these reserves thus reduces the potential loaning capacity of the commercial banks, tightening money conditions throughout the economy.

If, instead, the Fed decides to *buy* securities from commercial banks, then the process is reversed. The money from the Fed will enlarge the reserve accounts of the banks, and more "potential" money will be available for customer loans. Buying back securities from the banks may therefore result in more loans, an increase in the money supply, and (it is hoped) more spending.

The specific group that decides whether to buy or sell government securities to member banks is the **Open Market Committee.** It should be noted that open-market operations are used more frequently than the manipulation of the reserve ratio is adjusted. When the Fed changes the reserve ratio—(particularly upward), it causes great hardships for banks that are "all loaned up," or have already lent out their maximum amounts of money. The flexibility and ease of the open-market operation make it the number one monetary tool used by the Federal Reserve.

Our last major monetary control is called the **discount rate.** Remember from our earlier discussion that one of the Fed's services to member banks and other depository institutions is a borrowing privilege. These loans are discounts, and the interest rate on these loans is the discount rate. By *raising* the discount rate, the Fed discourages borrowing. Banks that reduce the amount of money they borrow from the Fed will have less money to lend out to their own customers.

On the other hand, *lowering* the discount rate encourages some bank borrowing; these banks will then have more excess reserves to meet the local demand for mortgages, installment loans, etc. Lowering the discount rate can also *indirectly* influence other interest rates throughout the economy. For example, when the discount rate is lowered, most banks are inclined to "return the favor" by lowering interest rates on their own loans.

These three controls—the reserve ratio, open-market operations, and the discount rate—are the monetary tools that the Fed uses not only to regulate the money supply but also to help stabilize the economy.

Now let's summarize what we learned about monetary policies and apply that to what we already know about supply and demand. First, we consider inflation. If our country were facing severe inflation, the Fed would probably do one, two, or all of the following:

1. Raise the reserve ratio.

2. Raise the discount rate.

3. Sell government securities.

This monetary policy leads to:

Less excess reserves.
↓
Less commercial loans.
↓
Less money.
↓
Higher interest rates.

If money becomes very scarce, overall interest rates can go "sky high," as they did in 1970, 1974, and the early 1980s. The combined impact of high interest rates and tight money conditions usually discourages business investment spending and dampens consumer demand for interest-sensitive durables, such as automobiles and housing. This sequence of events ultimately leads to a reduction in investment spending and is the basis of the Fed's anti-inflationary monetary policies.

We have come full circle. Our economic controls for influencing spending are now complete.

Recall our graphs of total supply and total demand in Figures 8-6, 8-7, and 8-8. There, we described the Keynesian fiscal policies that could raise or lower consumption spending C through changes in taxes and government spending G. The total

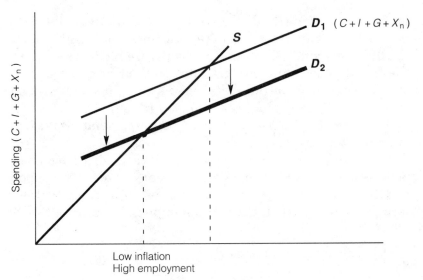

FIGURE 9-1 If the economy experiences high inflation due to excess de-mand (D_1), then the Federal Reserve can undertake *anti-inflationary* monetary policies to lower demand to a noninflationary level of GNP (D_2).

demand curve may rise or fall, depending on whether we are facing inflation or recession.

Now we know that monetary policies also have a profound impact on a third important component of total spending—investment spending I. Monetary policies that combat inflation will therefore affect our graph of total supply and total demand as shown in Figure 9-1.

In a recession, the appropriate monetary policies for easing credit are:

1. Lower the reserve ratio.

2. Lower the discount rate.

3. Buy government securities.

In theory, then, excess reserves will increase first. Then, as the money supply grows, credit will be easier to obtain. More money in the system will eventually drive interest rates down. Easier money and low interest rates should encourage investment spending, which, in turn, will help to lift up the total demand curve (see Figure 9-2).

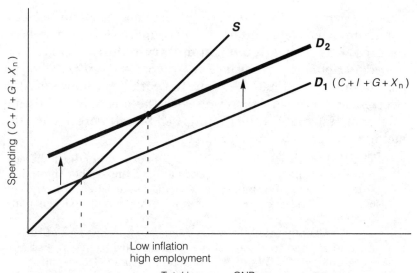

FIGURE 9-2   If the economy is sluggish as a result of too little demand (D_1), then the Federal Reserve can undertake *anti-recessionary* monetary policies to stimulate investment spending I, thereby expanding aggregate demand to D_2.

How closely do these theories match reality? Economists are quick to point out that monetary policies are more effective in combating inflation than recession. During an inflationary period, the monetary screw can be tightened until money and credit are actually squeezed off. In 1970 and again in 1981, we experienced some of the harmful side effects of *ultratight* money— for example, a "depression" in the housing industry when mortgage rates were driven to unreasonable levels.

On the other hand, lowering interest rates and making credit easily available does not force businesses to increase investments. During the Great Depression, for example, interest rates were very low, but the other negative factors—the stock-market slump, low incomes, loss of confidence, and general pessimism—far outweighed the expansionary effects of easy money.

The Federal Reserve is currently in a "Keynesian mode," as we described earlier. The Board of Governors is, in effect making a *conscious* effort to adjust credit, the money supply, and interest rates (which eventually impact on business investments and consumption spending) to forestall current or projected economic problems. This interventionist approach has also been referred to as **discretionary monetary policy.**

Paul Hellman, writing for *The Wall Street Journal's* editorial page (January 31, 1990), has some fun with Fed Chairman Alan Greenspan's incessant tinkering with the economy—adjusting this, adjusting that—as if he (or his Fed Board) were playing the metaphoric role of "auto mechanic":

> The Fed sometimes must roll up its sleeves and adjust the economic machinery. The Fed spends a lot of time either tightening things or loosening things, or debating about whether to tighten or loosen. Imagine a customer taking his car into Greenspan's Garage.
>
> Normally calm, Skeezik Greenspan took one look at the car and started to sweat. This would be hard to fix—it was an economy car: "What's the problem?" asked Greenspan.
>
> "It's been running beautifully for over six years now," said the customer. "But recently it's been acting sluggish."
>
> "These cars are tricky," said Greenspan.
>
> "We can always loosen a few screws, as long as you don't mind the side effects."
>
> "What side effects?" asked the customer.
>
> "Nothing at first," said Greenspan. "We won't even know if the repairs have worked for at least a year. After that, either everything will be fine, or your car will accelerate wildly and go totally out of control."
>
> "Just as long as it doesn't stall," said the customer. "I hate that."

All humor aside, this description does tend to approximate the school of thought that our economy needs an activist Federal Reserve. It should be noted, however, that there is a group of economists who feel that this tinkering (sometimes called "fine tuning") creates more problems that it solves. They call themselves **monetarists** and include, among others, Nobel Prize winner Milton Friedman and Allan Meltzer, who is affiliated with Carnegie Mellon University. Let's take a brief look at some of their arguments and suggestions.

Monetarism

Inherent in the **monetarist philosophy** is a distinct distrust of government in general and a specific distrust of the government's ability to know enough about current and future economic conditions to *time* its interventionist policies accurately to stabilize the business cycle. Friedman, for one, has looked at the historical data of monetary growth versus economic performance and concluded that the Fed's tendency toward frequent intervention has actually been counterproductive: Fed policies—undertaken in good faith—have produced even *greater,* not lesser, swings in the business cycle, according to Friedman.

For monetarists, money indeed "matters"; it is the chief determinant of current macroeconomic problems. On the other hand, money has the potential to contribute to macroeconomic solutions. The way to achieve economic stability, as the monetarist sees it, is by a simple **monetary rule:** increase the money supply at a relatively constant rate month after month, year after year.

Friedman advocates an increase of 3–5 percent per year—an expansion in the money supply commensurate with the potential long-run growth rate of overall economic activity. Surges in money growth will, according to Friedman, eventually result in inflation; discretionary cuts, after a time-lag, will move the economy toward recession. Given the monetarist's strict 3–5 percent rule, we would no longer use a "heroic" metaphor for the role of the Federal Reserve Chairman (even Hellman's "auto mechanic" would be inappropriate). According to the monetarist view, stable money growth creates the optimal conditions for long-run economic success—like a robotic dispenser feeding monetary nourishment on a predictable and steady basis to a healthy, growing economy.

In conclusion, whatever role the Fed takes or the dilemmas it faces, today or in the future, it will nonetheless continue to be a critical economic institution—hopefully one that helps to maintain a stable economy, a healthy financial system, and most importantly, a trustworthy monetary base from which we can all go about our private economic affairs with a feeling of confidence.

Questions for Thought and Discussion

1. Should a tight monetary policy or an easy monetary policy be used during stagflation?

2. A variety of events, including thrift deregulation and tax laws that encouraged risky real-estate investments (plus some outright fraud and financial mismanagement) has created the so-called "Savings & Loan Crisis" which, according to estimates, may cost the U.S. taxpayer somewhere between $300 billion and $500 billion. Question: How healthy are the S&Ls in your home town? Also, outline your own approach to solving the crisis that combines economic efficiency, fairness and also takes into account current political realities.

3. Could blades of grass be used as money? Why or why not?

4. *True or false?* The only way for a monetary system to work is for each unit of money (dollar, pound, yen, franc, etc.) to be backed by gold or silver equal to the *value* of that unit of money. Explain.

PART 2
Microeconomics

10

What Is Microeconomics?

From such large-scale, macroeconomic concepts as money and banking, or unemployment and inflation, we now return to the world encompassed by our "economic microscope"—the world of **microeconomics**. This time, however, we will be analyzing the subject in much greater detail than we did earlier. We will be asking—and answering—these questions: "What is micro-economics all about?" and, equally important, "Just how do we *begin* to think about the *inner world* of this fascinating area of economics?"

Design

I like to think of microeconomics as a problem in design. What we will be studying in Part II is how you and I, the grocer down the street, and even the large corporation—the "bits and pieces" of our economy—design our lives and organizations to meet certain economic objectives. Microeconomics is like a game with certain rules, constraints, and ultimate objectives. Consumers, for example, are constrained by their limited incomes. Businesses must work within the confines of their production costs, their competition, and the demand for their product or service. Both groups must obey the rules of the marketplace.

But what about the goals or objectives of our players? In microeconomics, the key objective is relatively uncomplicated: **maximization**. When we, as consumers, businesses, or workers, put on our respective "economic hats," we want to maximize the following economic goals:

- Consumers attempt to get the largest amount of *utility* (satisfaction) from their limited incomes.
- Workers want to maximize *income* and maintain or increase their *leisure time*.
- Businesses try to maximize *profits* within the constraints of production costs, demand, and competition.

Perhaps it is not surprising that economists have been criticized for developing and promoting the concept of economic maximization. When it is applied to consumers, workers, and businesses, "maximization" carries the connotation of operating with a kind of brutal efficiency while pursuing profits or enlarging an income base at any cost. In Chapter 2, we found that some people feel many of our social and economic ills—including worker exploitation, environmental pollution, wars, and the disappearance of craftsmanship, to name a few—originate from this maximization principle.

Sometimes we see attempts to promote greater worker satisfaction by developing alternatives to maximization goals. New experiments are tried all the time. I am intrigued, for example, by a little magazine called *Briarpatch Review: A Journal of Right Livelihood and Simple Living,* which suggests an alternative to profit maximization in small businesses:

> If you take "making a lot of money" off the list of reasons for being in business, you can pretty easily replace it with "fun," since you then have time to enjoy yourself by interacting with others.[35]

Or consider E. F. Schumacher's provocative book *Small Is Beautiful,* in which he describes a number of reasons (other than income maximization) why people work. The purposes of work, Schumacher explains in his chapter "Buddhist Economics," should be

> . . . to give a man a chance to utilize and develop his faculties; to enable him to overcome his ego-centeredness by joining with other people in a common task; and to bring forth the goods and services needed for a becoming existence.

> . . . To organize work in such a manner that it becomes
> meaningless, boring, stultifying, or nerve-racking for the worker
> would be little short of criminal; it would indicate a greater
> concern with goods than with people.[36]

Of course, the philosophy of "making work meaningful" is certainly not a new one. As Schumacher points out, these traditions can be traced back to various sources, including Buddhist philosophy and, more recently, the writings of Thoreau, Tolstoi, and Gandhi.

Maximization goals also tend to encourage people to see human beings and organizations in purely quantitative terms: the greater the profits, income, and utility, the better. Most economists would admit that there is some truth to this allegation.

Perhaps economists do promote the concept of maximization to an unnecessary degree. Yet I believe most of them recognize that monetary maximization is really only *part* of our total existence. Any business or individual who becomes totally obsessed with narrow economic goals is inviting social disapproval and possibly government restraint and regulation. On the other hand, if people or businesses totally disregard economic objectives, they undoubtedly will find their level of economic comfort—and perhaps their very survival—threatened. Most workers, consumers, and businesses tend to maximize goals. Economists' observations about microeconomic activity can thus help us to understand both ourselves and our organizations because their theories frequently *do* reflect the way the "bits and pieces" of our economic system actually behave.

We could also consider the maximization process to be symbolic of *any* activity or decision-making process that involves finite resources and freedom of choice. This returns us to the view of microeconomics as a method of designing our lives to achieve our objectives and, simultaneously, to recognize certain constraints. I think if we look at microeconomics in this light, we may well discover interesting and important insights into human behavior.

Micro versus Macro

Now let's take another look at the twin concept of micro and macro and find out just how they relate to each other. Meta-

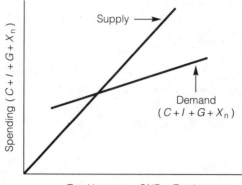

Total income = GNP = Total output

FIGURE 10-1 The aggregate supply and demand graph is a good visual representation of the world of macroeconomics.

phorically, the relationship is quite simple, as we see in Ho-o's brief poem, or haiku:

> A seedling shoulders up some crumbs of ground:
> The fields are suddenly green for miles around![37]

In other words, the macro view is nothing more than the sum total of the micro details.

Returning to economics, we can easily show the difference between micro and macro with graphs. In Chapter 8, we developed the Keynesian model of total (aggregate) supply and demand, which is redrawn in Figure 10-1. This graph represents the world of *macroeconomics*—the study of broad economic concepts, such as gross national product (GNP), unemployment, growth, and inflation.

In Chapter 3, we developed the simple supply-demand graph depicted in Figure 10-2. This single market is a good example of the smaller world of *microeconomics*. Two simple curves summarize a mass of information about the behavior of consumers (demand curve) and producers (supply curve).

Is there any way to relate the macroeconomic world of GNP to the microeconomic world of individual markets on one graph? Yes! It can be done with another old acquaintance, the circular-flow diagram from Chapter 4, redrawn here as Figure 10-3. Notice that households and businesses deal with each other through **resource markets** (*top*) and **goods and services markets** (*bottom*). As various markets deliver resources and

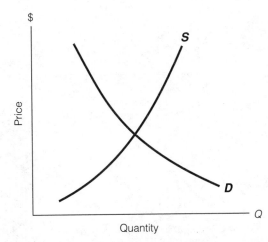

FIGURE 10-2 A supply-demand market for a particular good or service sums up a number of microeconomic ideas.

churn out final products, we begin to get a feel for the "piece by piece" make-up of our gross national product (GNP). (Recall that GNP, the key macroeconomic concept, is simply the summation of all the productive efforts of all individual businesses.)

Economists who study large-scale, macroeconomic flow patterns are primarily concerned with the health of the entire economic system; they spend much of their time devising policies intended to move our economy toward full-employment, economic growth, and stable prices (Chapters 7, 8, and 9). On the other hand, economists who study small-scale microeconomics spend most of their time analyzing the origin, make-up, and efficiency of individual markets and other smaller economic processes.

In our study of microeconomics, for example, we will determine where the supply curve comes from and analyze why a particular demand curve has a unique shape. You have already learned that an individual's demand curve for, say, corn or hamburgers is downward-sloping. Such a curve is "showing" us that when we reduce the price of the product, consumers demand greater quantities of it. This, of course, is a logical idea, but we have to *prove* that this negative relationship between price and quantity must normally be the case. Establishing such proof is one of our tasks in microeconomics.

Microeconomics can answer other questions as well. For example, why does your particular demand curve for hamburgers

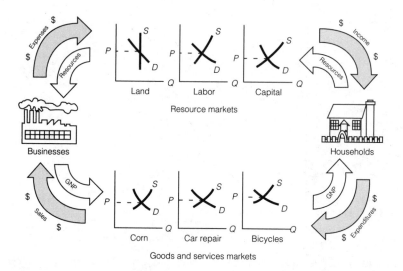

Figure 10-3 The familiar *circular-flow diagram* combines *macroeconomics* (large-scale flows of GNP, money, and resources) with *microeconomics* (individual markets).

look different from mine? Why are some people more sensitive than others to a price change? That simple looking demand curve expresses many subtle concepts that challenge us to look deeply into an individual's economic behavior.

We must do a certain amount of economic and psychological "snooping" to get at the fundamentals of microeconomics. We will have to take a close look at consumer incomes and preferences and at the prices of related goods, among other things. This is what "micro" is all about.

Finally, in microeconomics, we will carefully examine the supply curve. We will no longer be satisfied with saying, "It's logical that if corn prices go up, Farmer Brown will want to supply more corn." We must dig deeper now. To understand Farmer Brown's supply behavior, we have to study his production costs and revenues, which will help us determine how he operates to maximize profits at different prices. So, as you can see, the underlying concepts of microeconomics can be quite complex.

It should be worth the effort, though. By the middle of our microeconomic analysis, we will have "built" our first competitive market model; by the end, we will have explored the models of oligopoly and monopoly and differentiated competition in more detail. But first things first. In the following chapter, let's take a careful look at demand, tracing its origins and then following a typical consumer to discover its fundamental nature.

Questions for Thought and Discussion

1. Macroeconomic items, such as GNP, are said to be made up of the summation of the "microparts." Do the parts ever *not* add up to the whole? Is what is true for the part *always* true for the whole? Why or why not?

2. Why does the maximization process not apply if the decision-making process involves infinite resources and/or no freedom of choice?

3. Is it possible for a single individual to be a businessperson, a resource owner, and a consumer all at the same time? Explain and, if possible, give an example.

4. How would you fit net exports (exports – imports) into the circular flow diagram?

5. Do you "work to live" or "live to work"? Relate your answer to the concept of Buddhist economics.

11

Demand

Consider the source of our economic behavior. What exactly motivates us to engage in economic activity? A large part of the answer to this question lies in one word: ***consumption.*** We need to have goods and services to survive and also want to enjoy a standard of living commensurate with both our expectations and our dreams. For some people, a small amount of consumption will do, but most of us want to have more of the good things that our economic system can provide.

Utility

From this basic assumption about human behavior, we can infer that any level of consumption brings with it a certain amount of satisfaction—or, as economists say, ***utility.*** Utility can be a difficult thing to measure precisely. It is also difficult to make comparisons of utility between people. Your utility from consuming an automobile or a banana is probably going to be different from mine or from anyone else's. Indeed, we might discover some surprising results if we could actually measure utility between people. Depriving you of your fourth Cadillac, for example, might result in a greater loss of satisfaction to you than I would feel if I were to lose my one Ford. Even though you have four Cadillacs, the loss of one might depress you because all of your neighbors have five or six.

Nevertheless, we can say some important things about utility, as long as we confine our discussion to *one individual*. For example, Mary Smith might tell us that she "seems" to be getting about 5 units of utility from eating a hamburger and around 2 units from consuming a banana. To determine if she is accurate about her utility estimates, we will give her $0.70 and offer her the opportunity to buy fractions of hamburgers or bananas. If we price a full hamburger at $0.50 and a banana at $0.20 and Mary spends her $0.70 for one hamburger and one banana, we can assume that her rough utility ratio of 5:2 is correct.

Now let's make another utility observation, but this time we will only consider the consumption of one product, such as the Cadillacs you own. Even though we can't determine how much utility your fourth Cadillac gives you compared to the utility my one Ford gives me, we can say that you probably have received more utility from your *first* Cadillac than you will from your fourth. Or, to consider a more realistic example, Mary's third hamburger (in the short run) will probably give her less satisfaction than her second, and her second hamburger will probably give her less satisfaction than her first.

But since I know more about my own utility levels than yours, or Mary Smith's, I will turn to a more detailed illustration of this principle, using my own utility preferences. Thus, after considerable thought and experimentation, I come up with the following **marginal utility chart**:

Hamburger	Marginal Utility (MU$_h$)
1	7
2	3
3	1
4	0

From these figures, you can see that my first hamburger gives me 7 units of utility. The second provides 3 additional units, but by the time I eat my third, my *additional utility* is only 1 unit. Economists call this additional utility (which is assigned to the consumption of a specific unit) **marginal utility,** or simply MU. Obviously, I'm starting to get pretty full after two hamburgers; after my third hamburger, I am completely full, so the fourth will give me no marginal utility whatsoever. If somebody *gave* me that fourth hamburger, I'd leave it on my plate. What would your utility chart for hamburgers look like? You might want to construct one just for fun.

The Law of Diminishing Marginal Utility

Can we make any generalization about this utility pattern? Apparently, as a person consumes more of a given product, that

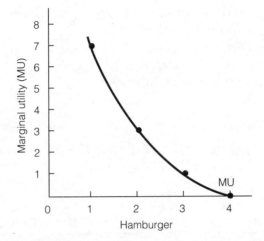

FIGURE 11-1 The *law of diminishing marginal utility:* as a person consumes more and more hamburgers, he or she experiences less and less marginal utility from each additional hamburger.

product has less marginal utility for that individual. This principle will probably be true, no matter what person or product we examine. Economists call this universal principle the **law of diminishing marginal utility**.

We can apply this principle to many types of human experience. Diminishing marginal utility is worth remembering if you happen to be on a diet, since that tenth spoonful of ice cream (or fourth cookie) will undoubtedly give you less satisfaction than the first. It may also help to explain why good marriages sometimes go bad or why that once "exciting" job eventually becomes boring.

Sometimes it's helpful to visualize economic relationships such as this one. Using the MU data just given, I can graph my *diminishing marginal utility curve* for hamburgers as shown in Figure 11-1.

Keep in mind that this graph is *my* MU curve for hamburgers; your curve, or someone else's, would probably look different. Spend a moment sketching different possible MU curves. Try one for a "Wimpy," who can lovingly eat a dozen hamburgers before he gets full. What about a vegetarian? What about your MU curve?

Now we can begin to make some interesting observations about how a consumer might behave when given a choice between two products. How, for example, would the law of diminishing marginal utility help me to maximize my satisfactions, given a limited income?

To see how this is done, let's add a second item to my menu—milkshakes. Let's assume that my marginal utility chart for milkshakes looks something like this:

MILKSHAKE	MARGINAL UTILITY (MU$_m$)
1	12
2	3
3	1/2

We will make this consumer example more realistic by adding an income constraint. To keep our example simple, we will assume that I am given, say, $4 per day and that the price of a milkshake is $1 and the price of a hamburger is $1. With this information, how do I go about maximizing my total utility? How do I spend my limited income in a way that I can enjoy the highest possible level of total satisfaction?

The best method of maximizing my utility would be to use what economists call *marginal decision making*—to make a separate decision for each dollar at my disposal. Thus, I take my first dollar and ask the question, "Where will this dollar give me the greatest marginal utility?"

If you compare the utility chart for milkshakes with the utility chart for hamburgers, you will see that I ought to spend my first dollar on a milkshake, because that first milkshake will give me 12 units of utility. (If I spend that same dollar on a hamburger, it will only give me 7 units of utility.) My marginal decision making now leads me to ask, "How can I best spend my second dollar?" "My third dollar?" "My fourth dollar?" A summary of my decisions follows.

My second dollar will be spent on a hamburger. The third dollar is a "toss-up," since both products will give me the same marginal utility (3 units) per dollar. (In the example, I will choose a milkshake for my third dollar.) My fourth dollar, in a sense, "balances things out," so that *once my total income of $4 is spent,* the marginal utility per dollar's worth of each product

MILKSHAKE			HAMBURGER	
dollar 1 ➤ 1	12 units	1	7 units ◄ dollar 2	
dollar 3 ➤ 2	3 units	2	3 units ◄ dollar 4	
3	1/2 unit	3	1 unit	
		4	0 units	

(3 units per $1) will be equal. Obviously, if I could obtain more utility from spending my last dollar on another product (french fries, for example), I would want to do so.

Let's assume that we have precise information about all the products we wish to consume (and therefore know the marginal utility of each product) and that we can spend our money exactly as we wish (even for fractions of hamburgers or milkshakes). Then we can attain the highest possible total satisfaction *if* the marginal utility per dollar's worth (marginal utility divided by product price, or MU/*P*) of product A is equal to the MU/*P* of product B, which is equal to the MU/*P* of product C, and so on. When these ratios are equal, so that

$$\frac{MU_A}{P_A} = \frac{MU_B}{P_B} = \frac{MU_C}{P_C} = \frac{MU_D}{P_D}$$

A = hamburgers
B = milkshakes
C = french fries
D = other things

then we, as consumers, have, in a sense, "solved" our maximization problem. We have spent our limited income in a way that gives us the maximum amount of utility.

So far, so good. But there are still people who are bothered by our inability to measure utility precisely, as we just tried to do in this example. Fortunately, we can use another method, called the ***indifference-curve*** *approach,* to determine consumer efficiency without giving actual utility values. Let's take a look.

Indifference Curves

Economists have a little of "the psychologist" in them, as well as a little of "the newspaper reporter." An economic researcher could conceivably run around asking people about their income levels, consumption habits, work preferences, personal values, and so on. The answers to these questions, in turn, would give the researcher insight into how consumers behave under various economic conditions. At some point, our economist-psychologist-reporter might even be able to discover some generalized principles (such as the law of diminishing marginal utility) that could become the basis of an important economic theory. The *indifference-curve approach* is such a technique. It allows us to ask some simple questions and derive some interesting generalizations and conclusions from the answers. Let's look at an example.

You are the economic researcher, and you ask me the following question: "If I gave you 1 milkshake and 3 hamburgers, you would derive a certain amount of utility from that combination, right?" I answer "Yes."

Then you go on: "Let's call that amount of utility your **total utility level** *Y*. Now if I reduce the number of hamburgers to 2, how many *additional* milkshakes would you need to keep yourself at total utility level *Y*?" Suppose I answer, "I will need an extra 1/4 milkshake to make up for the lost hamburger." This means that I am *totally indifferent* about whether I consume a combination of 3 hamburgers and 1 milkshake or a combination of 2 hamburgers and 1-1/4 milkshakes.

As a final question, you might ask me how many milkshakes I would need if I consumed only 1 hamburger but wanted to stay at total utility level *Y*? Let's say that I would need 2 full milkshakes to be indifferent to the other combinations. The following chart shows the results of your research (h = hamburger; m = milkshake):

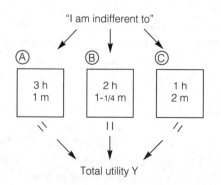

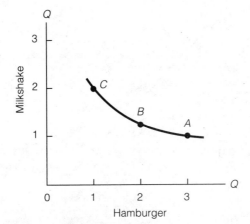

FIGURE 11-2 At points along the *indifference curve*, any combination of milkshakes and hamburgers offers the consumer an equivalent amount of total utility. The consumer is therefore indifferent to consuming at points *A, B,* or *C* (or at any other point on the indifference curve).

Thus, I would be equally well off with combination A, B, or C. I would be indifferent about consuming at any of these combinations because my total utility stays the same in each case. Now let's graph these "points" of indifference, measuring hamburgers on the horizontal axis and milkshakes on the vertical axis (see Figure 11-2). Connecting the points that represent combinations A, B, and C gives us a smooth **indifference curve** showing all the points of indifference. Suppose, for example, that you ask me, "Would you prefer to consume at point *A, B,* or *C* on the graph, or somewhere in between?" I would have to answer by saying, "I'm indifferent; all points give me equal satisfaction."

My indifference curve in Figure 11-2 might be described as having a "bow-like" or lazy C shape. Economists say that such a curve is "convex to the origin" (the origin is always in the lower left-hand corner of the graph). You may wonder why my indifference curve (or anybody else's, for that matter) has this general shape. Why isn't it a straight line or a "dome"? We will be able to answer this question once we understand the law of diminishing marginal utility. Let's see how it works.

Look closely again at point *A* in Figure 11-2, which represents the combination of 3 hamburgers and 1 milkshake. If I happen to be consuming at point *A*, I am obviously "full" of hamburgers; remember that this third hamburger added very little to my overall satisfaction. Since this third hamburger is

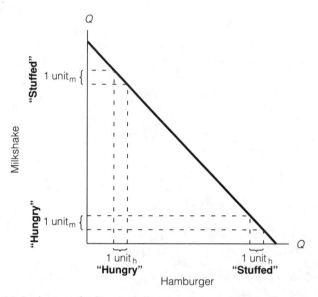

FIGURE 11-3 A straight-line indifference curve violates the law of diminishing marginal utility. It implies that consumers will trade off equal amounts of milkshakes, whether they are "stuffed" with hamburgers or "hungry" for them.

not that important to me, I am willing to "trade it off," or substitute it, for just one-fourth of a milkshake if I move to consumption point *B*.

Now let's look at point *C*, which represents 1 hamburger and 2 milkshakes. Here, hamburgers suddenly become much "dearer" to me, while milkshakes are less important due to the law of diminishing marginal utility. Thus, at point *C*, I am willing to give up a greater quantity of milkshakes (3/4 of a milkshake) to get that second hamburger.

If the law of diminishing marginal utility is working (and we are assuming that it is), then the indifference curve will have to be convex to the origin. An interesting test of this reasoning is to intentionally convert an indifference curve to a straight line (like the one in Figure 11-3) and then prove that this *cannot* be a valid shape.

Can you see why the line in Figure 11-3 violates the law of diminishing marginal utility? A straight line implies *equal* trade-offs of hamburgers for milkshakes, whether I am "hungry" for burgers or "stuffed" with burgers. But such a *continuous* one-for-one trade-off just doesn't conform to reality. The only configuration

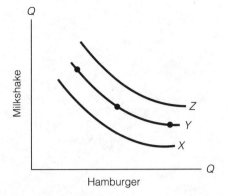

FIGURE 11-4 An *indifference map* is a unique "fingerprint," showing an individual's preferences—in this case, for milkshakes and hamburgers. In general, as indifference increases, total utility increases.

consistent with the law of diminishing marginal utility (and the actual behavior of consumers) is our original convex curve.

Indifference Map

Needless to say, we could draw thousands of indifference curves, each one reflecting the unique consumption preferences of a different individual. We could even show many *different levels* of utility for the same person. Up to this point, we have only discussed a single indifference curve that represents total utility at the *Y* level. There is also a curve somewhere below the *Y* level that would represent a lower total level of satisfaction (let's call it total utility at the *X* level) and another curve showing even higher satisfaction than *Y* (we'll call it total utility at the *Z* level). Of course, we could draw many other indifference curves above, below, and between these three curves. These different levels of utility, represented by a series of indifference curves, make up an **indifference map**—a kind of "consumer prefer-ence fingerprint"—on which each person displays a unique set of indifference curves. An indifference map for milkshakes and hamburgers is shown in Figure 11-4.

One important advantage of using an indifference map instead of our earlier marginal decision-making approach is that we now no longer need to assign actual utility values to the consumption of different products. For example, we really do not

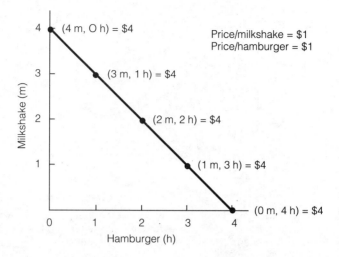

Figure 11-5 The *budget line:* here, a $4 budget allows the consumer to select from a variety of milkshake-hamburger combinations. If both milkshakes and hamburgers are priced at $1 per unit, then the budget line indicates all the consumption possibilities that a consumer can purchase with $4.

know how many *units of utility* the X curve represents, but we can still say with some certainty that indifference curve X is lower than indifference curve Y. Thus, all other things being equal, *an individual prefers to consume on the highest indifference curve.* The highest level of satisfaction in this illustration is indifference curve Z.

The Budget Line

Let's return to the example in which I have an income of $4 per day and hamburgers and milkshakes cost $1 apiece. If I spend all of my daily income on hamburgers and buy no milkshakes, I can buy 4 hamburgers. This means that my $4 budget allows me to operate at a consumption level of 4 hamburgers and 0 milkshakes. Of course my $4 could also buy 2 hamburgers and 2 milkshakes, or 3 hamburgers and 1 milkshake, or 3 milkshakes and 1 hamburger. These combinations all represent possible consumption levels, given my $4 income. Plotting these various combinations results in a **budget line,** which shows every combination of hamburgers and milkshakes that I can purchase for $4. Figure 11-5 summarizes these data.

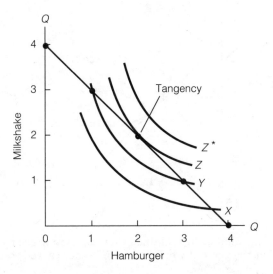

FIGURE 11-6 A consumer obtains the greatest total utility from a \$4 income at the point at which the highest indifference curve Z just touches (is tangent to) the \$4 budget line.

Sometimes it can be helpful to look at a budget line as if it were a kind of "economic straightjacket"—a visual representation of the "cruel world" of economic reality. Of course we would all like our budgets to be larger, but they are not. We have just so much money to spend, and we must limit our consumption to the possible product combinations that lie somewhere on the budget line.

So even though we are limited by budget restrictions, we still have a certain amount of *choice* in terms of selecting the right "bundle" of goods that will give us the greatest satisfaction. This is simply another way of looking at the fundamental economic problem of **utility maximization**. How do we solve the problem this time? How can I be sure I have chosen the best product combination with my \$4 income?

To answer these questions, all we need to do is combine the budget line with the indifference map. The combined system is shown in Figure 11-6.

The solution can easily be seen on the graph. First note that it *is possible* to consume on indifference curve Y. It crosses the \$4 budget line in two places. But why should the consumer stop on indifference curve Y when it is also possible to climb up to indifference curve Z? Notice that there is only one point where

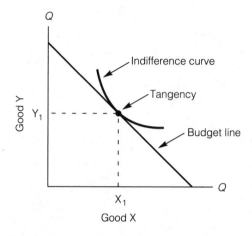

FIGURE 11-7 The total utility obtained from consuming good Y and good X is maximized at the point at which the indifference curve is tangent to the budget line.

the budget line is just tangent to indifference curve Z; this point of tangency represents the approximate consumption of 2 hamburgers and 2 milkshakes.

Yet someone might logically ask, "If higher indifference curves represent higher satisfaction, why don't you just move to the highest indifference curve of all (Z)?" The answer, of course, is that Z^* is not consistent with the $4 budget constraint. As you can see, the highest indifference curve does not coincide with the budget at any point on the graph. The very highest possible level of utility that I can attain with my $4 budget is the Z level shown by the point of tangency in Figure 11-6. Thus, we can say that *individuals maximize their utility by consuming at the point where the indifference curve is tangent to the budget line.*

Total utility will always be maximized at this point of tangency. It does not matter which indifference map we are looking at, what the dollar income constraint is, or what particular goods we are using in our example. In fact, it might be helpful to graph a more "generic" representation, using the more generalized X and Y goods (see Figure 11-7).

Now that we have established the point of utility maximization, or **consumer efficiency,** we can demonstrate a variety

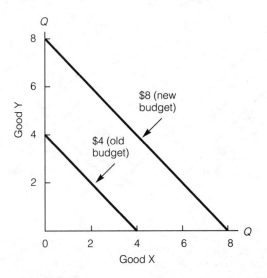

FIGURE 11-8 An expanding budget is represented by a parallel, rightward shift in the budget line.

of economic relationships. You'll be surprised to see how versatile the indifference-curve/budget-line format can be in describing consumer behavior. For example, how can we analyze a change in a consumer's income? Let's take a look.

Income Change

We will assume that our typical consumer (Chester Olson), who had an income of $4 per day, is given a raise to $8 per day. How do we show this change within the format we developed earlier?

Such an income increase can be shown by a *rightward shift* in Chester's budget line. Keeping the price of good X at $1 and the price of good Y at $1, we can see that the new point of reference on the *x* axis (for the $8 income) is now 8 units. This means that if Chester spent all his income on good X, he would be able to buy 8 units. The same is true of good Y. In Figure 11-8, we can easily see the difference between the old and the new budget lines.

Now let's take a variety of income levels and examine the points of tangency with their respective indifference curves. The points of tangency in Figure 11-9(a) show us exactly where Chester will maximize satisfaction at different levels of income.

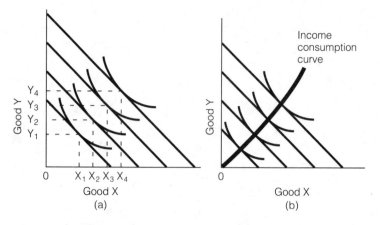

FIGURE 11-9 (a) Chester maximizes total utility as his income increases. (b) Connecting the points at which the indifference curves are tangent to the budget lines yields the *income-consumption curve.*

In Figure 11-9(b), note that we have connected all the points of tangency with a continuous line. A glance at this ***income-consumption curve*** shows the relative preference between the two goods as Chester's income increases.

In Figure 11-9(b), it looks as if Chester's preferences are fairly "balanced" between the two products. In other words, both good X and good Y in this example are what economists call ***normal goods***. When income levels increase, consumers tend to buy *more* of a normal good.

Economists also recognize the possibility that when income levels increase, consumers may purchase *less* of an ***inferior good***. Macaroni, powdered-milk, used cars over ten years old, retread tires, and used books are all inferior goods. Note that an inferior good does not always have to be inferior in terms of quality; powdered milk, for example, is highly nutritious and is often recommended for low-fat diets. Generally speaking, though, an inferior good tends to be a "poor person's product"; families tolerate these goods at low-income levels, but as their incomes rise, they tend to discard inferior goods in favor of normal goods. In Figure 11-10, we have expanded Chester's income from $2 to $8 per day. We can see that Chester purchases the inferior good (macaroni) less and less as his income expands. The income-consumption curve rises in a *leftward* direction, indicating that Chester is maximizing his satisfaction with fewer and fewer inferior goods as his budget increases.

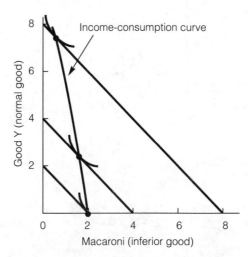

FIGURE 11-10 If income increases and consumers begin to buy less of a certain good, economists say that the product is an *inferior good*. Here, the consumption of macaroni, an inferior good, decreases as income increases.

Demand

Income changes are interesting microeconomic concepts but do not help us get to the heart of the demand curve, which is the major goal of this chapter. What is the key variable to understanding demand?

To answer this question, it might be helpful to review the fundamental nature of a demand curve. Recall from Chapter 3 that **demand** is the relationship between the *price P* of a good and the *quantity Q* of the good that is purchased. Can we derive a demand curve for hamburgers, using our friend Chester Olson as an illustration? Fortunately, this is not too difficult.

Perhaps the easiest method is to play "economist-reporter" and simply ask Chester how many hamburgers he will buy at different prices. Let's assume he tells us that he will buy 1 hamburger if the unit price is $2, 2 hamburgers if the unit price goes down to $1, and 4 hamburgers if the unit price drops to $0.50:

QUANTITY (Q)	PRICE (P)
1	$2
2	1
4	0.50

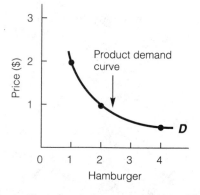

FIGURE 11-11 Information about consumer demand can be obtained by simply asking a person how much of a good he or she will buy at different prices and then plotting the price-quantity points on a demand curve.

This "direct research" method of determining Chester's hamburger demand gives us the curve shown in Figure 11-11.

We can also use the indifference-curve/budget-line format to determine Chester's hamburger demand. First, we find out what Chester's indifference map looks like; then all we have to do is *vary the unit price of hamburger* and observe how these price changes affect Chester's consumption.

To see how to show a price change on our indifference-curve/budget-line graph, let's return to our example of a $4 budget and an original price of $1 for a hamburger. If we lower the price of a hamburger to $0.50, Chester can buy a maximum of 8 hamburgers with his $4 income. We can also easily determine where the budget line intersects the x axis if we divide Chester's income by the price of a hamburger. Thus, if the price of a hamburger increases to $2, Chester can buy a maximum of 2 hamburgers with his $4 income ($4/$2 = 2).

Each time the unit price of hamburger changes, *the slope of the budget line changes.* At lower hamburger prices, it generally has a lower slope; at higher prices, the budget line becomes steeper. (We are assuming, of course, that the unit price of good Y does not increase or decrease.) We can see the slope changing in Figure 11-12.

Now all we have to do is trace Chester's indifference-curve map, drawing in the indifference curves that are tangent to the different budget lines. When we connect these points of tangency with a line, we have what economists commonly call a **price-consumption curve,** as seen in Figure 11-13(a).

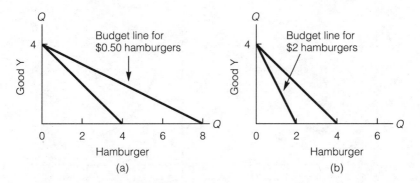

FIGURE 11-12 Changing the unit price of a hamburger: (a) if the price is lower ($0.50), then the $4 budget line is less sloped; (b) if the price is higher ($2), then the budget line is steeper.

Deriving the Demand Curve

After our long labors, we are now close to deriving a demand curve from an indifference-curve system. In fact, the last connecting link is really quite simple; perhaps you have already spotted it. All we need to do to find Chester's demand is to read off the number of hamburgers that he will consume at the different unit prices of hamburger, shown in Figure 11-13(a).Thus, at the $2 price (the steepest budget line), we see that Chester will demand 1 hamburger. If we draw a vertical dashed line down to the horizontal (hamburger) axis from the point of tangency of the lowest sloped line (representing $0.50 hamburgers), we see that Chester will demand 4 hamburgers.

These results, which are summarized by the product demand curve in Figure 11-13(b), are in exact agreement with our experimental method of finding demand by direct research (see Figure 11-11). Both of these approaches to finding Chester's demand are valid, but the indifference-curve method took us back to our study of consumption and was built up, in a sense, "from scratch." We began with the consumer's desire to maximize their utility within a budget limitation. We then observed the effects of the law of diminishing marginal utility, which became incorporated into the special C-shape (convex to the origin) of the indifference curves. At this point, we added budget lines (income constraints) to our indifference-curve graph and noted the point of consumer efficiency at the tangency of each budget line and indifference curve. Finally, we changed the price

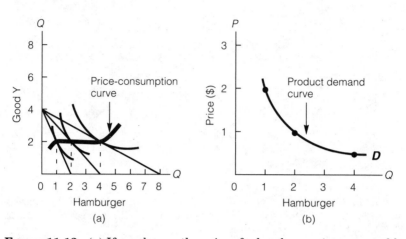

FIGURE 11-13   (a) If we change the price of a hamburger (represented by the three budget lines with different slopes) and then connect the points at which the budget lines are tangent to the indifference curves, we can derive three points on a *price-consumption curve*. (b) From the information given in the graph in (a), we can determine how many hamburgers will be purchased at the three different prices. When we graph these points, we obtain a *product demand curve* for hamburgers. Compare this method with the one used in Figure 11-11.

of good X (hamburgers) and noted the change in quantity demanded. From that information we derived the demand curve shown in Figure 11-13(b).

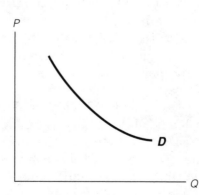

This completes our study of demand. We have discovered where a sample demand curve "comes from" and have learned some interesting variations related to maximizing satisfaction (inferior goods versus normal goods) when a person's income changes. We have also developed some valuable tools that will make our study of production theory much easier later in the book. But before we continue, let's look again at our accomplishment—an individual's product demand curve (a friendlier curve now)—and remind ourselves how far we have come.

Questions for Thought and Discussion

1. If you knew all the *individual* demand curves for a particular product, how would you construct a *total* (or "industry") demand curve for that product? (Hint: see bottom of p. 202)

2. Why can't the utilities of different people be added or compared?

3. Do people go around calculating MU/Ps when they make consumption decisions? If not, then why do economists use this method?

4. Does the law of demand (a negative relationship between price and quantity demanded) always hold? Why or why not? Give an example of such a good.

5. How "scientific" is the study of consumer demand? Review the tenets of scientific method—from developing hypotheses through constructing repeatable, controlled experiments— and evaluate the possibilities and limitations of using the scientific method in discovering micro-economic laws and principles.

12

Supply: Costs of Production

The Product Supply Curve

The simple **product supply curve,** which should be a familiar image to you by now, moves upward to the right, representing a positive relationship between the price of a product and the quantity of output that producers wish to supply. In other words, as the price of a product increases, a greater quantity of that product is supplied, as shown in Figure 12-1.

But *why* do you think the supply curve has this particular shape? In our first encounter with supply-demand theory, we often hear a common-sense explanation of supply, such as: "When farmers see an increase in the price of corn, they will logically want to supply more corn to the market. If the corn price goes up (has a higher unit price), then more corn will be supplied to the marketplace."

Although this statement is probably true, it doesn't *prove* much. For us to really determine the fundamental nature of a supply curve, we must first understand how a producer maximizes profits. Decisions about profitability will, in turn, take us into the financial regions, where profits (revenue minus production costs) are determined. Let's begin our exploration of supply with

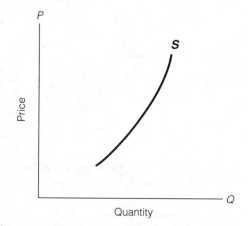

FIGURE 12-1 A simple *product supply curve* shows a positive relationship between price and quantity supplied. At higher prices, greater quantities are supplied; at lower prices, lesser quantities are supplied.

the subject of production costs, so that we can learn what really goes on "behind the scenes" of an average supplier.

Costs of Production

An interesting characteristic of product supply is that whenever we think we understand the fundamental concept, we suddenly discover, "Not quite!" We know that *production costs* play an important role in understanding profit maximization, but where do these costs come from? Think about it for a minute. You're probably saying, "Well, costs are determined by resource markets: the supply and demand for land, labor, and capital. From there, we get resource prices; from these prices, we derive costs." Supply and demand curves for the three major resources—land, labor, and capital—are shown in Figure 12-2. But now we are forced to ask, "What is the *origin* of the supply and demand for land, labor, and capital?"

Each question raises a new one as we travel backward into the heart of microeconomic theory. This process is reminiscent of Henry David Thoreau's attempt to find a "bedrock point of departure" from which he would begin his philosophical search for truth in *Walden* (1854):

> Let us settle ourselves, and work and wedge our feet downward through the mud and slush, . . . till we come to a hard bottom and rocks in place, which we can call reality . . . a place where you might find a wall or a state.

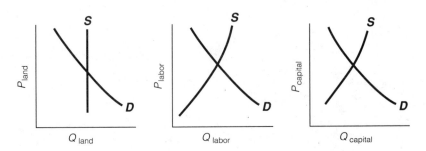

Figure 12-2   The supply and demand for resources determine the prices of land, labor, and capital. This information, in turn, becomes part of the supplier's production costs.

Can we find our bedrock concept—a solid principle of production from which we can build our "microeconomic wall"? The concept we are searching for is the well-known *law of diminishing returns*—one of the most important laws in all economics. Exactly how does this law relate to resource markets and production costs?

The Law of Diminishing Returns

Let's review the illustration of the law of diminishing returns in Chapter 4 (page 55) to see how it relates to production costs. We assumed that our hay-baling friend Chester Olson had a small farm of, say, 50 acres and a fixed amount of capital: one tractor, one baler, and one wagon. Recall that whenever we discuss diminishing returns, we *leave all resources fixed except one.*

Chester, working by himself, can bring in two loads of hay per day. When Jim joins Chester, Jim contributes an extra three loads of hay per day. Remember that the amount of hay that any one individual adds to the total is called his *marginal physical product* (MPP). So Chester's MPP = 2, and Jim's MPP = 3. Note that in this situation, the MPP is rising: Chester's operation is therefore experiencing *increasing returns.*

It is not difficult to see why Chester's hay-baling operation is in the stage of increasing returns. His fixed inputs (resources) are designed for two people. A simple two-person efficiency is achieved when one person bales hay while the other person stacks it on the wagon and when one person unloads the hay and the other person stacks it in the barn. But what happens when

Chester hires Steve, a third worker? What is Steve's MPP in relation to the other workers?

The addition of Steve to Chester's workforce increases the total daily output to six loads of hay. Therefore, only one unit (load) of extra output (MPP) can be attributed to Steve. With the addition of the third worker, the marginal physical product is beginning to fall (recall that Jim's MPP = 3). A declining MPP tells us that Chester's hay-baling operation has reached *the point of diminishing returns.*

Chester's total daily output is not lower because Steve is a less diligent worker but because the three-man crew is working with a limited amount of fixed inputs. One more tractor and wagon would make a major difference in Steve's productivity, but as a condition of our discussion of diminishing returns, we can't change any of the fixed resources.

Incidentally, diminishing returns would also occur if we held labor and land constant and added more capital. Diminishing returns is a universal law; it operates no matter what variable resource we are looking at.

You may enjoy, as I do, thinking through different kinds of production processes (like farming, teaching, raising children, operating a restaurant, studying for an exam, or operating a government department) and then trying to imagine at what stage the point of diminishing returns is likely to set in. For example, child-rearing (like hay-baling) is probably most efficient when it is conducted as a two-person operation. Or (to use perhaps a more relevant example for you) in cramming for an exam, you might observe, "I seem to have reached the point of diminishing returns," meaning that your most recent hour of study has produced a smaller amount of extra knowledge than the previous hour. You can see that the concept of diminishing returns can be applied to widely different situations!

Returning to Chester Olson's farm operation, can we now say that since Steve's low contribution is the result of the law of diminishing returns, Chester should not hire Steve? Recall that the answer to this question depends on the *monetary return* from Steve's contribution compared to the *wage* that Chester must pay him.

Steve's marginal physical product is only one load of hay. If that load of hay is worth $50, then the worth or value of Steve's MPP will be $50. We call this amount the **value of the**

marginal product of labor (VMP$_L$). The VMP$_L$ of any worker can easily be found by multiplying the MPP by the price P of the final product:

$$VMP_L = MPP \times P$$

Once Chester figures out the VMP$_L$ for *any* worker, all he has to do is compare this amount with the wage paid to that worker. Thus, the general rule for Chester to follow in hiring workers is to *keep hiring people as long as the VMP$_L$ is greater than the wage W.*

This process is similar to the marginal decision-making process (discussed in Chapter 11) in which a consumer takes each dollar of income, one at a time, and asks where that dollar will give her or him the greatest utility. Now Chester also makes marginal decisions, but in this situation he asks, "Should I hire the first person? (Does Jim contribute to profits by bringing in a revenue that is larger than his cost?) Should I hire the second person? Should I hire a third?" And so on. Chester must make a separate marginal decision based on each person's monetary contribution to the business versus the wage Chester will have to pay that particular worker.

Should Chester have hired Jim? Jim's MPP = 3 loads. At $50 per load, Jim's VMP$_L$ would be $150 per day. If we assume that Chester is paying the "going" wage of $20 per day, then the worth of Jim's output is obviously far greater than the wage Chester pays him. Thus, in regard to Jim's contribution to business profits, Chester's marginal decision (and the answer to our question) is a resounding "yes."

Should Chester have hired a third worker, Steve (VMP$_L$ = $50)? At a wage of $20 per day, Chester finds that it *is* still profitable to hire Steve, *despite diminishing returns,* because Steve's output earns Chester a $30 marginal profit.

What about a fourth person? Let's say that a fourth worker, Joe, brings in one-half load per day. Even at such a low productivity rate, it is worthwhile for Chester to hire Joe because the value of his daily output (VMP$_L$ = $25) is still greater than his daily wage ($20). Chester's marginal decision is now a more modest "yes" than before, but it is still a "yes." If the "going" wage were $30 per day, however, there would be no economic advantage to hiring a fourth worker.

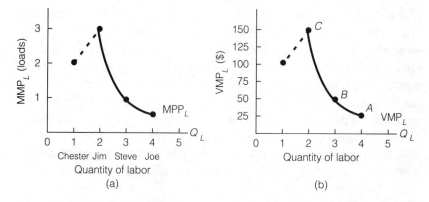

FIGURE 12-3 (a) A plot of the *marginal physical product* (MPP) for each worker (Chester, Jim, Steve, and Joe). (b) The *value of the marginal product of labor* (VMP_L) *curve* assigns a dollar value to each worker's contribution. These VMP_L values are based on the assumption that the hay that each worker produces can be sold for $50 per load.

Thus, in regard to the profitability of hiring workers, Chester should clearly continue to hire up to the point at which the daily VMP_L equals the daily wage W. Even if a worker's VMP_L is $20.01 and his wage is $20.00, Chester will still earn a small profit ($0.01) and should hire that worker. From now on, a general "rule of thumb," or profitability shortcut, will be to *continue to hire workers until the* VMP_L *of the last worker hired equals the wage* W *of that worker*. This shortcut, in turn, will offer us some insight into the nature of resource markets, including the demand for labor. Let's see how this works.

Demand Curve for Labor

The **demand curve for labor** is simply a series of points that tells us how many units of labor (the number of workers) will be purchased (by the producer) at different labor prices (wage rates). To see how the labor demand curve is related to the marginal physical product, let's graph Chester's MPP curve for labor (MMP_L) and the related VMP curve for labor (VMP_L) (see Figure 12-3), using the data we obtained earlier.

Based on the information given in the figure, we can easily work out labor demand. We can choose any wage; for example, let's choose $25 per day. How many workers will Chester "demand" if the daily wage for each worker is $25? The best way to answer this question is to go through the marginal decision-making process. Should Chester hire the first worker (himself)? Recall (page 182) that the answer will be "yes" as long as there is even a small amount of extra profit associated with that worker. The answer will also be "yes" for workers 2, 3, and 4. Our shortcut method gives us the same results: hire workers up to the point that $VMP_L = W$. In Figure 12-3(b), we see that a $25 wage is equal to a $25 VMP_L only when the fourth man is hired. Therefore, point A on Chester's labor demand curve is a $25 wage combined for four workers.

If, say, the wage rate is $50 instead of $25 per day, then Chester will hire up to and including the third man. (Remember that Steve's $VMP_L = 50.) Thus, point B on Chester's labor demand curve is a $50 wage combined for three workers.

Finally, at a wage rate of $150, it is obviously worthwhile for Chester to hire only two people (himself and Jim), making C the third point on Chester's labor demand curve. This information is plotted in Figure 12-4(a). When the three points are connected, as they are in Figure 12-4(b), we have Chester's complete demand curve for labor.

It should be no surprise that Chester's labor demand curve looks precisely like the VMP_L curve in Figure 12-3(b). In fact, as long as Chester maximizes his profits so that $VMP_L = W$, then *the VMP_L curve becomes the labor demand curve!* The VMP_L curve is, in turn, a monetary representation of diminishing MPP_L.

Why does the labor demand curve slope downward? We now know that this downward slope reflects a declining MPP or, more simply, diminishing returns! This conclusion is true for any resource that we choose to be the short-run variable; the demand curves for capital and land are the same as their respective VMP curves. Thus, other resources also have downward-sloping demand curves that reflect their compliance with the law of diminishing returns.

We have derived the demand curve for a resource. To discover the origin of resource prices, so that we can understand the nature of costs, we must also develop a supply curve to complete our resource market. So let's take a look at the basic structure of a single supply curve, using labor once again as our variable resource.

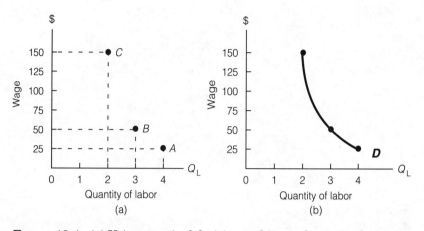

FIGURE 12-4 (a) Using marginal decision making to determine how many workers are hired at different wage rates, we are able to plot three labor-demand points. (b) These points are connected to form Chester's *demand curve for labor*.

Supply Curve for Labor

Labor supply is one of the more interesting topics in microeconomic theory, partly because it does not lend itself to a simple income-maximization process, as labor demand does. Instead, **labor supply** is influenced by psychological factors.

The subject of labor supply addresses different types of people and their unique preferences for work and leisure. How, for example, can we possibly use simple economic rules to explain why some people become "workaholics" and why other people seem to have nothing but free time to do whatever they want?

Obviously, all types of work attitudes must be taken into consideration when we discuss an individual's *willingness* to supply labor. Yet the general configuration of most people's **labor supply curves** would probably be somewhat similar. Let's see if we can construct this configuration.

Let's say you want to find out what Marsha's labor supply curve looks like. You will probably begin your investigation by asking her a question: "If you were given complete freedom to choose the amount of hours you wanted to work, how many hours would you choose to work per week if you received $2 per hour?" The answer will give you a single point on Marsha's labor supply curve. Next, you might ask, "How many hours a week

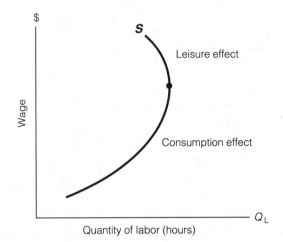

FIGURE 12-5 The *backward-bending labor supply curve.* As the wage rate increases, a person normally will want to work more hours; if this happens, then the *consumption effect* is dominant. If wage rates continue to increase, however, then a point will usually occur at which the worker voluntarily begins to cut the number of hours he or she works; if this happens, then the *leisure effect* is dominant.

would you work if wages were $3 per hour?" "If wages were $4 per hour?" And so on. You might also ask about Marsha's work preferences, even at very high wages. Each time she answers, you note the quantity of labor she is willing to supply under the stated conditions.

No doubt Marsha's response to a rising wage rate will probably be similar to most people's response. If the hourly wage is extremely low, she will probably be hesitant to "break her back" working a great many hours, unless she is forced to do so by necessity. As the hourly wage increases, the opportunity to earn greater income will probably be an incentive for Marsha to put in more hours. This direct, or positive, relationship (more hours worked at higher wage rates) we will call the **consumption effect.** It implies that a greater wage is a sufficient incentive to encourage Marsha to work longer to enlarge her income and to significantly improve her consumption level.

At some high wage level, however, a remarkable thing happens. Suddenly, "enough is enough"; any higher wage after this point results in fewer hours worked. Apparently, individuals want a greater amount of leisure time in which to enjoy a

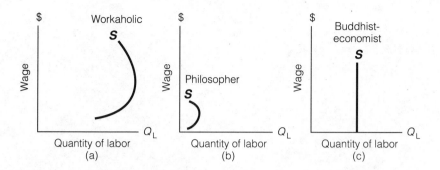

Figure 12-6 (a) The typical "workaholic" demonstrates a desire for large amounts of paid work. (b) The "philosopher" may move into a leisure pattern fairly quickly. (c) The "Buddhist-economist" may not be influenced by wage rates at all, whether they are low or high.

relatively higher income. When this happens, we might say that the *leisure effect*[38] has become more powerful than the consumption effect.

The leisure and consumption effects are graphed in Figure 12-5. Due to the consumption effect, the labor supply curve has a positive slope until a certain point; then it begins to turn backward and have a negative slope when the leisure effect takes over. Economists refer to this curve as the **backward-bending labor supply curve.**

It is sometimes interesting to experiment with different curve shapes, each of which demonstrates a variety of work attitudes and work-behavior patterns. Just for fun, let's try three radically different work models: the workaholic, the philosopher, and the Buddhist-economist.

The workaholic's labor supply curve will probably show high initial work loads that increase even more as the wage rate increases. Workaholics seem to need lots of work, and the opportunity to achieve higher and higher consumption levels prods them on as the wage rate increases. For such people, the leisure effect is evident only after extremely large quantities of labor have been supplied, as shown in Figure 12-6(a).

Next, we will look at the other end of the work spectrum, at the philosopher. In *Walden*, Thoreau advocates a simple, low-overhead lifestyle, saying his greatest skill "has been to want but little." This philosophy led Thoreau to something that was not quite voluntary poverty but was close to it:

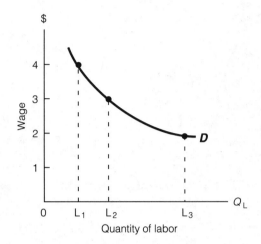

FIGURE 12-7 The *industry labor demand curve* is the summation of all workers hired by all employers in the industry at various wage rates.

> I found that by working about six weeks in a year, I could meet all the expenses of living. The whole of my winters, as well as most of my summers, I had free and clear for study.

What would Thoreau's labor supply curve look like? Apparently, it would bend back very quickly, like the one in Figure 12-6(b).

A final labor-supply model is the Buddhist-economist model, based on E. F. Schumacher's description (page 152) of an individual who is motivated not necessarily to earn wages but to develop personal character and lead a "dignified existence." Too much or too little work would not be an ideal situation for the Buddhist-economist. Thus, the supply curve would not have an upward slope or a backward-bending section; it would rise in a straight vertical line at the "ideal" level of labor, as shown in Figure 12-6(c).

You might want to draw an approximation of your own labor supply curve. Which one of the three models in Figure 12-6 does your curve resemble the most?

A Labor Market

So far, we have examined a single producer's demand curve for labor and a single person's labor supply curve. What we need to find out now is what the *overall* industry supply and demand

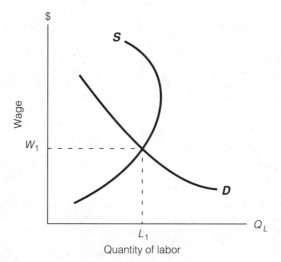

Figure 12-8 A typical labor market sums up the total quantity of labor demanded and the total quantity of labor supplied in a particular industry. The *equilibrium price* (wage W_1) is important information in determining production costs.

curves look like. This is not too difficult to do. To determine the industry demand for hay, for example, all we need to do is ask *all* the hay farmers the same question we already asked Chester Olson: "How much labor would you demand at different wage rates?"

Suppose that at a $4 hourly rate, Chester maximizes his profits with x workers; Jones, with y workers; Smith, with z workers, and so on. Then we simply add up the total numbers of workers $(x + y + z)$ at that particular wage rate. This information gives us the first point on the demand curve (see point L_1 in Figure 12-7). We go through the same addition process to obtain point L_2 at a $3 wage rate and point L_3 at a $2 wage rate. Connecting these three points gives us the **industry labor demand curve** in Figure 12-7.

The **industry labor supply curve** is determined in a similar way. We add up the total amounts of labor that all workers in that particular market are willing to put forth at different wage rates.

In Figure 12-8, the industry labor supply curve is combined with the industry labor demand curve. Together, they form our theoretical **labor market**—a unique supply-demand situation

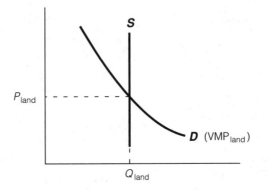

FIGURE 12-9 The *supply of, and demand for, land:* note the fixed (vertical) supply of land, implying that a land resource does not respond to changes in land price. Both land price and quantity will be used to calculate production costs.

that generates an *equilibrium price* (wage W_1) and an *equilibrium quantity of labor* (L_1).

We have derived demand and supply curves for the labor market, but what about the other two resource markets for land and capital? We had a brief look at these markets in Figure 12-2. How do we determine the prices of these resources?

We can apply a similar analysis to both land and capital. The **demand curve for land** is land's VMP curve. It slopes downward due to diminishing returns, just as the labor demand curve does.

The other half of the land market is the **supply curve for land**. We know, by definition, that the supply of land is fixed; there are only so many land resources, no matter how much the price of land varies. Thus, supply curve for land is simply a vertical line at the fixed quantity of land resources. The combined supply-demand market for land, with an equilibrium price (P_{land}), would look something like the graph in Figure 12-9.

The **demand curve for capital** is the its $VMP_{capital}$ curve; the **supply curve for capital** is determined by the available capital stock at any one time. The equilibrium price $P_{capital}$ is often expressed as a rate of interest. Thus, a short-run market for capital would be similar to the graph in Figure 12-10.

We have now reached the conclusion of this chapter on production costs. We have traced short-run production theory from the law of diminishing returns through simple resource

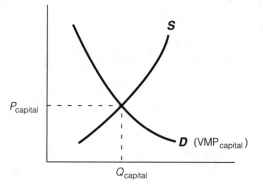

FIGURE 12-10 A *short-run market for capital:* the supply curve intersects the demand curve at an equilibrium price and quantity, supplying capital-cost information to businesses.

markets and, from this, have learned how resources are priced. From these prices, we can calculate a producer's costs of production!

In Chapter 13, we will combine these production costs with the concept of producer revenues. This knowledge will, in turn, lead us to the product supply curve.

Questions for Thought and Discussion

1. Are workers being exploited if they are paid less than the value of their marginal product (VMP_L)?

2. Have you experienced the leisure effect; that is, have you ever decreased your labor when your wage was high?

3. Is it possible for the marginal physical product (MPP) of labor to be negative? If so, when, if ever, would it be logical to hire these units of labor?

4. Explain how a fixed supply of land resources is related to global environmental issues.

5. *True or false?* The demand for any input used in a production process is independent of output markets for final goods and services. Explain.

13

The Short-Run Supply Curve

Before we move on, let's take a minute to look back and see how far we have come. Keep in mind that one of our primary objectives in microeconomics *is to build a model of a simple market.* We began by exploring the origins of the familiar supply and demand curves that make up a typical competitive product market.

In Chapter 11, we analyzed the product demand curve. The origin of demand, we learned, can be traced to the law of diminishing marginal utility and to the desire of consumers to maximize utility within their limited incomes. To find the origins of the product supply curve (Chapter 12), we had to first learn about a producer's costs, which, in turn, are based on the markets for economic resources (land, labor, and capital). We also discovered that resource demand curves are explained primarily by the law of diminishing returns and the desire of producers to maximize profits.

But we have yet to make the important connection between the production costs and the actual supply curve *for a product—* the major objective of this chapter. By the end of Chapter 13, we will have constructed a real-world product supply curve, which, when combined with the product demand curve, will complete our model of a competitive market.

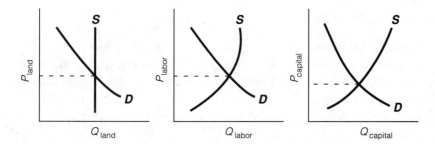

Figure 13-1 From the *resource markets* of land, labor, and capital, we obtain resource prices, which help producers calculate their overall production costs.

The Idea of Costs

Based on our work in Chapter 12, let's derive Chester Olson's production costs. First, we determine the prices of land, labor, and capital by observing the equilibrium price of each resource indicated by the supply and demand curves for the respective market (see Figure 13-1). Once these prices (P_{land}, P_{labor}, and P_{capital}) are known, we can use them to interpret a variety of interesting cost concepts. Let's begin with fixed costs.

Fixed Costs

Fixed costs result from the fact that, for Chester, supplies of land and capital do not change in the short run. Chester's total cost of these two resources will therefore be the "going" industry prices multiplied by the quantities of these fixed resources that he decides to use. To illustrate this point, let's say that Chester's fixed costs are:

$$P_{\text{land}} \times Q_{\text{land}} = \$50$$

$$P_{\text{capital}} \times Q_{\text{capital}} = \$50$$

Adding these costs together gives Chester total fixed costs of $100. Of course, we are greatly simplifying this example. In reality, Chester would have many kinds of fixed or **overhead costs** on his farm. Land rental, tractor, wagon, baler, barn depreciation, insurance, and taxes are just a few of the fixed costs for a typical farm.

Variable Costs

Chester's variable resource has always been labor. Therefore, his *variable costs* will be the "going" industry wage rate multiplied by the amount of labor that Chester decides to use (based on the procedures outlined in Chapter 12). Again, in reality, a farmer's variable costs are far more extensive than labor; they also include such expenses as fuel, seed, and fertilizer. In general, *any input that is directly connected to output is a **variable resource**.*

To summarize Chester's situation, his total costs (TC) so far are his fixed costs (FC) of $100 plus his variable costs (VC). Thus, TC = FC + VC. These are the *obvious costs* to Chester that will involve an apparent outlay of money. Such out-of-pocket costs are often called ***explicit costs.***

There may also be other costs that are not so obvious but that should be included in Chester's overall production costs. Economists call these expenses **implicit costs.** Let's look at some examples.

Implicit Costs

Frequently, a single operator like our friend Chester Olson forgets to consider his own labor as part of his costs, or he may simply undervalue the long hours that he spends working on his farm. This is also true of the many owners of "mom-and-pop" stores, single proprietorships, and partnerships, who often fail to recognize the full value of the total hours they spend on the job. Logically, these implicit costs should be included in the overall production costs of the business.

How do we estimate an implicit labor cost? In Chester's case, we could ask how much money he might be able to earn elsewhere for working the same number of hours. An alternative method is for Chester to assess how much money he would have to pay someone else to replace him. Adding this implicit labor cost to Chester's other expenses will reduce Chester's profits.

Another implicit cost that Chester has probably not fully accounted for is some fair return on his land and capital investment. If, for example, he has invested $100,000 in farm assets, he is foregoing a certain rate of return he could be earning on this money if it were invested in something else.

Thus, when economists look at production costs, they should include both implicit and explicit costs.

Social Costs

Other costs that should be included in production costs (but usually are not) are called *social costs*—the financial costs that the production of a product creates for society, usually in the form of direct or indirect pollution costs. If, for example, Chester Olson pollutes his neighbors' water supply by applying a heavy application of nitrogen fertilizer to his land, his neighbors must pay the cost of drilling a deeper private well when they discover their water is unfit for drinking.

An economist looking at this situation would argue that the financial cost of drilling a new well is really a legitimate production cost for the farmer and that Chester should pay the well-drilling expense. Our economy, however, has yet to recognize the logic of social costs fully and to institute policies that would force producers to *internalize* (bear the financial burden of) these costs themselves. (For more details, see Chapter 4.)

Let's call the sum of all the costs just discussed *total economic costs,* so that

Explicit costs + Implicit Costs + Social costs =
Total economic costs

Marginal Costs

Assuming (for the sake of simplicity) that no social or implicit costs result from Chester's hay-baling operation, let's look at an example of how production costs change as Chester's output increases. We will also assume that Chester can hire both part-time and full-time help, so that he can figure out exactly how much extra money it will cost him to produce one extra load of hay. Economists call this *extra cost of producing one more unit of output the **marginal cost** (MC).

After looking at the table on the next page, we can now say, "The marginal cost of Chester's fourth load of hay is MC = $6," or "the marginal cost of the fifth load is MC = $4." Once the total economic cost is known, then the marginal cost of producing the

Output Quantity (loads)	Total Economic Cost ($)	Marginal Cost ($)
1	110	—
2	130	20
3	140	10
4	146	6
5	150	4
6	170	20
7	210	40
8	270	60

second unit of output (load 2 of hay) is simply the difference between the total economic costs of producing loads 1 and 2, the MC of load 3 is the difference between the total economic costs of producing loads 2 and 3, and so on.

The next step is to graph the **marginal cost curve,** using the data from this table. Chester's MC curve is shown in Figure 13-2.

What does this MC curve show? At a glance, it tells Chester how much *extra* money it will cost to produce any particular load of hay. A striking feature of the MC curve is its characteristic U shape. First, marginal costs go down; then (around the fifth load of hay in Figure 13-2) they begin to go up. This common configuration implies that Chester must pay more and more money for extra loads of hay after the fifth load. What do you think causes the MC to go down and then up?

You have probably guessed correctly: it's our old acquaintance, the law of diminishing returns. Recall that when Chester hired Jim, he increased his total daily production to five loads. Jim's marginal physical product was three additional loads (MPP = 3), compared to Chester's two loads (MPP = 2), as shown in Figure 12-3(a); in other words, up to and including load 5, Chester's hay-baling operation is in the stage of increasing returns. Jim's *higher* productivity, therefore, leads to *lower* marginal costs.

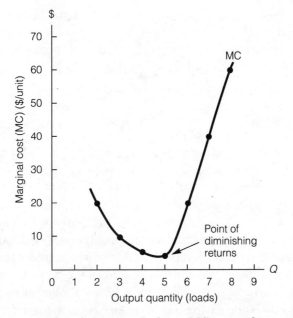

FIGURE 13-2   At a glance, the *marginal cost* (MC) *curve* shows us how many extra dollars it will take to produce one additional unit of output. When the MC curve begins to rise, the operation is producing at the *point of diminishing returns.*

To get an extra load after the fifth load of hay, however, becomes a very expensive proposition for Chester. Remember that Steve's MPP is only one load, due to diminishing returns; but Chester must still pay Steve *the same wage that he pays Jim* ($20 per day). This explains why Chester's marginal cost literally "shoots up" after his fifth unit of output and continue to rise rapidly from that point onward. In short, the MC curve begins to rise at the point at which marginal physical productivity begins to fall (the point at which diminishing returns set in).

After two chapters on the nature of costs, we have at last arrived at our most important cost concept so far: the derivation of the MC curve, which has its roots in the law of diminishing returns. This U-shaped curve will, in turn, become the basis of the product supply curve.

But we still have one more idea to pursue before we are able to put everything together. We need to know something about Chester's *revenues* so we can determine his total "profitability."

What does our microeconomic theory tell us about revenues within the setting of a competitive market structure? Let's answer this question by reviewing what we mean by the term "competition."

Competition

The structure of a **competitive market** is precisely the opposite of a monopoly structure. A **monopoly** (Chapter 2) is the most concentrated market structure; a competitive market is the least concentrated. A monopolist is a one-firm industry—a single seller of a product that has virtually no close substitutes—and therefore has undisputed control over industry price. In contrast, the perfect competitor is just one of many thousands, or even hundreds of thousands, of sellers—simply a drop in "an ocean" of producers, all supplying exactly the same product. Thus, the lone competitor has virtually no control over industry prices, and any attempt to differentiate his product is obviously not worthwhile.

"Competition" can be a confusing term. Ask any person you meet to name a competitive industry and, judging by the TV ads, his or her response might be the automobile, breakfast-cereal, or steel industry. Indeed, there may be a lot of *rivalry* between, say, Ford, Toyota, and General Motors, but they are not true competitors because the automobile industry does not exhibit the competitive characteristics we just outlined.

In addition, purely competitive industries have one attribute—*easy entry into, and easy exit from, the market*—that automobile manufacturers would never wish to share. A single seller in a truly competitive market can move into the industry without exotic skills or a great deal of capital. This easy entry means that any excessive industry profits are threatened by new profit-seeking firms, which can easily move in, depress prices, and squeeze out existing profits. This is obviously the kind of competition the large car and processed-food industries wish to avoid. So what is a good example of pure competition?

After careful study, economists have found that the agricultural industry best represents a competitive market structure. Of course, certain "big-business" farm operations, such as a modern dairy farm, are not so easy to establish. In addition, the

prices of certain grain crops are supported by government programs, and these subsidies tend to dilute the pure competitive-
ness of some segments of American agriculture.

Perhaps the best illustration of farm competition is the hog
or hay industry. For example, hundreds of thousands of hog
producers (many of them quite small) can move in and out of the
industry with relative ease. Thus, when prices are good, they
"move in." The cumulative effect of this influx is a rapid increase
in the supply of hogs and, very likely, a decrease in the overall
price of hogs. Once prices drop significantly, many of the more
inefficient hog producers exit the industry as quickly as they
entered it.

Now let's return to our earlier question: exactly how are
revenues determined under competitive conditions? Generally
speaking, to determine the revenue of a competitor, we multiply
the "going" industry price by the units of output that the competitor has to sell. For example, a single hog producer might sell
1000 or 10,000 pounds of pork at the industry price. Thus, no
matter how much a single competitor has to sell, it cannot affect
the overall market price in any way.

Since these characteristics also apply to hay producers,
let's see if we can illustrate Chester Olson's individual situation.
If Chester can sell any amount of hay at the "going" industry
price, then Chester's individual demand curve will be *flat* (or
perfectly elastic), showing that the market will take all the hay
he is willing to produce. At an overall market price of $60 a
load, Chester's demand curve would look like the one shown in
Figure 13-3.

Once we know Chester's revenue situation, (which is defined by his demand curve), we are equipped with all the information we need to derive his product supply curve. Let's give
it a try.

Competitive Supply

Recall that a **product supply curve** is *a series of points that
shows how much output a producer is willing to supply to the
market at alternative prices*. For example, Chester's supply curve
for hay will indicate how many loads he will want to supply if the
"going" price of hay is, say, $60 a load, or $40, or $20, or any unit

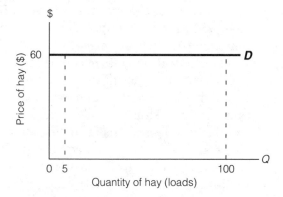

FIGURE 13-3   An individual seller in a perfectly competitive market "sees" a horizontal demand curve for its product. The single seller, whether it sells a lot or a little, is simply too small to influence the overall industry price.

price in between. The line that connects these points becomes Chester's product (hay) supply curve.

Obviously, Chester's decisions about how much hay to produce at different prices will be based on profit maximization. Chester will want to produce x amount of hay at $60 per load, because that amount will give him the maximum amount of profits at that price. Exactly how will Chester know when he has arrived at that maximum profit quantity?

To find out, Chester must go through a marginal decision-making process similar to the one he went through when he was trying to decide how many workers to hire. This time, however, he will be asking himself, "Will the first load be profitable?" and "Will the second load be profitable?" and so on. As a general rule, Chester should *continue to increase output as long as each additional load adds something to profits.*

Assuming (as we did in Figure 13-3) that the market price of hay is $60 per load, is it profitable for Chester to produce any hay at all? He answers that question by comparing the costs of the first loads of hay with the revenues he will receive if he sells them. To find out what his costs are, Chester refers to his MC curve, shown in Figure 13-4. We can now see that the production costs of these early loads are significantly lower than the $60 revenue Chester receives from selling each load. Thus, it is profitable for him to produce these first loads.

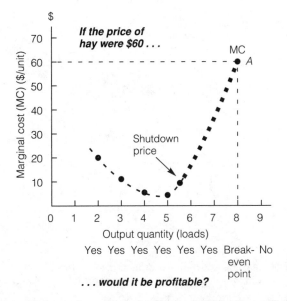

FIGURE 13-4 If the price of hay is $60 per load, then Chester should produce hay as long as the extra (marginal) cost is less than the $60 selling price per unit of hay. Note that all the units of hay under consideration (up to unit 8) will add something to Chester's profits.

Now let's move along the *x* axis of Chester's MC curve until we get to the seventh load. Again, Chester asks his question, "Is it profitable to produce and sell load 7?" The marginal cost of this load is $40, but the extra revenue he receives from producing it continues to be $60; thus, Chester's marginal decision is still "yes" (to produce load 7). Now what about load 8? This particular load is obviously a **breakeven point.** The marginal cost of any load past load 8 will be >$60 and should not be produced. Therefore, Chester ought to continue producing *up to and including* the eighth load; if he goes beyond eight loads, the extra marginal cost will be greater than the extra revenue (*P*). Our "profitability rule of thumb" is therefore *stop producing at the quantity Q at which price P = marginal cost* (MC).

In Figure 13-4, we use this rule to obtain the first point (point *A*) on Chester's product supply curve (also note point *A* on the completed supply curve in Figure 13-5). To find another point, we must begin all over with a new price. For example, how much hay is Chester willing to produce if the market price is $40 per load? Going through the same marginal decision-making

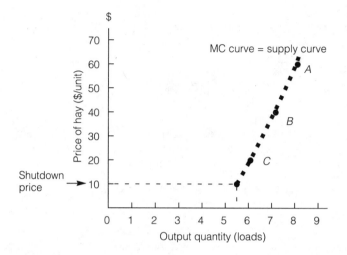

FIGURE 13-5   Chester's short-run supply curve for hay is his marginal cost curve above the *shutdown price*. It rises upward and to the right due to the *law of diminishing returns*.

process he did before, Chester would obviously maximize his profits by producing and selling up to and including load 7. (In Figure 13-4, note that the eighth load now represents a $20 loss; MC = $60, but *P* = $40.) A marginal cost of $40 and a quantity of 7 loads gives us our second point on Chester's product supply curve (point *B*).

Finally, if the price of hay is $20 per load, we can easily see that Chester will produce up to and including load 6 at point *C* on his product supply curve.

Perhaps you are noticing a consistent pattern. The three points we derived on Chester's product supply curve are *the same three points we derived on his* MC *curve.* This is no mere coincidence. It should be obvious that as long as we determine profitability points in this way, Chester's MC curve *becomes* his supply curve!

We should note that the industry price of hay could decline to such a low point that it might not be worthwhile for Chester to initiate production (produce *any* hay), at least in the short run. In terms of committing resources, however, Chester cannot get out of paying a fixed amount of short-run costs, even by shutting down his operation! What would this **shutdown price** be for Chester? By shutting down, Chester would lose his $100 in fixed costs (using the figures from our earlier example).

Suppose that the price of hay is so low that Chester's revenues do not even cover his variable costs. This means that poor Chester will lose not only his fixed costs ($100) but also *some* money from the variable costs that were not matched by sufficient revenue. In this case, it is wise for Chester to shut down and minimize his losses ($100) from the unavoidable fixed costs.

In summary, we can say that Chester's shutdown price is the price at which revenues generated from total sales do not quite cover variable costs. Chester's product supply curve (see Figure 13-5) can therefore be defined as *his* MC *curve above the shutdown price* (see Figure 13-4).

Now that we have derived Chester's product supply curve, we are near the completion of our task. All that we have left to do is to work out the so-called **industry supply curve**. In our example, the industry would include *all* producers of hay in Chester's particular area. Therefore, to find the industry supply, we simply add up the total quantities of hay that all of the producers in the area are willing to supply at different unit prices. The other producers' supply curves will probably look something like Chester's, because their marginal decision-making processes will be similar to his.

The only major difference between an individual's supply curve and the industry supply curve is that the quantities of hay on the industry curve are much larger; the unit prices remain the same. Instead of 8 loads at $60 per load, the industry in our example may produce 8 million loads of hay at $60 per load, but the slope of the industry supply curve will still look very much like Chester's positively sloped individual supply curve.

Building a Market

So far, we have used Chester's hay-baling example to demonstrate the fundamentals of production. We moved along with Chester from the basic law of diminishing returns, to resource pricing, to profit maximization, and on up to the derivation of the industry supply curve. Obviously, Chester and his compatriot hay producers are just simple illustrations of the activities of *all* competitive suppliers. Thus, in *any* short-run competitive market, the product supply curve reflects rising marginal costs and therefore slopes upward and to the right.

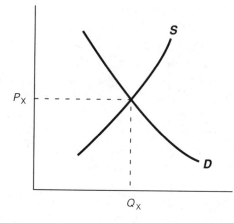

FIGURE 13-6 A typical market for industry X.

In earlier chapters, we derived a simple product demand curve. In the case of demand, our starting point was the law of diminishing marginal utility, which eventually contributed to a downward-sloping demand curve. We can now say that *all* product demand curves have a similar downward-sloping shape.

With these theories of supply and demand behind us, it now seems appropriate to construct a more generalized market, using a typical supply-demand curve from virtually any competitive market. We'll simply call it "industry X." This sample market is shown in Figure 13-6.

We have completed our major objective for the first half of Part II—building a complete product market. As we admire this "basic building block" of our market economy, we can now appreciate the many microeconomic principles and concepts that lie behind these simple lines.

Questions for Thought and Discussion

1. Are all implicit costs also fixed costs? Why or why not?
2. Assume that you live in a small city in which 35 pizza restaurants operate. How closely do the competitive characteristics discussed in this chapter describe the pizza "industry" in your city?

3. What happens to the theories in this chapter if firms have goals other than profit maximization?

4. *True or false?* Marginal costs are calculated only from changes in variable costs, not from changes in fixed costs. Explain.

5. If you own a car (or know someone who does), then list the fixed and variable costs associated with owning and driving the car. Are any social costs associated with driving the car? If so, what are they?

14

Using the Markets

One of the rewarding things about microeconomics is that after we have made the time-consuming effort to develop the underlying concept of economic markets, we have some useful tools at our disposal that are more than just abstract theories. These markets have now become practical instruments that can help us understand real-life issues and problems. In Chapter 14, we will explore some of these possibilities.

First, we will learn about how labor markets can help us understand the age-old problem of income distribution; later, we will use our knowledge of product markets to better understand the U.S. farm problem. By the end of this chapter, you should gain a respect and appreciation for how versatile and useful market theory and market models can be in helping us to explain and gain insight into interesting, real-world situations.

Income Distribution

Who reaps the rewards of economic activity? Why do some individuals get more than others? What mechanism divides up income in our society? What part of the economic pie goes to the labor force, compared to the resource markets for capital and land? All of these questions are related to the issue of *income distribution.* Indeed, they are questions that have not always been easy to answer in relation to a modern market economy.

In older, traditional economic systems, production and distribution were based on well-established patterns, so the question "Who receives the output?" was fairly easy to answer. Once you understood the traditional source of power in a particular culture (often based on land control), then you pretty much understood how the income was distributed.

But what about a market system? If traditional patterns do not determine who gets the rewards of production, then what does? A precise answer to this question, based on resource markets, was formulated around the turn of the current century. This solution is now known as **Clark's Theory of Distribution,** after its proponent, American economist John B. Clark (1847–1938).

In its simplest form, Clark's theory attempts to show how much of the total economic pie is distributed to labor resources and how much is distributed to land resources. Clark's conclusion is fairly simple, once we grasp the underlying concept of a labor market. To demonstrate, let's redraw a typical labor market. Recall that a labor demand curve represents the worker's value of the marginal product of labor (VMP_L). We will simplify labor supply in this example, making it a vertical line as shown in Figure 14-1.

Clark observed that under normal economic conditions, each worker receives a *market equilibrium wage* (a wage equivalent to the "last" worker's VMP_L). In Figure 14-1, the eighth worker's VMP_L is $20 per day. At this point, the supply curve crosses the demand curve; therefore, *all* workers receive a wage equivalent to the eighth worker's wage ($20 per day). Thus, labor's share of the total economic pie (the monetary return on labor) is $20 × 8 workers, or $160 (represented by the shaded area in Figure 14-1).

But what about the owner of the other resource, land? According to Clark's analysis, the landowner receives what looks like a "surplus," represented by the unshaded triangular area under the demand curve. If the landowner adds workers on a one-by-one basis, the law of diminishing returns (Chapter 4) indicates that the first worker will contribute the most to total output and that subsequent workers (all the way down to worker 8) will contribute less and less to total output. In theory, the first

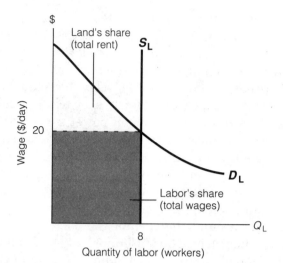

FIGURE 14-1 *Clark's Theory of Distribution* graphically helps us to "see" what portion of total output goes to the worker and what portion of total output goes to the landowner.

workers contribute *more* to total production than they receive (remember that *everyone* receives a wage of $20 per day). Clark concluded that this "surplus" (the upper unshaded triangle) is actually not a surplus but an economic return—or *rent*—to the owner of the land resource.

It should be obvious that the labor wage rate (and labor's share of the total economic pie) will generally depend *on the positioning of the supply-demand curve.* This knowledge, in turn, can help us answer some intriguing questions about what takes place in our market economy, such as "Why do very hard-working individuals frequently receive the lowest wages?" Let's look at a typical example of this problem.

Mike Jones, a waiter at the Bixby drive-in, had to see his dentist, Dr. Franklin, last week. When he received his bill in the mail, Mike was first surprised and then angered to discover that his dentist had completed $50 worth of work in 30 minutes, the equivalent of three full days of the wages Mike earns as a waiter. "How in the world could my dentist make 40–50 times my hourly wage?" Mike wondered.

This large differential in wages can be partially explained by a simple resource-market analysis. To demonstrate, we have

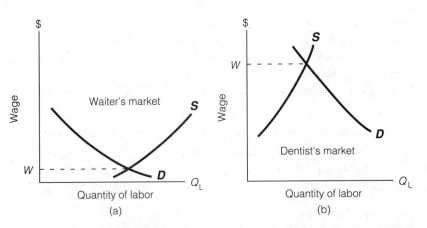

FIGURE 14-2 The positioning of labor supply and demand often determines which professions offer high wages and which professions offer low wages. A comparison between the labor markets for waiters and dentists provides an exaggerated example.

drawn separate markets for dentists and waiters in Figure 14-2, where W is the equilibrium wage rate.

Let's look at the waiter's market first. In Figure 14-2(a), we can see how supply-demand positioning makes Mike's wage rate low. However, these demand and supply curves do not tell us why the supply of waiters (and waitresses) is so great and the demand for their services is so small. Some possible explanations for the large labor supply are:

- Too many relatively unskilled individuals (both men and women) are willing to do this kind of work.

- Entry into the waiter-waitress labor market is relatively free; no unions, licensing, or certification is required.

The waiter's labor market is also inhibited by low demand. Possible reasons for the small labor demand are:

- The value of the marginal product of labor (VMP_L) is low, especially compared to a dentist's VMP_L, because work as a waiter or waitress is relatively *labor intensive;* very little technology or capital is required to do it.

- The demand for the final product (a restaurant meal) is relatively low.

On the other hand, Dr. Franklin's labor market, shown in Figure 14-2(b), has, from the viewpoint of wages, a more favorable supply-demand configuration: a high demand for dentist labor and a relatively low labor supply. Note that the high wage rate is created because *both* supply and demand are in favorable positions. What are the possible explanations for this situation? First, let's consider the reasons for the small labor supply:

- There are relatively few qualified dentists because they must complete a long and expensive training period.
- Entry into the field is restricted. Entrants are approved by the professional associations that control licensing examinations, certification requirements, and so on.

On the demand side, dentists benefit from the following factors, among others:

- A dentist's productivity (VMP_L) is relatively high because of labor-saving dental technology (high-speed drills, X-ray equipment, auxiliary services, and so on).
- There is a relatively high demand for dental health care.

If, by some quirk of fate, all waiters and waitresses (as a group) were required to complete strict schooling and licensing programs while dentists built more dental schools and lowered entry barriers to their profession, then the gross wage differential between these occupations would undoubtedly be reduced.

This analysis includes only the *market reasons* for this wage differential. In the real world, there may be other explanations. For one thing, waiter and waitress work has usually been considered "woman's work," and traditional "female" occupations (teaching, library work, nursing, and so on) generally have poor pay scales. Other social factors that can (but should not) affect a particular individual's wage include race, ethnic origin, religion, age, and whether that person was fortunate enough to have parents who could pay for expensive professional training. Also, "who you know" and "just plain luck" can play important parts in determining any particular individual's life-time earnings.

Unions

We can also apply our understanding of resource markets to an analysis of the economic impact of **unions.** Generally speaking, unions are formed because of the inherent weakness of individuals who work for very large, powerful, and often impersonal employ-

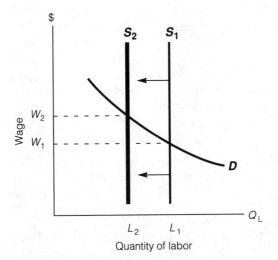

FIGURE 14-3 *Unions* and other labor or professional organizations intentionally restrict the supply of labor in their industry or profession to raise their members' wages.

ers. In large-scale businesses or industries, where workers might be unsuccessful in promoting their individual interests, a unified group—with the power to strike—can often promote the group's interest quite effectively. What is often overlooked when discussing unionization, however, is that this organizational power can "manipulate" labor markets, usually for the express purpose of raising the wage rates of the people they represent. We now have an excellent background to help us understand how this is accomplished.

Basically, organized labor can raise wages in one of three ways. Let's begin with the union policies that can shift the labor supply curve to the left (see Figure 14-3).

As we saw before, entry barriers (or, simply, upgraded entry requirements) erected by any organization can often shift the labor supply curve to the left. A variety of professional organizations, including barbers, doctors, teachers, and accountants, insist that individuals complete apprenticeships or years of schooling before they begin to work. Over 200 years ago, Adam Smith recognized a genuine (but often overlooked) purpose of these "regulations" when he wrote:

> The intention of both regulations is to restrain the competition to much smaller number than might otherwise be disposed to enter

the trade. The limitations of their number of apprentices restrains it directly. A long term of apprenticeship restrains it more indirectly, but as effectually, by increasing the expense of education.[39]

Smith was unhappy that many of these artificial barriers (apprenticeships, long schooling, licensing, and so on) prevented individuals from freely exercising their skills and entering into productive relationships with a potential employer:

> The patrimony of a poor man lies in the strength and dexterity of his hands; and to hinder him from employing this strength and dexterity in what manner he thinks proper without injury to his neighbor is a plain violation of this most sacred property. It is a manifest encroachment upon the just liberty both of the workman and of those who might be disposed to employ him. . . .
>
> To judge whether he is fit to be employed may surely be trusted to the discretion of the employers whose interest it so much concerns.[40]

Note that the same restrictive impact can be accomplished by simply establishing *fixed quotas* on the number of workers who are allowed to join a union. The more direct technique of quotas characterizes many of the building trade unions. Unions also may support legislation to limit the foreign immigration of certain workers who might compete in their workers' particular labor market, thereby indirectly restricting entry in certain areas.

A leftward shift in the labor supply curve does result in higher wage rates for unionized workers, but it also reduces the number of workers who can enjoy those high wages. (Note that the number of workers employed is reduced from L_1 to L_2 in Figure 14-3.) In addition, these barriers and restrictive policies may reduce the efficiency of the overall economy by preventing individuals from entering the more specialized job arena. In turn, the price of the final product becomes higher to the consumer than it would be if a free-entry policy were in effect.

Another method of increasing wage rates is by expanding the labor demand curve, as shown in Figure 14-4. How would an upward shift in the labor demand curve from D_1 to D_2 be accomplished? Recall that the labor demand curve reflects the VMP_L curve. Therefore, any increase in productivity—working harder, adding more capital, or utilizing more advanced technology—will eventually shift the labor demand curve upward.

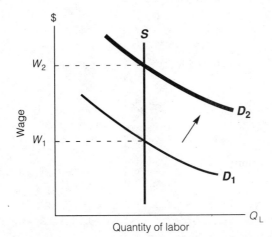

Figure 14-4   By improving productivity or by promoting product demand, unions can help to shift the labor supply curve up and to the right, increasing wage rates (from W_1 to W_2) without sacrificing industry employment.

This is the major reason why wage levels in **capital-intensive** Western countries are significantly higher than wage levels in less-developed Third World countries.

Another way to raise the labor demand curve would be for the unions to encourage workers to purchase their own labor output (for example, Ford autoworkers to buy Ford cars). This strategy recognizes that the VMP_L curve reflects not only worker productivity but also *the demand for, and the price of, the final product.*

Some unions help to advertise their workers' products ("Buy the union label"); others tend to put their promotional energies into political channels. For example, construction workers often push for lower mortgage rates, autoworkers lobby for the construction of highways, and textile workers urge further restrictions on imports. These are just a few examples of how unions help to shift the labor demand curve upward and to the right.

A final method of raising wage rates reflects the sheer collective power of the union organization. To avoid a strike, management may be forced to offer *wage-supports* (similar to price-supports) to workers through the **collective bargaining process.** Graphically, wage supports create a somewhat higher wage rate than the equilibrium wage *without* shifting the supply curve or the demand curve. In Figure 14-5, note that the equilibrium wage is at W_1 but the agreed-on wage can reach up to W_2.

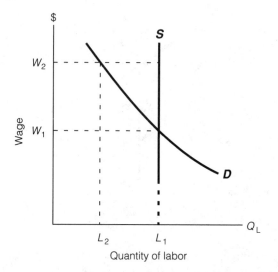

FIGURE 14-5 A *wage support* raises wages (from W_1 to W_2) without shifting labor supply or labor demand. Organizational power, *collective bargaining,* and, ultimately, the threat of a strike may force management to raise workers' wages.

Raising wages to W_2 appears to defy the labor market; at this wage, it looks as if unionized workers are getting "something for nothing." But as is true of most economic benefits, there is a cost involved. What is the drawback? Notice that the higher wage rate W_2 intersects the labor demand curve at L_2, which indicates a lower quantity of labor than the former equilibrium labor quantity L_1. In practical terms, this means that some people who where formerly working will lose their jobs after the wage-rate increase.

On the other hand, it is often asserted that nonunion labor in equivalent or similar industries frequently benefits from union wage rates. Employers may attempt to prevent unionization by offering higher wage rates to workers than they would if no unions existed.

We now turn our attention to the subject of product markets, with particular emphasis on the farm problem in the United States. We choose the agricultural industry because of the ease with which we can apply the knowledge of competitive supply and demand that we developed in previous chapters.

What is our "farm problem"? How did it begin, and what are some possible solutions to this problem? Let's take a look.

The U.S. Farm Problem

Although there is no example of *perfect* competition, the farming industry comes the closest to our earlier definition. For example, competition is usually considered healthy for the economy. In theory, a competitive industry operates efficiently and provides relatively low prices for the consumer. Indeed, these characteristics are beneficial to all of us. Yet from the viewpoint of the producer, American farming has greatly suffered from an inability to control both agricultural output and prices—a characteristic that is especially unfortunate when we consider that most American industries *do* have some control over their prices. This imbalance has often worked to the disadvantage of the U.S. farmer.

To see more clearly how this situation works against farm producers, we must go back to the "root problem" of agricultural prices. Economists look at this price dilemma from two vantage points: as a historical problem, and as a short-run problem. Let's use our supply-demand tools to help us understand the historical difficulties that U.S. farmers have faced over the years.

The Historical Problem

American farmers are incredible food producers. Through the exploitation of natural resources and the intensive use of energy, farm chemicals, large-scale machinery, hybrid seeds, and other enhancing factors, our agricultural producers have amazed the rest of the world with their productivity and the sheer magnitude of their output.

The average U.S. farmer can feed himself and about 100 other people. Ironically, however, this amazing and enviable productivity is also a source of the historical farm problem.

How can "too much" be a problem? The high state of farm technology has, in effect, shifted the raw-food-and-fiber supply curve far to the right of the historical supply-demand graph. Agricultural product demand has not kept up with this large shift in supply, however. Of course, our population has grown, as have incomes, but these increases have simply not matched potential U.S. food production.

Economists say that if, for example, our food fits the general category of an *income-inelastic* product, then when income increases by a certain percentage, a corresponding increase in the consumption of an income-inelastic product (like food) will not be proportionately as large. Thus, food demand has increased over time, but it has not increased enough to match the large increases in food supply. Nor has the population growth rate made up the difference. The ultimate result, therefore, is *depressed agricultural prices relative to prices elsewhere in the economy.*

A final factor compounds the problem. Recall that agricultural products are *price inelastic* (see Chapter 3): the quantities of these products that are demanded are relatively *insensitive* to a change in price. Inelastic demand curves, in turn, have a rather steep slope, making low farm prices possible (see Figure 14-6). In summary, the historical U.S. farming problem stems from:

- A large rightward shift in supply (technological advancement).
- A relatively small shift in demand (income inelasticity).
- A steep demand curve (price inelasticity).

When we put all of these factors together on a graph, we can easily visualize the farmer's price problem as it developed over the years.

In Figure 14-6, P_2 is the equilibrium price from an earlier period. Over time, the supply and demand curves shift to positions S_2 and D_2, respectively, resulting in the new, lower equilibrium price P_1. Admittedly, this example is somewhat exaggerated. The absolute prices of agricultural commodities may not actually fall. What happens is that farm prices drop *relative* to the prices of the consumer goods that farmers buy and to the prices of farm inputs, such as land, fertilizer, seed, and machinery.

This relative price disadvantage is sometimes referred to as a *parity problem*. A poor parity situation means that it now takes more bushels of a given commodity (wheat, corn, soybeans, or whatever) to purchase a certain bundle of consumer or producer goods than it did in an earlier period. To bring farmers up to a higher level of parity (say 90 percent), some economists suggest government subsidies, primarily in the form of price supports. We'll take a look at price supports and some other

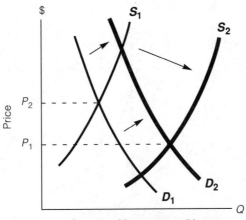

Quantity of farm commodities

FIGURE 14-6 The historical farm problem includes, among other things, low prices due to the fact that farm-commodity prices are depressed relative to other prices in the economy. Note the exaggerated increase in supply over time compared to the more modest increase in demand.

government programs a little later in the chapter. Now let's briefly examine what economists call the "short-run" problem in the U.S. farm industry.

The Short-Run Problem

If deteriorating parity summarizes the farmers' historical problem, then their short-run problem can be summarized as *unstable farm prices, output, and income on a year-to-year basis.* Obviously, no farmer knows ahead of time what his or her year-end production will be, or what the total production or the market product price will be for the industry as a whole (all suppliers). There are simply too many variables: lack of rain; damage from insects, fungus, or an early frost; and so on. These factors may result in higher food prices for that year but, at the same time, may leave the farmer with very little product to sell.

On the other hand, perfect growing conditions can result in a *bumper crop*, which, ironically, can be just as much of a headache as too little output. Perhaps this can best be explained in terms of a home garden. Has your family ever experienced a true bumper crop? Maybe there were times when you had twice as many beans or tomatoes as you needed—or three, four, or five

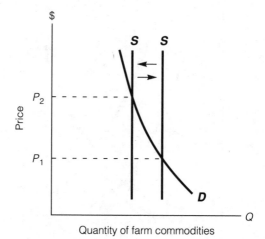

FIGURE 14-7 The *short-run farm problem:* widely fluctuating prices, due to weather and other uncontrollable environmental factors, result in industry-wide price and income instability.

times as many. Unfortunately, everyone else is probably in the same situation at the same time. As hard as you try, you have trouble even giving your tomatoes away. Now imagine that your yearly income is dependent on the price of your beans or tomatoes! You may have a lot of product to sell, but you may be able to sell it only at a very low price—or not at all.

Figure 14-7 summarizes these short-run pricing problems. Notice the substantial variation in price. The major causes of this situation are a widely fluctuating product supply and an inelastic (steep-sloped) demand curve.

Price instability leads to income instability. Even small changes in commodity prices, a few cents up or down, can have a dramatic effect on the farmer's annual income. When nonfarmers hear the "noon price report," they probably wonder why anyone would be interested in relatively small changes in the price of corn, wheat, hogs, or any other commodity. Yet these modest changes can easily make the difference between profit and loss for the average farm producer. Few industries face an equivalent situation of income uncertainty on a year-to-year basis.

Our discussion of the two related farm problems leads us to ask, "What, if anything, can be done about them?" Unfortunately, a "sure fire," low-cost solution has yet to be discovered for either the historical or the short-run problem. Various

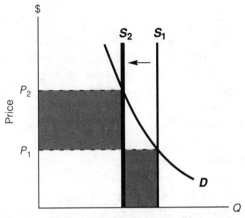

FIGURE 14-8 *Crop-restriction programs* offer financial incentives to farmers who do not plant crops. These programs are designed to raise prices, improve farmers' revenues, and avoid the accumulation of excessive commodity *surpluses.*

government programs have been designed to help the American farmer. With the aid of our supply-demand tools, we will examine how some of these programs work, noting their strengths and weaknesses.

Farm Programs

Let's look first at the government's **crop-restriction* program,** which essentially pays each farmer (either in cash or in surplus grain) to keep a certain amount of land *out of production.* Now that we know much of the farm problem stems from oversupply, it is easy to see the logic of restricting the number of acres that each farmer is allowed to plant. If we look at the impact of this program on a graph (see Figure 14-8), we can see that crop restriction shifts the supply curve backward (to the left), which brings about higher agricultural prices.

*In the 1950s, this program was called "Soil-Bank"; later, it was referred to as a "Set-Aside" program. Beginning in the mid-1980s, the federal government initiated the Conservation Reserve Program (CRP), which not only restricts agricultural output but also has the added benefit of limiting production on lands that are considered to be "highly erodible."

Farmers receive a higher price P_2 for their products, as well as greater total revenue for producing less output. How do we know this? In Figure 14-8, the total revenue lost (the smaller shaded area) is smaller than the total revenue gained (the larger shaded area). This will always be true whenever we deal with a price-inelastic demand curve (see Chapter 3 for more details). In summary, the farmer's benefits from crop restrictions are (1) a subsidy from the government for keeping land out of production, and (2) higher commodity prices and a greater total revenue.

However, crop restriction has some major drawbacks for both taxpayers and consumers. These disadvantages include (1) higher taxes to support the crop-restriction program, (2) higher food prices, and (3) less food available for consumption.

In another form of intervention, the **price-support program,** government attempts to deal more directly with the price- and income-instability problems of the farmer. Basically, a price support does two positive things for the farmer: it increases *and* stabilizes farm-product prices above the normal equilibrium price.

In Figure 14-9, the government's **support price** is P_S, a price above the original equilibrium price P. This higher price also gives the farmer a greater total revenue because the food demand curve is inelastic. In addition, the higher support price cuts back the quantity demanded from Q_2 to Q_1, while supply remains constant at the original level.

The inevitable result of this situation is the creation of a **surplus** that must be bought up by the government at the support price P_S. The quantity of this surplus is the difference between Q_1 and Q_2; the cost of the surplus is represented by the shaded area in the figure. When the government buys up these farm surpluses, it distributes bonus incomes to the farmers at the taxpayers' expense. Taxpayers not only purchase these farm surpluses, but also pay to store them. And, as before, the consumers find higher food prices in the grocery store.

Finally, government is attempting to enhance the *demand side* of the farm market through various programs and policies. The large Federal Food Stamp Program is one example. Also, high on the list of U.S. foreign policy objectives is the creation of a favorable international climate in which to sell U.S. agricultural commodities (and sometimes surpluses). Such efforts, if successful, will improve prices for the domestic farm producer.

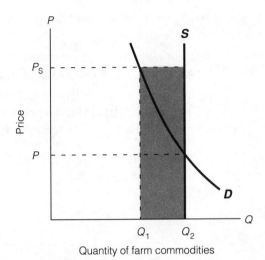

Quantity of farm commodities

FIGURE 14-9   In the *price-support program,* government offers subsidized *support prices* (P_s) for farm-grown commodities. If P_s is greater than the equilibrium price P, then a surplus (shaded area) is generated that must be purchased and stored at the taxpayers' expense. Farmers benefit both from stable prices and from greater total revenue (than they would earn at the equilibrium price).

In conclusion, our government is still searching for effective programs that will help the farm industry, but so many important criteria must be met. These programs must be cost-effective, fair, and still offer U.S. farmers incentives to continue to provide raw food and fiber to home and foreign markets and, at the same time, not abuse or deplete our nation's world-class land and water resource base. The search for effective policies and specific programs should be made by men and women who have a working knowledge of environmental relationships (ecology) and an understanding of traditional supply and demand markets and the other intricacies of microeconomics.

Questions for Thought and Discussion

1. Have unions outlived their economic usefulness? Why or why not?

2. "Economic power is reflected in political power." Are agricultural programs the result of such influences?

3. How is the monopoly power of large corporations related to the distribution of income?

4. Is a minimum wage enacted by a government similar to a price-support program for an agricultural product? Explain.

5. What is the difference between a relative price and an absolute price? In this chapter, has the relative price or the absolute price of most farm products decreased over time? Why?

15

Long-Run Supply

Until now, our discussions of competitive supply have been primarily concerned with the short run. The resources of Chester Olson, our hay-baling friend, were essentially fixed except for one variable resource (labor). Under this strict condition, the well-known law of diminishing returns evolved.

But what would happen if we suddenly dropped this condition? If we allow Chester to expand or contract the amount of land he farms, to add more capital, or to alter some other resource, then we will be looking at what economists call the "long run." The long run is a "whole new ball game," and its analysis involves a somewhat different approach than we used in our earlier microeconomic discussions. Let's see how this new idea works.

The Long Run

Perhaps it is easiest to think of the **long run** as a time period that is long enough to *allow all resources to become variable resources.* In the short run, Chester could not get out of paying for things like land costs, insurance, depreciation, and taxes. In

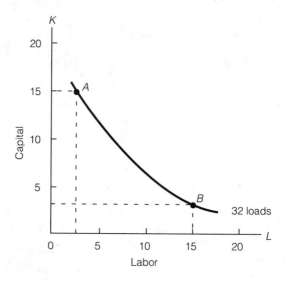

FIGURE 15-1 At a glance, the *equal-product curve* shows the many combinations of capital K and labor L that will produce a fixed amount of output or "equal product."

the long run, however, we are assuming that Chester can reduce or expand any resource that was formerly fixed.

Thus, at one extreme, the long run gives Chester the opportunity to leave farming altogether (if he cannot meet his economic costs); at the other extreme, Chester can purchase entire new farms and double or triple the size of his operation. Economists use the phrase "changing the scale of operation" to indicate an enlargement or a reduction of all resources.

To show the long run on a graph, we must therefore have some way of indicating scale changes. Economists do, in fact, use such a technique—one that is surprisingly similar to the indifference-curve/budget-line system we developed in Chapter 11. Our new technique is called the **equal-product curve system**.

The Equal-Product Curve

Note, for example, that the curve in Figure 15-1 looks very much like an indifference curve. This time, however, instead of plotting two goods on the horizontal and vertical axes (hamburgers and milkshakes), we plot two resources: capital K and labor L.

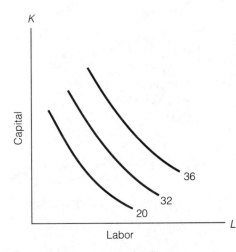

Figure 15-2 *An equal-product map* shows the various combinations of capital K and labor L that will produce different levels of output. Three levels or representative equal-product curves are shown here.

Our indifference curve showed a constant level of *utility*. Our equal-product curve shows a constant level of *output*.

Assume, for example, that Chester's equal-product curve (shown in Figure 15-1) represents an output of 32 loads of hay per day. This curve indicates *all the combinations of capital K and labor L that would generate 32 loads of hay*. At point A, for example, the combination of 15 units of K and about 2 units of L will produce 32 loads; so will point B, which represents 15 units of L and about 3 units of K. Any point in between A and B will generate precisely the same output!

There are, we will see, some other interesting similarities between the indifference and the equal-product curves. For example, in the long run, Chester has the opportunity to move onto higher and higher equal-product curves, just as the consumer (in Chapter 11) can move onto higher and higher indifference curves. Each new equal-product curve (moving upward to the right) therefore represents a higher level of output. When a number of curves are placed together on one graph, this **equal-product map,** or **production function,** shows us the many, many resource combinations that will produce a variety of production levels. A partial production function with three possible levels of output is shown in Figure 15-2. Of course, we could

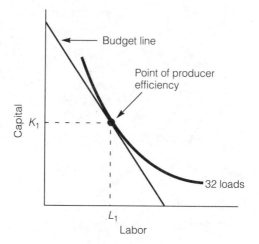

FIGURE 15-3 *Maximum producer efficiency* implies that the producer is getting the highest possible output from a given production budget. Graphically, this level of efficiency occurs at the point at which the highest equal-product curve just touches (is tangent to) the budget line.

enlarge this graph to include other possible production levels as well.

The budget line is another point of similarity with our earlier indifference-curve analysis. In our current example, this line represents a specific budget for production costs. The producer's budget line is drawn exactly the way the budget line is drawn for the consumer. (Reread the explanation in Chapter 11 on pages 168–169 now, if you feel uneasy about how these lines are derived.) Once a budget line is drawn for any specific budget, we can easily find the point at which Chester *maximizes output* (just as the consumer maximizes utility) with a given budget. Of course, when we say the producer is "maximizing output with a given budget," we are also saying that this producer is minimizing costs when producing a specific amount of output.

Let's assume that Chester spends a fixed amount and then determine at which point he maximizes output with that fixed budget. Take a close look at Figure 15-3. The point of **maximum producer efficiency** is really not surprising: the solution is similar to the one we obtained earlier in demand theory using indifference curves. Here, however, the producer maximizes output (or minimizes costs) at the point at which *the equal-product curve is tangent to the budget line.* In Figure 15-3, that "optimal" point is obviously point A. From this point of tangency, we can move horizontally over to the K (capital) axis and vertically down to the L (labor) axis from that point to find the "best" or most efficient combination of resources that Chester can use to produce 32 loads of hay. The ideal resource mix is therefore K_1 and L_1.

One reason we are being so careful to compare demand theory (indifference curves) and production theory (equal-product curves) is to highlight the similarities between them. As we saw in Chapter 11, the consumer attempts to maximize total utility within a limited budget; here, we see that the producer tries to obtain the highest output within a budget constraint.

The major *difference* between demand and production theory is that the producer is trying not only to use resources efficiently but also to maximize long-run profits. Profit maximization makes supply a somewhat more complex topic than demand, as we will see a little later in this chapter.

Chester Goes to India

Let's return to Chester's efficiency position, shown in Figure 15-3, and try an experiment. We will transfer our hay-baling friend to India—a labor-intensive and relatively capital-poor country.

The extremely large, unskilled, rural labor supply in India contributes to a labor market of depressed wages. On the other hand, India's capital-goods shortage makes capital prices relatively high compared to capital-goods prices in the United States. Different resource prices will force Chester into a different pattern of production than he followed in the United States, which is a high-wage, industrialized country. We can see some interesting aspects of Chester's new production situation if we work with his equal-product curve.

First, we will assume that equal-product curves are probably the same in India as they are in the United States. The resource "mix" that can produce a certain level of output is more or less a "mechanical arrangement": a specific input anywhere in the world results in the same output. So what is the major difference in production costs between the two countries?

In Figure 15-4, we can see that this difference in production costs is indicated by *the slope of the budget line*. For example, a

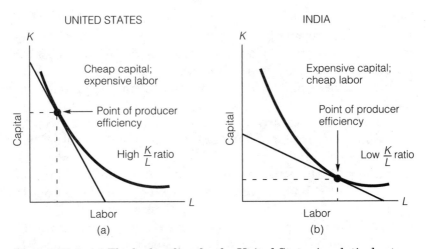

FIGURE 15-4   (a) The budget line for the United States is relatively steep, implying a high cost of labor and a low cost of capital. The point of tangency between the budget line and the equal-product curve therefore tends to favor production techniques with *high* capital-labor (*K/L*) ratios—techniques that employ few workers and lots of capital. (b) The budget line for India, where labor is relatively inexpensive, has a lower slope. The point of efficiency implies the use of production techniques that favor *low K/L* ratios compared to those of the United States.

$300 budget in India can obviously buy a great deal of labor because labor costs in India are relatively low. However Chester can't buy very much capital in India because capital costs are so high there. His budget line for production in India will therefore have a low slope. Note that in the budget-line comparison between the United States and India shown in Figure 15-4, the budget line for the United States has a relatively steep slope due to our country's high labor costs and relatively low capital costs.

What is so interesting about these two graphs is that they show the dramatic impact that different resource prices have on the way a country produces its products. ***Production efficiency*** in the United States, for example, is defined by a resource mix that represents a *high* capital-labor (*K/L*) ratio. This is not unexpected; U.S. businesses frequently use more capital-intensive methods in an economic climate of relatively high labor costs.

Production efficiency in India is just the reverse. Chester will produce the maximum output in India with a low *K/L* ratio—a highly labor-intensive technique. It is easy to jump to the conclusion that the labor-intensive method of producing hay in

India is less efficient than the U.S. capital-intensive system. This may not be correct, however. To find out which country's production method is more efficient, we must compare *overall* production costs. If we assume that Chester is operating on the same budget and producing the same level of output, then the two countries will be *equally efficient* from an economic perspective.

The Expansion Line

Now let's bring Chester back to his original farm and offer him what we originally promised: the chance to use a wide variety of budgets and the long-run freedom to change any or all of his resources. Then we can watch him expand his scale of operation and note the points of tangency between his equal-product curves and new budget lines. We will connect these points of tangency with what is called an ***expansion line,*** which will show Chester precisely which combinations of capital and labor most efficiently produce a large variety of output levels.

A sample expansion line, using five equal-product curves, is shown in Figure 15-5. With the expansion line in place, it is now possible for Chester to choose a level of output, find the point of tangency between the applicable equal-product curve and budget line, and move over to the horizontal and vertical axes to determine the most efficient combination of capital and labor. For example, at output level E in Figure 15-5, Chester finds that L_1 and K_1 turn out to be the most efficient resource mix.

From the expansion line we can also see how this long-run situation differs from the short-run conditions in our earlier discussion. Note, for example, how Chester is now varying *both capital and labor.*

Long-Run Average Cost

We are now in a good position to discuss one of the most important ideas of this chapter—the derivation of Chester's ***long-run average-cost (LAC) curve.*** You might be wondering why we are interested in discussing yet another cost concept; didn't we spend enough time and energy developing numerous cost theories (Chapter 13), culminating in the critical concept of marginal cost?

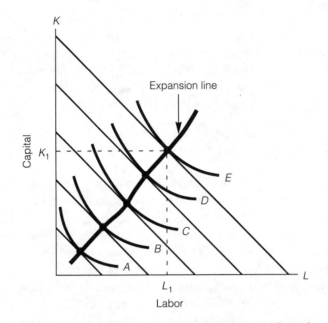

FIGURE 15-5 The *expansion line* indicates how a typical producer, with ever-increasing production budgets, would expand its operation. Note that all points on the expansion line conform to the various points of producer efficiency.

Marginal cost is still an important and useful tool, because it helps us to determine the point at which a producer maximizes profits. The LAC curve, on the other hand, is our best measure of *output efficiency*. Although we analyzed "efficiency" when we discussed the point of tangency, this is only one *kind* of efficiency (the best combination or mix of resources in which to produce *A*, *B, C, D,* or *E* levels of output).

What we don't yet know is *which of the different levels of output* is the **optimal output level**. As an example, level *A* may be only one load of hay per day (see Figure 15-5). Although we now know the "best" combination of resources required to produce that one load, certain *efficiencies of size* may nevertheless occur at some higher output level. (Large-scale operations can often produce goods more cheaply than small-scale operations.) These size efficiencies are referred to as **economies of scale**. It is important for the producer (Chester) to calculate the level of output (*A, B, C, D,* or *E*) that maximizes his economies of scale (gives him the lowest average cost). Let's figure it out for Chester.

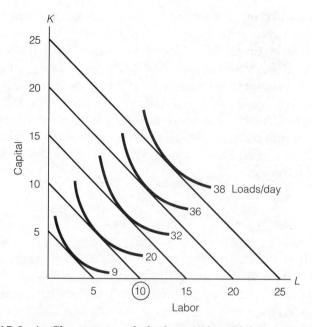

Figure 15-6 As Chester expands *both* capital and labor as his operation gets bigger and bigger, he can identify points of producer efficiency where the budget lines are tangent to the equal-product curves.

For simplicity's sake, we will assume that a unit of capital costs $20, and a unit of labor also costs $20. We now have sufficient data to find Chester's average costs. To start off, let's give him a budget of $100. At $20 per unit of labor, the maximum potential quantity of labor that Chester can purchase with this budget is 5 units; thus, the budget line would strike the labor axis at the 5-unit level. On the other hand, if Chester spends all of his $100 on capital and purchases no labor, he can buy 5 units of capital, so that the budget line would strike the capital axis at the 5-unit level. This budget line is shown as the smallest budget line in Figure 15-6.

Next, we give Chester a budget of $200 and work out a budget line for that amount. Then we give him budgets of $300, $400, and $500. Each new and higher budget is represented by an expanding budget line in Figure 15-6. Finally, we draw the relevant equal-product curve that is tangent to each of these budget lines and note the output level associated with each equal- product curve. From these figures, we can derive Chester's long-run average costs.

Let's work out a specific example, using this information. Look carefully at the particular budget line that strikes the labor axis at 10 units. (Note that the number 10 on the labor axis is circled.) Remembering that a unit of labor is priced at $20, we know that this budget must be worth 10 × $20 = $200.

Next, we read off the maximum output possible for this $200 budget, which is represented by the equal-product curve tangent to this budget line. The maximum output level with 10 units of labor is 20 loads of hay. The average cost of producing 20 loads of hay is

$$\frac{\$200}{20 \text{ loads}} = \$10 \text{ per load}$$

Using the same method, we can figure out the average costs at the other points of tangency as well. Each average cost (in relation to a particular quantity) is one more point on Chester's LAC curve. Rounding off to the nearest half dollar gives us the following average costs at the five points of tangency in Figure 15-6:

POINT (See Figure 15-7)	$ BUDGET / LOADS	=	LONG-RUN AVERAGE COST (LAC) (ROUNDED TO NEAREST HALF DOLLAR)
①	$\frac{\$100}{9 \text{ loads}}$	=	$11 per load
②	$\frac{\$200}{20 \text{ loads}}$	=	$10 per load
③	$\frac{\$300}{32 \text{ loads}}$	=	$9.50 per load
④	$\frac{\$400}{36 \text{ loads}}$	=	$11 per load
⑤	$\frac{\$500}{38 \text{ loads}}$	=	$13 per load

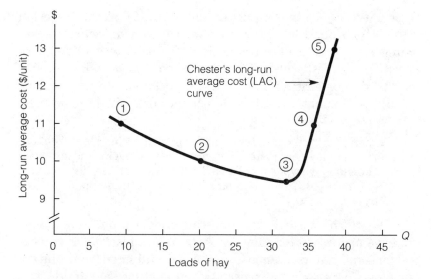

FIGURE 15-7 With the aid of a *long-run average cost* (LAC) *curve,* Chester Olson can determine which output level (or scale of production) is the most efficient. The bottom of the U-shaped LAC curve indicates the optimal size or scale of operation (32 loads at $9.50 per load).

Using the data in this chart, we are able to graph five points on Chester's LAC curve (see Figure 15-7). This LAC curve has a special shape to it, which raises an interesting question. Why do you think it turns down first and then, at 32 loads (point 3), begins to turn up? Answering this question will force us to examine a fascinating and important topic that we touched on earlier: economies of scale.

Economies of Scale

Inspecting Chester's LAC curve a little more closely, we see that when he produces only 9 loads of hay a day, his average cost per load is $11. As Chester expands production, however, he is able to reduce his average costs to a low of $9.50 per load due to a shift in his economies of scale to 32 loads. What are these mysterious "economies?"

Economies of scale are various cost-cutting efficiencies that are created as the scale of a business operation grows. Certainly, the most common economy of scale results from the *specialization and division of labor.* When workers specialize, they learn to do their specific jobs more quickly and accurately than a worker who shifts around from job to job (as Chester did when he was baling hay by himself). In addition, you have probably experienced the difficulty of "getting going" on a new task (studying for an exam or writing a term paper, perhaps?) or moving from one project to another. Adam Smith once described the problem this way:

> A man commonly saunters a little in turning his hand from one sort of employment to another. When he first begins the new work he is seldom very keen and hearty; his mind, as they say does not go to it and for some time he rather trifles than applies to good purpose.[41]

When Chester enlarges his scale of operation, he is able to increase not only the number of workers but also the number of tractors and balers, wagons, and other equipment and materials. One worker can now specialize in loading hay; another, in driving the tractor with the baler; another, in taking loads back and forth; and another, in unloading. After a while, Chester's baling crew will be able to operate much like an assembly-line operation.

Also, consider the economy of scale that results from the use of larger machinery. A baler that costs $2000 could easily be *more than twice as productive* as a baler that costs $1000. You can see such economies of scale at work on many large farms in the form of giant tractors, plows, and other large-scale pieces of machinery.

Economies of scale can also be observed in other industries. For example, if someone tried to produce automobiles on a scale of 100 cars per year, the average cost per car would obviously be extremely high. If, however, the producer can "up the scale" of output to 30,000 cars per year, many little efficiencies will bring average costs down. In addition, large businesses often operate dozens of separate plants to take advantage of specialized expertise at various managerial levels, as well as *the efficiencies of purchasing large versus small quantities* of raw materials and other resources. Good examples of such businesses are McDonald's restaurants and K-Mart retail stores, where economies are passed on to consumers in the form of relatively low prices. From Henry Ford's original assembly line to large-scale farming to fast-food restaurants, the average consumer benefits from production techniques based on economies of scale.

Returning for a moment to Chester's U-shaped LAC curve in Figure 15-7, note what happens when his scale of operation becomes even larger. At a certain key point (32 loads), the LAC curve turns upward. Economists say that when long-run average cost begins to rise, production has reached a point at which **diseconomies of scale** tend to outweigh economies of scale. Sometimes it can be interesting to assess what these diseconomies might be for different organizations. Let's look at some examples.

In Chester's case, diseconomies of scale probably begin to emerge when he finds himself *wasting time and fuel* hauling his tractors and machinery around his enlarged farm operation. Another diseconomy is the additional difficulty Chester has in *coordinating* all the diverse factors of his business operation (workers, machines, etc.) to maintain production efficiency. Related to this is the increasing problem of *getting accurate information* about what is happening around the farm as the size of the operation increases; without this information, Chester finds himself making decisions based on inadequate data—decisions that cost him money. In addition, Chester's large machinery will probably be more costly to repair, and "one sunny day's breakdown" will be far more expensive to him than it was when he ran a smaller operation.

In large businesses, diseconomies frequently crop up in the form of *bureaucratic red tape* and layers and layers of hierarchical decision making. Upper-level managers in large businesses often do not know precisely what is going on at the lower levels of the operation; some organizations are simply too big and too spread out. To obtain the information they need, middle- and upper-level managers find themselves spending more and more time in meetings and conferences. They also often must solicit the opinions of a growing army of management specialists, but hour-to-hour sessions with these highly paid executives take their toll in costs. Smaller companies, on the other hand, can frequently avoid these information-gathering inefficiencies.

Larger companies may also be *less flexible* in making necessary changes, such as altering a product line or adapting a new technology, or they may just be more rigid in their overall policies, such as approving the extra money to hire particularly gifted employees. Perhaps you can think of certain types of jobs that relate specifically to large companies—jobs that would probably not exist if the organization were smaller. (Possible examples might be security personnel, parking-lot attendants, or legal and public-relations departments, all of which add to production costs.)

Of course, diseconomies are often little, but they do add up. At some point, they begin to outweigh the more commonly known economies of scale. When this eventually happens, the LAC curve begins to rise.

Double Efficiency

Now let's summarize and tie together what we have learned about economic efficiency. We discovered that as he enlarges his operation, Chester will experience economies of scale up to a certain point (32 loads of hay per day) and that he can produce hay for the lowest possible average cost ($9.50 per load) only at this quantity. Thus, 32 loads is the output level at which Chester's economies of scale are apparently maximized.

This, in fact, would be the correct capacity for *any* producer who uses the same hay-baling technology that Chester does. This type of efficiency—*the efficiency of scale*—is represented by the *bottom point* on an LAC curve. The low point on an LAC curve also represents another kind of efficiency, *the right mix of resources,* which is represented by the point of tangency between the equal-product curve and the budget line.

A kind of "double efficiency" therefore takes place at the bottom of the LAC curve. These two efficiencies are combined in Figure 15-8 to show how the two systems are related to one another. In summary, the output level of 32 loads and the average cost of $9.50 per load represent double efficiency: (1) the most efficient mix of resources (for that level), and (2) an optimal output or scale (considering all possible output levels).

An important question now arises. If this double-efficiency point on Chester's LAC curve is such an ideal situation economically, will Chester, in fact, operate there? Before we can answer this question, we need to find out how Chester intends to maximize his profits. Only if the point of efficiency is the same as the point of profit maximization can we be sure that our competitive model is working to promote an efficient use of resources in the long run.

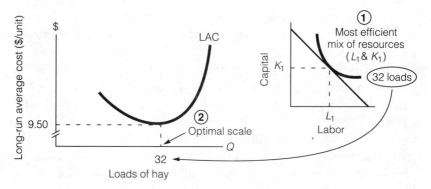

Figure 15-8 *Double efficiency.* The first element of an efficient operation is to obtain the most output from a certain budget. The point of tangency tells the producer the correct mix of capital and labor that is needed to produce that particular level of output. A second element of producer efficiency is to determine which output level offers the lowest average cost. This is the output level associated with the bottom of the LAC curve.

Efficiency and Profits

Fortunately, we have already worked out a technique for determining profit maximization. Recall (pages 199–201) our general principle that Chester should increase his output as long as the marginal cost (MC) is less than the price of a load of hay? Chester should stop adding to his output only when the extra cost of hiring another worker exceeds the value of a load of hay. We concluded earlier that Chester will maximize his profit position *when the marginal cost equals the unit price* (MC = *P*).

Nothing has changed this theory, even though we are now in the long run. We do have one problem, however; we have not yet worked out what Chester's MC curve—or, more specifically, his ***long-run* marginal cost (LMC) curve**—will look like. Our only long-run data is summarized by the LAC curve we developed earlier; without knowing the long-run marginal cost, we have no way of calculating Chester's profitability. It is possible, however, to roughly work out his LMC curve from his LAC curve.

One of the best ways to see how the concepts of "marginal" and "average" relate to one another is to look at a topic that is familiar to most of you: grade-point averages. The secret to connecting average with marginal data is to recognize that your grade-point *average* is made up of many *marginal* grades; in fact, these marginal values raise or lower your average.

For example, let's assume that you take economics as an "extra" course and get an "A," but the overall average grade for all of your courses combined is a "C." The "A" is your marginal grade; it is the grade you receive for taking an extra course. If your marginal grade is *above* your overall average grade, then it will pull the average up to some degree. (Of course, that marginal "A" will not lift your overall average grade to an "A.") On the other hand, if your marginal grade is a "D," it will obviously pull your overall average grade down.

Now let's return to the world of economic costs. Assuming the grade-point analogy holds, we know that if the average cost (the LAC curve) is moving downward, it means that the marginal cost (the MC curve) lies below it. Just as very low marginal grades will pull your grade-point average down, low marginal costs will pull the average cost down. On the other hand, at output levels at which the LAC curve is moving upward, the MC curve must lie above the LAC curve (just as your "A" pulls up your overall average grade).

One important characteristic of this relationship is that as soon as the long-run marginal cost is a fraction of a dollar above the long-run average cost, *it begins to pull the* LAC *curve up.* This, in turn, means that the LMC curve must strike through the LAC curve *at the bottom of the* LAC *curve* (at the most efficient scale of output). Since long-run marginal cost—the guideline to maximum profitability—is equal to long-run average cost at its most efficient point, it is a good omen. This unique relationship is shown in Figure 15-9.

As you can see, however, there are many other points on Chester's LMC curve as well. If the price of a load of hay happens to be above or below the $9.50 level, then Chester will maximize profits at some *nonoptimal level.* What we need is some kind of guarantee that the overall industry price of hay will settle at the $9.50 level. Chester will then equate price with long-run marginal cost (the point of maximum profitability), which coincides with the bottom of his LAC curve (the point of maximum efficiency).

Is there any unique characteristic of a competitive market that will guarantee this "correct" price? Fortunately, there is: *easy entry into, and easy exit from, the market* (recall our discussion on page 198). The fact that small competitors may easily enter or leave the hay-baling industry in our example guarantees

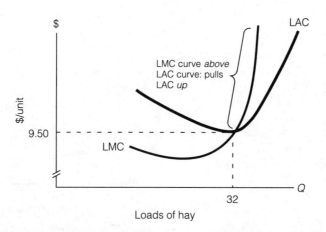

FIGURE 15-9 If the *long-run marginal cost* (LMC) *curve* lies below the long-run average cost (LAC) curve, then the LMC curve tends to pull the LAC curve down. If the LMC curve lies above the LAC curve, then the LMC curve slowly pulls the LAC curve up. This relationship between the two curves means that a rising LMC curve will, at some point, strike through the bottom of the LAC curve.

the $9.50/load price, because this is the only unit price at which there will be no excessive long-run profits.

Suppose the price in the short run is $12 per load—a price that will give hay producers a temporary profit because it is greater than average costs. This profit, in turn, will be a signal for a "swarm" of small producers to move into the industry, increasing overall supply and driving the price back down to $9.50—the only *no-profit point* (where price equals average cost).

Perhaps you object to the fact that Chester is going to wind up at a breakeven unit price in the long run even though he is pursuing maximum profits. Keep in mind, however, that we are assuming that *all* of Chester's economic costs are being met. Therefore, a "no-profit" situation means that Chester is paying himself a fair wage and earning a normal rate of return on his investment. Outside of this return, however, he has virtually no control over other hay producers who wish to move into the market when the price of hay increases above average costs. Thus, in the short run (not a long enough period for new producers to enter the market), Chester may make extra profits, but we assume that a glut of producers will move into the hay-baling industry in the long run.

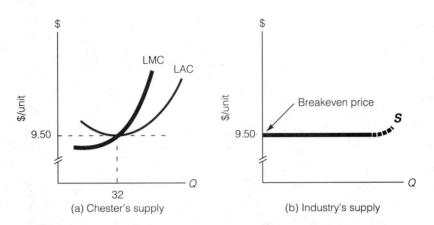

(a) Chester's supply   (b) Industry's supply

FIGURE 15-10   (a) The *easy-entry* characteristic of perfect competition implies that in the long run any above-normal, short-run profit will be a signal for new producers to enter the market and drive the unit price down to a long-run breakeven point. If industry losses occur in the short run, the *easy-exit* characteristic of perfect competition allows firms to leave the market and force the product price up. (b) Thus, the *long-run* supply curve for the competitive industry becomes a horizontal line at the breakeven price.

This situation operates in reverse, too. For example, a dip in the unit price of a load of hay below the $9.50 level will result in some losses within the industry, because the price of hay will be lower than average costs. Again, the long run is a long enough period of time to allow some of the losing hay producers to move out of the market, which will cut back overall industry supply and eventually increase the industry unit price to $9.50. It is important to see how the easy-entry/easy-exit characteristic of the competitive market model *forces* suppliers to operate exactly where consumers want them to operate—at the output level at which the LAC curve is lowest and the maximum economies of scale are in effect (Figure 15-10a).

Therefore, in the long run, we have a rather strange-looking supply curve for a perfectly competitive industry (Figure 15-10b): a horizontal line emanating from the vertical axis at the lowest possible point ($9.50) on the LAC curve. Of course, if an industry's output grows *too* large, it may take more money to attract additional resources. When basic industry costs rise, we can expect an eventual upward turn in the industry supply curve at some large output level. This situation is represented by the dashed portion of the *S* curve in Figure 15-10b.

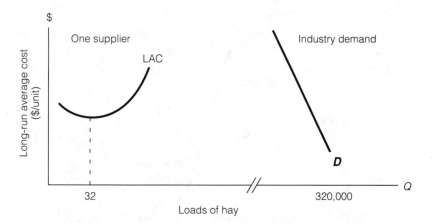

FIGURE 15-11 When a single supplier like Chester operates efficiently but still supplies only a minimal percent of total industry demand, the market is likely to be very competitive. Here, the demand is sufficient to "fit" 10,000 efficient hay producers.

In conclusion, we can say that purely competitive industries meet consumer demands in the long run by supplying the level of output demanded, generally at the lowest possible cost. Not only does our long-run competitive solution promote economic efficiency, but it also offers the consumer a product for a price that reflects maximum economies of scale. These are some of the reasons why economists find the competitive model so attractive.

Competition versus Monopoly

Farming is a good illustration of competition, partly because its ideal scale is relatively small compared with the overall demand for the product. The agricultural industry can accommodate thousands and thousands of small, efficient operators, making it an ideal setting for competitors, as we can see in Figure 15-11. (Note the change in the horizontal axis from 32 loads to 320,000 loads.)

But what would happen in some other industry that *had to have* a very large operation to be relatively efficient? In an extreme example, the electric-utility industry's regional demand is usually insufficient to meet the optimal scale requirements of more than one supplier. This situation is graphed in Figure 15-12.

Note the continually dropping LAC curve, indicating that there is "room" for only one producer in the market. This situa-

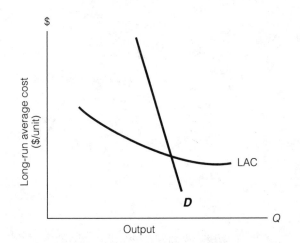

Figure 15-12 When a single supplier (for example, an electric utility) can singlehandedly and efficiently meet total product demand, then the market will probably be supplied by a *natural monopoly*. (Compare this monopoly model with the competitive model in Figure 15-11.)

tion is precisely the opposite of our competitive model. We now have an environment made to order for a monopolist. Such a situation is called a **natural monopoly** because *even one* additional supplier is economically unnecessary.

How do monopoly industries operate in regard to pricing and efficiency? Are monopolies good or bad for the overall economy? We will examine the answers to these and other questions in Chapter 16, when we zero in on the monopoly market structure.

Questions for Thought and Discussion

1. When the capital part of the *K/L* ratio embodies more advanced technology, does that affect the nature of the ratio? The quantity of labor? Explain.

2. Does a firm ever "operate" in the long run? Why or why not?

3. How are the scale of operation, the optimal level of output, and economies of scale interrelated?

4. Should a natural monopolist be regulated? Why or why not? If so, how?

5. Does a firm ever know if it is operating at the lowest point on its LAC curve? Why or why not?

16

Monopoly

To get a perspective on the subject of monopoly, first we'll take a look at a broader concept that encompasses monopoly markets as well as other *market structures* that are *not* perfectly competitive. As a broad group, economists refer to these more concentrated structures or industries as **imperfect competition.** Let's take a moment to review this important idea briefly.

Imperfect Competition

Just why, in reality, are so many U.S. industries *not* perfectly competitive? Recall from the end of Chapter 15 that some types of production require such a large scale or size to operate efficiently that there is room for only *one* firm in the industry (for example, an electric utility). Other production systems, including automobile, steel, and computer manufacturing, also require large-scale facilities but can accommodate a number of firms (although not the thousands necessary to classify them as truly competitive).

In addition to this scale requirement, existing firms in an industry may discourage potential rivals from entering the market. Barriers such as patent protection, monopolization of raw

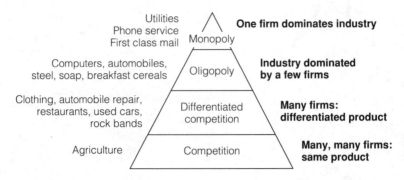

Figure 16-1 The top three market structures or types of industries in the *market structure pyramid*—monopoly, oligopoly, and differentiated competition—are considered to be imperfectly competitive.

materials, brand-name recognition, and aggressive price cutting are often erected to ward off newcomers.

With these entry barriers, we begin to move into the "real-world" economic environment that we briefly examined in Chapter 2. In addition to the noncompetitive models of monopoly and oligopoly, we will be looking at a new model called **differentiated competition.** Let's look at the **market-structure pyramid,** which shows how all of these markets and pure competition are related to each other in terms of degree of concentration (see Figure 16-1).

If we are going to get an accurate picture of how our economy actually functions, we must now go beyond pure competition. Fortunately, this does not mean that we have to begin all over again with resource pricing and cost curves. Our cost theory for noncompetitive systems is pretty much the same, since *all* firms in any one of the four market structures have similar-looking long-run average cost (LAC) and long-run marginal cost (LMC) curves, based on their resource use and productive capabilities. So what is the difference between the competitive market structure and the three noncompetitive structures: monopoly, oligopoly, and differentiated competition?

The major difference between these markets is reflected in the *individual firm's demand curve.* The demand curve, in turn, is based on the firm's relative *control* over the industry market. Recall that the perfect competitor faces a horizontal demand curve, reflecting the competitor's inability to influence the overall industry price. The monopolist, however, controls the entire industry demand and therefore can select one price (from a variety of prices) that will maximize profits. We will examine the oligopolistic and competitively differentiated market structures in Chapter 17; for now, let's focus our attention on the pure monopolist.

A Definition of Monopoly

Perhaps the easiest way to define a monopoly is simply as a *one-firm industry*. In theory, there are no close substitutes for the monopolist's product. Consumers have no choice: they either buy from the monopolist or they don't get the product or service. The monopolist may attain its unique status by scale requirement alone; if the market cannot economically support more than one producer (as in the case of an electric utility), then this is a ***natural monopoly.***

On the other hand, in some cases, as occurred during the formation of the original Standard Oil Company, the monopoly attains a dominant position in the industry by mergers or ruthless price-cutting practices, which "freeze out" the competition. Economists call this a ***predatory monopolist.*** Monopolies can also be formed through the discovery and use of new technology (Polaroid instant cameras) or the exclusive ownership or control of raw materials (DeBeers Diamonds of South Africa). But no matter how a monopoly is formed, the monopolist always winds up with industry demand all to itself.

Of course, there are some limits to the monopolist's power. Even though a monopoly can exert considerable control over the price of its product, it must still operate within the confines and constraints of consumer demand. If it charges an outrageous price for its product, the monopolist will discover (as is true in any other business) that consumers will learn to do without its product and nobody will buy it.

Nevertheless, price control does work to the monopolist's advantage because it "fine tunes" the industry price to gain maximum profits. Unlike the perfect competitor, which is a "price-taker" economists say that a monopolist is a "price-maker" or, more accurately, a "price-searcher"—searching for that one price that will earn the highest net income or, in business vernacular, maximize "bottom-line" profits. Certainly, no other market structure enjoys so much flexibility.

To show how a pure monopolist can use price controls to maximize profits, let's devise a new example. We will assume that Chester Olson is fed up with the risks and uncertainties of baling hay. He decides to manufacture a new baler that is so efficient and technologically advanced it will make all other hay balers virtually obsolete. Despite some start-up problems, Chester establishes a huge baler factory and successfully markets his baler nationally. Farm trade journals, in turn, praise Chester as "the new Henry Ford" of hay-baler manufacturing.

As an effective monopolist, Chester now finds himself in a much more favorable position than he did when he was just plain "Chester Olson, competitive hay supplier." Then he had to abide by the industry price, no matter what it happened to be. Now Chester can set his own price, geared to make maximum profits within the constraints of market demand and production costs. Just how does Chester search for his "ideal" price?

The procedure is not much different from the earlier method Chester used to maximize profits. He first looks for the output level associated with the greatest profits. Thus, he will continue to produce balers as long as the extra cost, or marginal cost (MC), of producing a baler is lower than the extra revenue, or **marginal revenue** (MR), of selling that particular baler.

The marginal revenue is the extra revenue gained from selling an extra unit of output. When Chester was a competitive hay supplier, the marginal revenue was exactly the same as the price of a load of hay; if Chester sold an extra load, he received an additional amount of revenue equal to that price. Now, however, as a monopolist, Chester is dealing with *total* industry demand; he is undoubtedly facing a *downward-sloping demand curve* with a marginal revenue that varies from the price. To understand this point more clearly, let's work through a simple example, which will also help to illustrate how Chester chooses the "ideal" quantity and price at which to maximize profits.

First, let's figure out Chester's industry demand curve. We will assume that if Chester charges $1000 for a baler, he won't sell any, but that he will sell one baler at $900. If Chester drops his unit price to $800, he will sell two balers; to $700, three balers; and so on. The first two columns of the following table contain Chester's demand-curve information. To work out Chester's **total revenue** (TR), in the third column, we multiply price by quantity.

From the total-revenue column, we can now calculate Chester's additional revenue from the sale of one extra unit

Baler Quantity (Q)	Price (P)	Total Revenue (TR)	Marginal Revenue (MR)
0	$1000	$0	$0
1	900	900	900
2	800	1600	700
3	700	2100	500
4	600	2400	300
5	500	2500	100
6	400	2400	−100

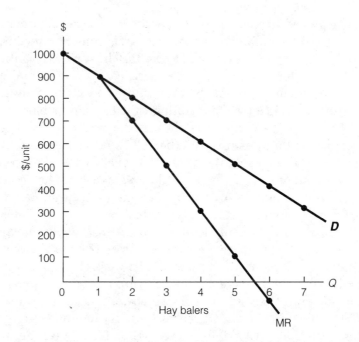

Figure 16-2 Chester's *marginal revenue* (MR) *curve* shows how much extra revenue Chester will earn when he sells one additional product unit.

(baler). This is Chester's marginal revenue, shown in the fourth column. For example, the marginal revenue of unit 2 is $1600 (total revenue from selling unit 2) minus $900 (total revenue from selling unit 1), or $700; similarly, the marginal revenue of unit 5 is $2500 – $2400 = $100. Note the interesting relationship between the marginal revenue of a given unit and its price. In each case (except for unit 1), marginal revenue is lower than price (MR < P). By graphing Chester's MR curve against his demand curve, we can actually see these relationships (see Figure 16-2).

Chester now knows what his demand and MR curves look like. But to make profit-maximizing marginal decisions, Chester must determine his marginal costs. In Figure 16-3, all of the relevant curves (including the LAC curve) are shown on the same graph. This figure provides Chester the monopolist with all the information he needs to maximize his profits using the old marginal decision-making approach.

The first question Chester asks is, "Is the first unit profitable?" Since we can see that unit 1 earns Chester far more

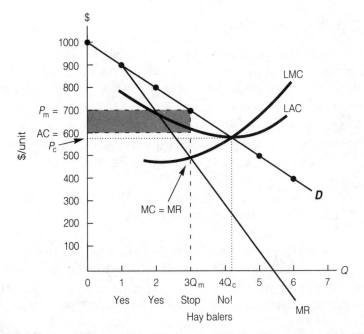

FIGURE 16-3   A *monopolist* maximizes profits at the point at which MC = MR. Below this point is the maximum profit quantity of 3 units. The maximum profit price is the price (read from the demand curve) associated with 3 units, or $700. If the average cost (read from the LAC curve) is $600, then Chester will make a profit of $100 per unit, or $300 ($100 × 3).

revenue than it costs him to produce it, the answer is a very profitable "yes." It is also profitable for Chester to produce unit 2, but he will receive a smaller marginal profit on this unit because MR is dropping rapidly. Chester obviously ought to stop producing at unit 3, where his marginal cost equals his marginal revenue (MC = MR). Past unit 3, there is no hope that any more units will be profitable; the MR curve is dropping too fast, while the LMC curve is rapidly climbing upward.

This example shows the logic behind marginal decision making, but we can simplify this process by using a more direct method: *maximum profits are achieved at the quantity at which MC = MR*. From now on, we will simply note the point at which the LMC curve crosses the MR curve and then move directly down to the horizontal axis to locate the quantity Q_m associated with maximum profits.

Pricing and Efficiency

Once we know that Chester maximizes profits at 3 units (Q_m), we can trace the other important information concerning his monopoly operation. It is possible to derive the following information from Figure 16-3:

- **Monopoly price P_m:** Move vertically up from the profit-maximizing quantity Q_m to the demand curve; then move horizontally over to the price axis. In this example, P_m = $700 per unit.

- **Average cost (AC):** Move vertically from Q_m to the LAC curve; then move horizontally over to the price axis. Here, AC = $600.

- **Per-unit profit:** In this example, each unit sells for $700 and AC = $600, so the per-unit profit is $100.

- **Total profit:** Selling 3 units at a per-unit profit of $100 means that total profits (shaded area) are $300 ($100 × 3).

Figure 16-3 also shows what the output and price would have been in a long-run competitive situation. From Chapter 15, we know that a competitive market forces a long-run price equivalent to the lowest possible average cost (lowest point on the LAC curve). In Figure 16-3, the **competitive price** P_c would be just under $600; the **competitive quantity** Q_c, which is a little more than 4 units, can be found by moving directly down to the horizontal axis from the lowest point on the LAC curve.

Thus, a competitive market has some advantages over a monopoly. Competition offers a lower unit price to the consumer and increases output to a level more in line with the optimal scale of operation. The monopoly, in contrast, often creates an "artificial scarcity" of the product it is supplying and simultaneously charges a higher price than the competitive price. The net result is a misallocation of the economy's resources.

Consumers are often irritated by the unusually large profits they believe monopolies make simply because they control a considerable portion, if not all, of a market. It might surprise you to know that monopolists sometimes do not make such excessive profits, because profits earned by a monopoly are dependent on a favorable average cost situation in relation to the demand curve. As an example, Chester could become such a complacent businessman that he allowed his LAC curve to creep up above the market price of the baler. If this happened, monopolist Chester Olson would actually lose money (admittedly, an unusual situation).

Assuming that Chester earns a significant profit as a monopolist, can we say that this profit is unjustified? Some consumers would probably answer "yes," but there may be reasonable justification for both monopolists and other businesses operating under imperfect competitive situations to earn large profits. For example, it is generally acknowledged that profits can be a legitimate return on *innovation*. In Chester's case it is difficult to argue that he does not deserve some financial reward for creating his superior hay-baling machine. In addition, Chester should probably receive some kind of monetary recompense for the *risk* involved in undertaking this financially hazardous venture. Finally, economists generally recognize that a certain amount of profit should be earned for *entrepreneurial skills* (the effective coordination of resources).

Nevertheless, economists are still concerned that any degree of monopoly within a market, compared to a more competitive situation, will ultimately result in a less efficient use of society's resources. Furthermore, monopoly profits are not always the result of innovation, risk, and efficient resource coordination. Monopolists often profit by barring new firms from the industry. Illegitimate profits can also result from the formation of a **trust, cartel,** or **shared monopoly,** in which producers form an alliance to carve up markets and fix prices, acting as if they were a single monopolist. (For more details on how cartels operate, see Chapter 17.) Recognizing that monopolies can create economic problems for society, economists search for ways to reduce the harmful effects of these market structures. Let's take a look at some of their strategies.

Dealing with Monopoly

Perhaps the easiest type of monopoly to recognize and to deal with is the natural monopoly. As we learned earlier, natural monopolies result from scale requirements; a telephone or electric company can be allowed legal status as a monopolist as long as it consents to *regulation* by some publicly appointed commission. The regulators then establish a unit price and quantity more in keeping with what would be true under competitive conditions.

Another method of eliminating unjustified monopoly profits is to "tax them away" with a *fixed* or *lump-sum tax.* If, for example, the government decides that all of Chester's monopoly profits are unjustified, it can tax him the full $300 profit by raising his LAC curve equal to $100, so that monopoly price equals average cost (P_m = AC) and Chester earns no profit. The drawback to this "solution" is that it leaves Chester's old MC = MR intact; thus, he will continue to produce at the artificial-scarcity level of Q_m (see Figure 16-3).

Cartels and predatory monopolies present a slightly different situation. These monopolies are often difficult to recognize; once they are detected, the government must legally prove their anti-competitive behavior under U.S. antitrust laws. Firms that violate these laws may be penalized with stiff fines, and the individuals responsible for the illegal decisions could be sentenced to jail terms.

Other types of monopolies are even more difficult to detect and monitor. In *Tools for Conviviality,* Ivan Illich identifies what he calls "radical monopolies," which dominate large product systems:

> I speak about radical monopoly when one industrial production process exercises an exclusive control over the satisfaction of a pressing need. . . . Cars can thus monopolize traffic. They can shape a city into their image—practically ruling out locomotion on foot or by bicycle in Los Angeles.[42]

Illich has also written about radical monopolies in schools in *Deschooling Society* (1970) and modern medicine in *Medical Nemesis* (1976)—monopolies so powerful and pervasive that they leave us with very few practical alternatives. If Illich's conclusions are correct, radical monopolies may pose greater problems for an economic system than industrial or corporate monopolies do. This is one important area of economics that needs further research.

An understanding of an economic monopoly can help us deal with this problem in other guises; for example, a political dictatorship or a one-party state is a form of monopoly. The parent-child relationship can also be considered a monopoly, a theme explored in John Holt's book *Escape from Childhood* (1984).

In whatever way we look at the concept of monopoly—whether in purely economic terms or in a broader context, it is usually a no-alternative situation for the "consumer" because the competitive system of checks and balances is all but absent. Without regulation or mitigating circumstances, a monopoly can easily become exploitative and gain an inordinate amount of profits and power. Understanding the monopoly—identifying it in operation and, when necessary, evolving strategies to reduce its injurious effects—in economics, politics, and elsewhere—is important to us all.

A monopoly is the extreme form of concentrated economic power. Now let's descend the market-structure pyramid in Figure 16-1 to examine the other two imperfectly competitive models: oligopoly and differentiated competition.

Questions for Thought and Discussion

1. Are the antitrust laws in the United States *really* effective in controlling monopolies? Why or why not?

2. Compare and contrast free enterprise with pure competition.

3. Does free enterprise mean that monopolies should not exist? Explain.

4. *True or false?* Monopolists have no reason to advertise, because they have no competition. Explain.

17

Oligopoly and Differentiated Competition

We now move away from the extreme ends of the market-structure pyramid (see Figure 16-1) and shift more toward its center. Here, we find businesses closer to the real world; we see them day in and day out—from our favorite delicatessen down the street to the major corporations of the world.

In this middle range of market structures, it often becomes harder for economic theorists to accurately describe what happens. Biology may offer the most appropriate metaphor: we must try to understand a kind of *ecology* in the form of vast, complex interactions *among* businesses and how larger forces of change, often worldwide in scope, affect these relationships. These forces can be changes in energy supplies or exchange rates, regional droughts or new political regimes groping for more effective economic policies, domestic and international debt, government regulation, the quality of the workforce, dramatic shifts in consumer tastes, and large currency flows between the major financial centers of the world.

Some of these factors are short term; while can only be measured in decades. Much of this interlocking "economic ecology" is poorly understood and therefore difficult to integrate into a single theory. It is not surprising that no one framework can explain and predict economic behavior in this complex, real-world "middle ground."

Still, it is the job of economists to try to simplify these conditions. To do this, they must, as we have done before, hold some factors constant while they search for common patterns from which to construct a workable theory about how such enterprises maximize profits. Let's begin by reviewing the most prominent class of business in our economy, commonly known as oligopolies.

Oligopoly

In Chapter 2, we learned that the key word in our definition of "oligopoly" is the word "few": an oligopoly is a market or industry dominated by a *few* firms or producers. But how do we actually measure this key characteristic of "domination"?

One approach is to take the total revenues of a single industry and calculate the percent of total sales taken in by the largest four firms. Economists call this percent the four-firm *concentration ratio.* If, for example, a certain industry has total sales of $10 billion and the so-called "Big Four" companies have sales of $8 billion, then the four-firm concentration ratio is 8/10 = 0.80. Examples of industries that approximate this 0.80 ratio include laundry soap and vacuum cleaners. Other industries with relatively high four-firm concentration ratios include farm machinery, tobacco, breakfast cereals, and domestically manufactured automobiles. Obviously, when foreign competition is factored in, this ratio declines in certain industries, such as the automobile industry.

Although some oligopolists sell pretty much the same product (as is true in the gasoline and steel industries), most oligopolists make an attempt to *differentiate* their product or service from that of their closest competitors. Promotion, however, is usually accomplished *not* by lowering price but by a variety of techniques that economists call *nonprice competition.*

Nonprice competition includes differences in fashions and styles, brand-name recognition, advertising, service, quality, and special, convenient locations. This kind of competition can be as honest as a "five-year, unconditional warranty," quality craftsmanship in construction, and low frequency of repair or as devious as projecting an improbable image of sexual conquest or financial success. Price cutting, however, is generally frowned on by the industry because it tends to destabilize corporate earnings.

It is also common for many oligopolies to maintain their market domination by setting up a variety of **entry barriers.** You might take a moment to think through the probable obstacles you would face if you tried to establish a competing automobile company, market a new breakfast cereal, or manufacture your own brand of an over-the-counter drug. You would obviously need a relatively large production unit to take advantage of economies of scale (Chapter 15), which would, in turn, require a *large capital investment.*

In addition to the problem of establishing large-scale production, you would also need to gain access to, and earn the confidence of, financial lenders, researchers and engineers, specialized production experts, and many other suppliers of essential resources during the various production stages, including regional distributors and, ultimately, the consumers themselves. At each stage of operation, you would probably face enormous difficulties as you attempted to enter your competitors' "turf," break down established arrangements with consumers and suppliers, and rearrange traditional patterns of operation. You would also have to fend off the defensive ploys of the dominant producers in the industry, which could take the form of legalities (for example, defending patent rights), high-powered advertising campaigns, or temporary price cuts. Entry barriers, in short, can be quite formidable.

Another characteristic of an oligopoly is **mutual interdependence**—complex interactions among producers to ensure their survival and profit maximization that approximate an economic ecology. Recall that when Chester Olson was only one hay producer among many (in the competitive model), he really didn't care what the other hay producers were doing. Essentially, Chester sold the same product (hay) at the "going" market price. Sure, he might have been curious, possibly even envious, if his neighbor bought a new tractor or built a new barn; but what his neighbor (or any other hay producer) did, did not change Chester's financial situation.

In contrast, oligopolists are vitally concerned about their rivals' pricing, packaging, styling, advertising, new technologies, and other product-related activities. At times, this mutual interdependence can become as complex and mock warlike as a grand-master chess game.[43] The inherent nature of mutual interdependence makes it difficult to design an appropriate theory that offers a clear, consistent, predictive model of oligopolistic behavior. One model that does seem to work well (but under unique and sometimes hard-to-maintain conditions) is the classic cartel. Let's take a closer look.

Cartels

A **cartel,** as we saw in Chapter 16, is a group of oligopolists that combine forces to fix industry prices and act as if they are a single monopolist. The ultimate impact of a cartel on the economy and society is much the same as that of a monopoly. Of course, domestic cartels are illegal under U.S. anti-trust laws, but that doesn't prevent conspiracies from taking place; the great electrical conspiracy of the 1950s and the decades-long paper-company cases (and convictions) are examples.[44]

International cartels, such as OPEC (the Organization of Petroleum Exporting Countries), are not under the jurisdiction of U.S. anti-trust laws and consequently offer us a transparent view of how cartels can, at times, price like a single monopoly. In 1972, for example, the price of a barrel of crude oil was about $2.50. By 1980, a barrel of oil cost the nations of the world roughly $34. The cartel didn't last, however. In 1982, international pricing "discipline" became lax as oil demand softened, giving "cheaters" an opportunity to cut prices and temporarily raise their revenues. By the mid-1980s, oil prices had dropped so far that the entire oil industry, including OPEC, was in a severe slump.

Price-Leadership

Another oligopolistic theory revolves around the concept of **price-leadership,** whereby one of the dominant producers establishes an industry price and the other producers simply follow along. Because no formal agreement regarding the pricing structure is made among these producers, the price-leadership method does not fall into the category of an illegal cartel. There is, however, an element of *parallel pricing* among producers, based on price information obtained from speeches, press releases, trade-journal publications, and other legal intraindustry communications.

Price leaders of recent history include such companies as General Motors, U. S. Steel, R. J. Reynolds, Kelloggs, and IBM. A price leader may obtain its special status simply by being the largest firm and/or the lowest-cost producer in the industry. In theory, a price leader tries to work out its individual demand curve based on possible pricing arrangements. Any business that is not absorbed by the price leader is divided up among the so-called "fringe" firms. Once the price leader approximates its demand curve, then the firm follows the standard price-searching practice we examined in Chapter 16. First, the price leader maximizes profits where its marginal costs equal its marginal revenue (MC = MR); from that point, the firm can easily determine its profit-maximizing quantity and price. The price, once announced, then becomes the overall industry price.

Price-leadership helps us to understand why there is frequently a large degree of *price rigidity* within oligopolistic industries, giving them the go-ahead to engage in various forms of nonprice competition. A related oligopolistic theory that also explains industry price rigidity is represented by the "kinked-demand" curve. Let's take a look at an example in detail by bringing back Chester Olson, who was last seen in Chapter 16 operating a hay-baler monopoly.

The Kinked Demand Curve

After a number of years, assume that Chester loses his former monopoly position due to technological changes in the hay-baling industry. Old stand-bys, such as John Deere, reestablish themselves in the marketplace and continue to manufacture their innovative hay balers with relatively high efficiency, based on economies of scale. For argument's sake, we'll also assume that John Deere becomes the price leader. Chester is now just one of three or four other "fringe" manufacturers in the industry. Soon the price leader moves ahead to establish an industry price, which we will call P_a, the administered price.

Once P_a becomes the prevailing price, how can it affect Chester's own demand curve? If Chester takes it upon himself to *raise* his unit price, then the rest of the industry producers probably won't be too concerned; they will gladly watch Chester lose much of his old business as a result of unilateral price-raising. The very fact that Chester will lose a large part of his

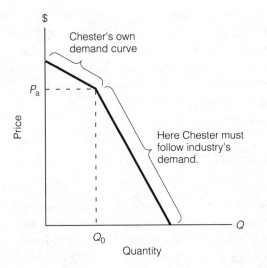

Figure 17-1 *The kinked demand curve:* the kink in Chester's demand curve indicates that when Chester the *oligopolist* increases his price higher than P_a), the rest of the industry will let him "go it alone." However, if Chester tries to reduce his price below P_a, then other oligopolists will join in the price cutting and Chester will be forced to follow the more inelastic industry demand curve.

market share implies that he is on the elastic portion of the demand curve, which we will call "Chester's own demand curve." Naturally, our friend should think twice about raising his unit price.

Another strategy would be for Chester to *lower* his unit price and hope to capture a larger share of the market for himself. This plan might work as long as the rest of the industry leaves him alone, which is unlikely. But the other producers simply aren't willing to lose their market shares to the "Olson Baling Company." Thus, if Chester lowers his price, the other sellers *will follow right along,* forcing Chester to move onto the industry demand curve. This curve, in turn, will be much less elastic than Chester's own demand curve. Chester might gain some additional customers after lowering his price, but his gains will be minimal because other producers will be lowering their prices, too.

Chester is therefore faced with two distinctly different demand curves: the demand curve above the administered price P_a will be highly elastic; the demand curve below P_a will be less elastic. When these two curves are combined, the **kinked demand curve** that results represents all of Chester's price-quantity options (see Figure 17-1).

Perhaps you already have a feeling about why Chester would be reluctant to make a price change. Instinct tells us there is no practical reason to raise or lower the unit price, but we have yet to *prove* (via profit maximization) that this instinct is correct. Now let's see what kinked-demand theory tells us about profit maximization specifically.

Profit Maximization

To find out where the oligopolist maximizes profits, we again refer to the standard price-searching strategy, whereby profits are maximized when the marginal cost is equal to marginal revenue (MC = MR). What does Chester's MR curve look like in relation to his kinked demand curve?

Chester's MR curve as an oligopolist will be quite similar to the MR curve we developed for Chester as a monopolist (see Figure 16-2), implying that the MR curve lies somewhere *below* the demand curve. The only difference is that we are now dealing with *two* demand curves and, therefore, with *two* MR curves, each of which lies below its respective demand curve and reflects a different demand-curve slope.

Referring to Figure 17-1, we can say that up to output level Q_0, the relevant MR curve is the one associated with the relatively elastic individual demand curve; after Q_0 the relevant MR curve is the one associated with the less elastic industry demand curve. Figure 17-2 shows the two MR curves and some additional sample MC curves to help us find the price-quantity point at which Chester will maximize his profits. Note that because the kinked demand curve has two distinct slopes, it causes a *discontinuity* between the two separate MR curves: a long break in the curve occurs directly under the kink and above Q_0. This discontinuous section provides the basis for price rigidity in oligopolistic markets.

Chester will achieve his maximum-profit position (MC = MR) in the vertical plane, where the MC curve intersects the discontinuous MR section. Chester then moves down from this point to the horizontal axis to find the maximum-profit quantity and then up to the demand curve and over to the vertical axis to find the maximum-profit price.

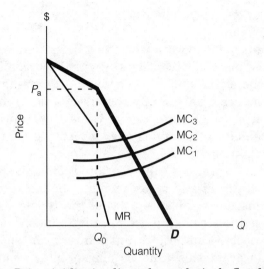

FIGURE 17-2 *Price rigidity in oligopoly:* a relatively flat demand curve above the kink and a relatively steep curve below the kink give rise to two marginal revenue (MR) curves separated by a discontinuous (vertical) segment directly under the kink. If an MC curve crosses this vertical segment, then the maximum profit price associated with MC = MR will be the same as the administered price P_a.

For each MC curve shown in Figure 17-2, the most profitable quantity is Q_0, and the most profitable price is P_a (the industry leader's administered price). Therefore, *maximum profitability is consistent with a large degree of price rigidity.* In short, price competition usually doesn't pay.

In many oligopolistic industries, we find pricing policies that may be closer to the monopoly model than to pure competition. There is certainly fierce rivalry in design, workmanship, packaging, advertising, and service among oligopolists, but their consumers very rarely benefit from good, old-fashioned price competition.

As we approach the end of our microeconomics section, we should examine one more market structure—an industry often referred to as **monopolistic competition.** This term, however, makes this market structure appear to be related more closely to a monopoly, when such industries are actually much more similar to decentralized competitive markets. We will therefore call this market structure by a slightly different name—**differentiated competition**—to more accurately reflect its true nature.

Differentiated Competition

It's always enjoyable to work with the differentiated competitive model because many of us can identify with these smaller business operators who strike out on their own, attempting to become "their own bosses." This partly romantic notion reminds us of the old ideal of free enterprise—a value that continues to be deeply ingrained in the minds of many people throughout the world today.

Who exactly are these differentiated competitors? They are the small restaurant and resort owners, the barbers and beauticians, the used-car salespeople, and the repair-shop owners. They are also the struggling artists, rock bands, freelance photographers, poets, craft potters and painters, and small publishers. A producer in this kind of market may compete in an industry containing dozens and dozens, perhaps hundreds, of other producers.

Differentiated industries share with their purely competitive cousins the easy-entry/easy-exit characteristic; thus, scale requirements are usually not an important factor in entering a differentiated market. Easy entry also implies that differentiated competitors face an uphill struggle to achieve anything more than a modest profit in the long run (if they are lucky!). Indeed, these smaller operators contribute disproportionately to overall business mortality statistics.

It would not be unusual for you to be thinking about starting a differentiated competitive business someday as, say, a restaurant manager, artist, photographer, store owner, or small-scale manufacturer. Many people, young and old alike, find the idea of controlling their own destinies appealing and dream about the possibilities of taking an entrepreneurial "fling" at the universe—risking their savings, working long days, and sometimes bringing in partners or their families for extra help.

Perhaps you are thinking that this sounds a lot like a purely competitive market: many, many sellers, easy entry and exit, high risk, and little (if any) long-run profits. In the differentiated market, however, each producer has a *slightly* different product, service, and/or location. There is almost always some difference between Frank's and Joe's barber shops or bars, or "Super Sally's Roast Beef" and "The Village Cafeteria," or the many makers of designer clothing. In short, differentiated

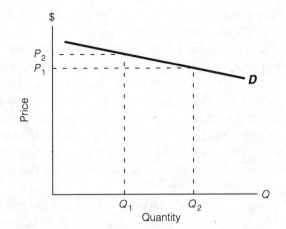

FIGURE 17-3 The single seller in a *differentiated competitive market* faces a demand curve that is fairly flat (or elastic) but not perfectly horizontal, as in perfect competition. Its modest slope is due to the fact that sellers have a slightly differentiated product or service and enjoy some degree of consumer loyalty in the face of small price increases.

competitors have an identifiable product or brand name that attracts *some degree of consumer loyalty.*

Consumer loyalty, in turn, means that the producer has a *slight* amount of control over the price of the good or service being offered. A competitive seller of corn can't get away with selling this product for even one cent above the industry price. In contrast, the differentiated competitor usually has a *small amount of price flexibility.* However, if prices increase too much, even loyal customers will turn away and take their business to one of many alternative producers.

Therefore, a differentiated competitor's demand curve would probably be quite elastic but not perfectly so. A sample curve is shown in Figure 17-3. Note that the differentiated competitor can raise its price from P_1 to P_2 without losing all of its customers (Q_1 will still be demanded). Thus, some people will continue to patronize the differentiated producer because of its brand name or an individualized product or service.

Returning to the odyssey of our friend Chester, rumor has it that he has sold the Olson Baling Company—bailing out after a firm developed a revolutionary new baler, as he had done years before. Chester decides to move to Los Angeles and operate a small, neighborhood bicycle-motorcycle sales and repair shop. A glance at the metropolitan Yellow Pages tells him that there are many, many other shops like his in the city, but he hopes to gain an element of customer loyalty over time, derived from his innate friendliness and mechanical expertise. Chester has now made the rounds—from competitor to monopolist to oligopolist; now he is comfortably settled into a differentiated competitive market. Since we have already approximated a demand curve for this type of market (see Figure 17-3), we will now assume that this curve represents the demand for Chester's standard motorcycle tuneup. How does Chester maximize profits under these new conditions?

First, he figures out his MR curve. As in our earlier example, the MR "curve" would be a straight line that falls below the very elastic demand curve. Next, Chester computes his long-run marginal cost (LMC) curve. Figure 17-4 shows approximations of both of these curves.

At what price-quantity point does Chester maximize profits? Like a broken record, repeating itself over and over, "Profits are maximized at the quantity at which MC = MR." Thus, Chester's profit-maximizing quantity is Q_1. We move from Q_1 on the horizontal axis up to the demand curve and over to the vertical axis to find out that Chester will charge $33 for output level Q_1.

Next, let's look at the extent of Chester's profits. Our standard procedure to determine profits is to move up from Q_1 on the horizontal axis to the LAC curve to find the average cost (LAC) and then compare this cost with the price P. When Chester does this, however, he is unhappy to discover that his average cost *equals* his price (LAC = P), leaving him no long-run profits. What characteristic of this market structure denies a producer a long-run profit?

The answer, as it was for the pure competitive model, is the easy-entry/easy-exit factor. The fact that Chester has no excessive profit still implies that he is earning a fair wage and receiving some normal rate of return on his investment. Just as when Chester was in the purely competitive hay-baling business, there is no way that he can keep other firms from easily moving into the bicycle-motorcycle repair market. For anyone who is interested in becoming a differentiated competitor, this easy-entry market characteristic should raise a red warning flag! As the saying goes, "Hope for the best, but expect the worst."

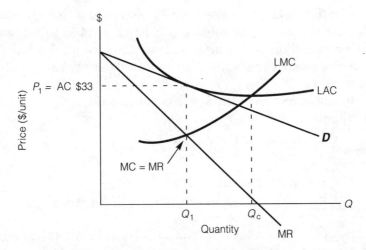

FIGURE 17-4 Differentiated competitors also maximize profits at the point at which MC = MR. Here, Q_1 is the maximum profit quantity and P_1 ($33) is the maximum profit price. Note that in the long run, however, the easy-entry characteristic of this market will, in theory, squeeze out above-normal, short-run profits, forcing the price down to the point at which the selling price is equal to the average cost.

There is, however, another more optimistic side to this model: the possibility of creating a unique product—a fantastic restaurant, a book store that provides unequaled service and selection, an incredibly good repair shop, or popular photographs or songs—that will reap "quasimonopoly" profits. But don't count on it! Those who make it big against competitive odds are few and far between.

Now if this model has some advantages and disadvantages from the producer's viewpoint, how does it fare in terms of overall economic efficiency? To find out, we must take another look at Figure 17-4. Note that Chester's output is not the ideal-scale output, which is represented by the bottom of his LAC curve. The optimal quantity is Q_c, the quantity that prevails under purely competitive conditions.

Differentiated competitors may build less than optimally efficient plants or operate their businesses at less than optimal capacities. We can observe workers in gas stations, barber shops, bars, and other small businesses spending many relatively idle hours during each day. Even when this condition is obvious, or seems to be obvious, some "brand new" seller can easily enter the scene, diluting the market even more.

A differentiated competitive industry does not offer the consumer the lowest possible price; however, due to a highly elastic demand curve, the price will not differ too markedly from the purely competitive price. You can easily verify this point in Figure 17-4.

In summary, differentiated competition tends (in theory) to have the following long-run drawbacks:

- A tendency toward low or zero long-run profits for the producer.
- Some underutilization of resources.
- A price slightly higher than the competitive price.

However, let's remember that this type of market has some advantages, too. If you live in a modern city, just look around you. For one thing, these differentiated businesses offer consumers a *variety of suppliers*. Who, for example, would like to have only two or three restaurants to choose from? Particularly in large, urban settings, these little businesses add a considerable degree of interest, variety, and novelty to city living.

Another advantage, alluded to earlier, is a symbolic one. It stems from the free-enterprise dream. Unlikely? Yes, but still possible. What we have here is a group of relatively small-scale business possibilities that provide an opportunity to escape from a hierarchical existence—from large, bureaucratic institutions or from the boredom of the factory assembly line—if that's what an individual wants to do. It is a small slot within a basically large-scale economic system, where you can still organize your own resources, test your entrepreneurial strength, and—just possibly—not only survive but prosper.

Questions for Thought and Discussion

1. What would happen in an oligopoly if the competitors decided *not* to follow the price leader?
2. Justify the slightly higher price charged by a firm in a differentiated market.
3. What is the relationship between the number of available consumption substitutes and the shape of the demand curve?

4. Relate this relationship to the demand curves of firms in each of the four market structures.

5. How would the nature of nonprice competition differ in a firm making steel compared to a firm manufacturing automobiles?

6. *True or false?* All cartels will break up after a long enough period of time. Explain.

PART 3
The World Economy

18

The Benefits of Trade

It has become commonplace to hear businesspeople, economists, and government officials speak of a "global economy." They proclaim that our jobs, our markets—indeed, our very material comforts—are becoming more and more dependent on international economic arrangements. Representative of this reality is the emergence of world *multinational* corporations, which take advantage of business opportunities with minimal regard for, or loyalty to, their country of origin. Consider, for example, the following press release:

> General Motors Corp. is going to put a French name on a German car that will be built in South Korea for export to America. GM's Pontiac division will resurrect the Le Mans name and put it on the subcompact economy car. The car was designed by GM's West German subsidiary, Adam Opel AC, and will be built by Daewoo Group Ltd., which is 50 percent owned by GM.[45]

At the root of these changes is, of course, a growing desire among nations to engage in international trade. Perhaps it is time to explore some very basic questions in economics that reflect this expanding global reality: "Why do countries like the United States, Japan, Mexico, Germany, and the Soviet Union trade? What's in it for them? What's in it for us? How do we benefit?" Let's examine some possible answers.

Why Is Trade Necessary?

The most obvious reason to trade is to get essential or highly desirable *raw materials* that cannot be obtained domestically. For example, the United States must import most of its bauxite (for use in aluminum smelting), chromium, manganese, cobalt, and, to a lesser extent, oil, potash (for use in fertilizers), zinc, nickel, and tin. Add to this list some nonessential (but desirable) food imports, such as coffee, tea, bananas, and cocoa, and you can begin to see how important international trade is to the United States. And what is true for our nation is even more true for countries that are less endowed with the basic raw materials of industrial production.

Another reason to trade is to *promote competition* in highly concentrated oligopolistic industries. Consumers almost always benefit from having a greater choice of products. Imported products frequently offer American consumers more variety and better quality at lower prices. Of course, this kind of international rivalry may annoy or even hurt some domestic industries. In the end, however, healthy competition and a greater degree of consumer choice usually improve an individual's overall standard of living.

Also remember that *trade is a two-way street:* it benefits the exporting industries as well as the importing industries. Consumers and businesses in foreign countries purchase tremendous quantities of American agricultural commodities, as well as many products manufactured in the United States, including computer, plastics, farm machinery, paper products, chemicals, and aircraft. When discussing the pros and cons of trade, we should not forget that approximately one out of every eight American jobs depends on healthy trade arrangements with the rest of the world.

International trade also creates a sense of *interdependence* among world nations and can have the side effect of enhancing world peace. "We need you, and you need us" is the unspoken theme, as a continuous flow of imports and exports ties countries together with invisible threads of mutual benefits and often enhanced mutual trust. Free trade among the formerly antagonistic Common Market countries (primarily Germany, Britain, France, Italy) provides a good example. The "binding effect" of trade, however, is sometimes no match for the explosive forces of nationalism. During the 1979 anti-Western revolution in Iran, for example, the mutual benefits of foreign trade did not overcome a deep-seated Iranian hostility toward, and mistrust of, the United States and others, despite the mutual benefits of trade.

Some critics of international trade feel that mutual interdependence may create an unhealthy dependence on critical imports, particularly defense-related goods and services. This problem is compounded when the essential import is controlled by a monopolistic country (the sole supplier) or, in the case of oil, by a cartel (OPEC). Thus, the huge increase in oil prices during the 1970s alerted Americans to the need to promote conservation and to develop alternative energy supplies. Keep in mind, however, that such monopolistic situations are unusual and should not distract us from recognizing the overall benefits of free trade.

Perhaps you are still not convinced. The following thoughts could still be running through your mind: "Sure, trade is a good outlet for our own surpluses, and it does provide us with some essential raw materials. It may even create some healthy rivalry in certain industries. But if our nation is good at producing certain products yet, over time, finds itself losing out to imported substitutes at the expense of domestic jobs, then how can free trade be favorable for the United States?"

This question is often on the minds of workers, business owners and managers, and elected representatives. The answer, surprisingly, is that free trade is *still* a positive economic influence in the long run, even though it may create punishing short-run dislocations. British economist David Ricardo made this discovery about 150 years ago when he began to question the benefits of the growing volume of trade between his home country and nearby Portugal. Ricardo observed that even though both Britain and Portugal were relatively good producers of wine and cloth, each country began to specialize in the production of one of these products over time, resulting in short-run unemployment in the respective "weaker" industry. Ricardo felt that both countries were "better off" as a result of this free-trade arrangement and set out to prove this intuitive judgment. Out of observations and analyses came Ricardo's famous **theory of comparative advantage.** Let's take a closer look at this startling economic principle.

The Theory of Comparative Advantage

Let's see how Ricardo's theory might pertain to trade between Japan and the United States. Instead of wine and cloth, we'll use television sets and rice. We know that Japan is quite good at manufacturing TVs because Japanese labor is relatively inexpensive, but it may come as a surprise that the United States is quite efficient at producing rice due to its relatively abundant land and farm-capital resources. In fact, rice is a major U.S. food export!

Let's assume that both Japan and the United States have the capability to produce both products (which they do). We can even assume that Japan has a slight edge—an *absolute advantage*—in terms of the prices of both products. Even under these conditions, however, we will see that both countries will still benefit from specialization.

To determine which product each country should produce, we must examine a simplified version of each country's **production possibilities curve** (remember the old "guns-and-butter" curve in Figure 1-1?). Figure 18-1 shows straight-line production possibilities curves for television sets and rice in both countries.

First, let's look at the United States. Notice that the domestic trade-off is 1 for 1: if the United States wants to produce 1 additional ton of rice, it must give up 1 TV set. For Japan, in contrast, the trade-off is 1 for 2: if Japan wants to produce 1 additional ton of rice, it must give up 2 TV sets. Even though each country is capable of producing both products, their *opportunity costs* are significantly different. For example, we can say that rice is *relatively cheap* in the United States (costing only 1 TV set), whereas TV sets are cheap in Japan (costing only 1/2 ton of rice). If David Ricardo were looking at these trade-offs, he would say that the United States has a *comparative advantage* in the production of rice.

Now it should be obvious that each country has something to gain from producing its own specialty product and trading it with the other country. Looking first at Japan, wouldn't Japan "jump" at the opportunity to trade 2 TVs to the United States and receive 2 tons of rice in return? Recall that before trade, these 2 TVs would be worth only 1 ton of rice domestically. Similarly, the United States, envious of the terms of Japanese domestic trade, would jump at the opportunity to trade 1 U.S.

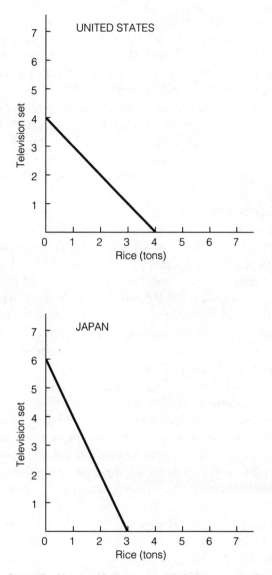

FIGURE 18-1 Straight-line production possibilities curves for the United States and Japan show the trade-off (or *domestic terms of trade*) between television sets and rice. For example, in the United States, the trade-off would be 4 TVs for 4 tons of rice (or 1 TV for 1 ton of rice); in Japan, the trade-off would be 6 TVs for 3 tons of rice (or 2 TVs for 1 ton of rice).

ton of rice to Japan and receive 2 TVs in return—a much better deal than the 1-for-1 U.S. trade-off. But now you may be wondering, "Is there something wrong here? Exactly what advantage is there to having each country make exchanges on the basis of its own internal trade-off ratios? What's in it for the United States if, for example, it gives Japan the *same* terms of trade (1 for 1) that it can get for itself without trade, and vice versa?"

Ricardo would probably suggest, "Why not compromise with an international term of trade—something between 1 for 1 and 1 for 2." A likely candidate for the compromise (depending on the demand for each product) might be 1 ton of rice for 1-1/2 TV sets (or the equivalent ratio of 2 tons of rice for 3 TVs). Now the United States can trade 2 tons of rice for 3 TVs (better than 1 for 1!); Japan, in turn, only has to give up 3 TV sets (instead of 4) to receive 2 tons of rice.

We'll assume that both countries find this compromise satisfactory, which, as we shall see, will bring about some very positive end results. For example, the United States now has the *potential* to increase its total TV consumption by 50 percent; in Figure 18-1, note that if the United States wants to export all of its rice (4 tons), it can import as many as 6 TV sets. Japan's total rice potential has increased by 33 percent: if Japan exports all of its 6 TVs, it can receive as much as 4 tons of rice, instead of the original 3. These new trade possibilities can be shown on an *expanded production possibilities curve* for each country (see Figure 18-2).

These expanded production possibilities curves indicate that the consumers in each country have the opportunity to enjoy *more* of both products. On the average, their standards of living have improved, but not due to an enlargement of either resource base; each country is simply using its original resources more efficiently by specializing in the area in which it has a comparative advantage.

According to David Ricardo, free trade gives countries this unexpected bonus. Therefore, he was not saddened when he saw the cloth industry in Britain grow at the expense of its wine industry and the cloth industry in Portugal decline as its wine production expanded. Although these trade-offs certainly caused short-run economic dislocations (unemployment, bankruptcies, etc.), the net long-run change was positive.

Actually, the benefits of international trade are really no different than the benefits of local or regional trade. Think, for example, about the obvious advantages of trade within the United States. There is a significant difference, however, between international trade and domestic trade: the dislocations caused

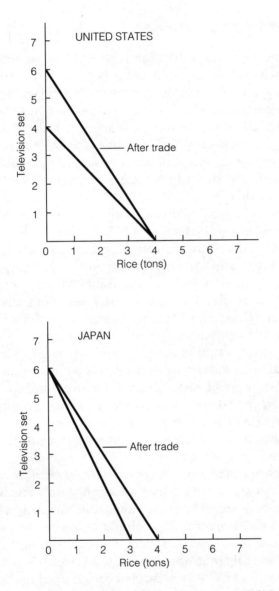

FIGURE 18-2 The expanded after-trade production possibilities curves for the United States and Japan imply that specialization and trade based on comparative advantage provide higher standards of living in both countries.

by foreign imports are usually *more abrasive politically* than the dislocations caused by purely domestic trade. This issue, in turn, brings us to the heart of an important and sensitive subject—*protectionism*.

Trade Protectionism

One of the best ways to illustrate the pressures to restrict imports (without losing sight of the benefits of trade) is to draw up an exaggerated example of trade between two states. Imagine that a particular state—say, Wisconsin—is actually a small, self-reliant "country," producing most (if not all) of its essential economic requirements. We'll further assume that the people of Wisconsin have an unusual craving for citrus fruits and that, over the years, a thriving orange and grapefruit industry has grown up in this "country."

At this point, you might be wondering, "How could Wisconsin, way up there along the northern U.S. border, grow citrus fruit?" The answer is that if the domestic demand is great enough (if the people of Wisconsin are willing and able to pay high prices for citrus fruit), then it will be profitable to grow oranges and grapefruit in artificially heated hothouses. Let's say that fruit grown under these conditions will be priced at $3 for an orange and $4 for a grapefruit.

Now assume that once Wisconsin establishes its large and thriving citrus industry, some enterprising individual discovers that the "country" of Florida can grow an orange for $0.10 and a grapefruit for $0.15. Adding another $0.05 for shipping, our entrepreneurial friend finds that he can make a good profit selling these fruits in Wisconsin at a fraction of the industry prices there.

It does not take any imagination to guess what will happen after the "cheap Florida imports" began to roll into Wisconsin. First, there is shock and dismay among the "domestic" (Wisconsin) citrus growers. Horror stories circulate, resulting in corporate bankruptcies, loss of tax revenues, and long unemployment lines. A powerful trade association, the Wisconsin Citrus Growers Association (WCGA) is formed and immediately begins to exert political pressure to help save the Wisconsin industry. Soon the political machinery begins to respond, undertaking measures to promote Wisconsin fruit consumption and to discourage the importation of Florida fruit.

The first measures take the form of *nontariff barriers,* subtle methods of dealing with the import problem without resorting to the more common tariffs and quotas. First, massive advertising campaigns praise the virtues of "domestically" grown fruit and might imply that some of the "cheap Florida imports" have been determined to be unhealthy. We'll assume, however, that the Wisconsin consumer finds the "imported" fruit just as tasty and wholesome as the home-grown variety. The next tactic is to pass a law stating that all imported fruit must be dyed blue. But even that strategy doesn't work—the price is too good!

Sooner or later, the Wisconsin growers convince their legislators to take more drastic steps, such as setting tariffs and quotas. We will examine these measures in greater detail, but first let's take a look at what we have learned about the real world from this example.

The first lesson is that cheap imported products almost always cause some economic dislocation in directly affected industries. Assertions of comparative advantage are not very comforting to workers who have lost their livelihoods and incomes. Their first reaction is almost always shock, followed by intense anger. Consider the following story from a St. Paul, Minnesota, newspaper:

> Workers at the Teledyne Wisconsin Motor firm, which was playing host to Japanese businessmen, hauled down a Japanese flag in front of the plant and raised an American flag on the same pole.
>
> They sang the "Star Spangled Banner" as the American banner was raised.
>
> One worker tried to burn the Japanese flag but could not ignite it. He then slashed it with a pocket knife, took it across the street, and shoved it down a sewer opening.
>
> John Claffey, president of Local 283 of the United Auto Workers, said . . . the transfer of the so-called Wisconsin Robin engine business to Japan had cost "50 percent of our engine business" and the 350 people had been laid off at the West Milwaukee plant as a result.[46]

These intense feelings are understandable. Compassion tells us that workers who are adversely affected by sudden shifts in international trade arrangements need help to offset the pain of sudden unemployment and to shift their skills and resources to new industries in which they do have a comparative advantage.

This point brings us to the second real-world lesson in our illustration. It should be clear that despite the economic hardship, Wisconsin really *has no business growing grapefruit and oranges*. Its land, resources, and climate are far more ideal for producing dairy products. Once Wisconsin begins to specialize

Hi. I used to own the largest orange-growing hot house complex in Wisconsin. We grew our oranges even during the harshest Wisonsin winters. Sure they weren't cheap because of high fuel costs. But they sure tasted great!

One day my neighbor Chester Olson, Jr., came back from a vacation in Florida with a load of oranges which sold for a tenth as much as mine. He sold out in Hours, then went back to get more. Well that got us Wisconsin orange growers thinking. Soon we had a law passed that required all Florida oranges to be dyed blue.

We did this for our customers' convenience, err . . . that way they wouldn't accidentally buy inferior Florida oranges. Well that didn't help too much, so we tried to reduce our costs by putting cows in our hot houses (the cows seemed to generate quite a bit of heat).

Even that didn't help our orange business. Then one day Chester, Jr., came by asking if he couldn't buy some of my milk to take back to Florida. He says milk there costs $10 a gallon while I can sell it to him for a dollar a gallon. Hmmm, maybe I really ought to be producing milk instead of oranges.

Sure enough, my cows were producing milk cheaper here in Wisconsin because they seem to like the cooler Wisconsin weather and our rolling pastures. This makes it possible to ship my cheap milk to Florida. By the way those inexpensive Florida oranges aren't really that bad after all.

Well that's about it. I'm now a prosperous Wisconsin dairy farmer. One thing I wonder about though . . . why does Florida make me dye my milk green?

and to trade dairy products for inexpensive Florida citrus fruit, both Wisconsin and Florida will enjoy higher standards of living compared with the days before trade.

Thus, the most productive reaction to the import threat is for Wisconsin to start promoting a dairy industry. To facilitate this change, the government may have to offer temporary, low-cost loans for certain types of farm investments, set up research facilities, and help to seek out potential markets for dairy products. Indeed, it would be economically disastrous to hold on to citrus production at all costs. Such a reaction *would lock Wisconsin's resources into the wrong industry for years and years.*

Strong protectionist reflexes are, however, far more common than attempts to adjust to new economic realities. We therefore need to take a closer look at the nature of these restrictions to see how they work and how they affect the consumer.

Tariffs and Quotas

Certainly, the most common strategy for discouraging imports is to levy *tariffs*—taxes on specific imported goods. Although tariffs are sometimes justified by the claim that they will generate tax revenues, their real intent is almost always to choke off foreign competition. Indeed, if revenues were the issue, there would be no point in specifically discriminating against foreign manufacturers and levying such taxes just on them.

The economic effect of a tariff is the same as that of an excise tax on any product: it *lifts* the supply curve precisely by the amount of the tax. The degree to which this hurts the consumer depends on *demand elasticity.* Figure 18-3a shows a fairly elastic demand for Mexican tomatoes; Figure 18-3b illustrates an inelastic demand for Canadian natural gas. In each case, the supply curve has moved a *vertical* distance equal to the amount of the tariff ($0.50 per unit). But due to the different demand elasticities, the tariff on the tomatoes increases the final price to the consumer only slightly while the same tariff on natural gas translates into a large price increase. The explanation for this can be traced to the fact that imported tomatoes are a "non-necessity"; several other vegetables can be substituted for tomatoes. Natural gas, however, is a necessity that has few substitutes. The consumer, therefore, has little or no choice but to absorb most of the $0.50 tariff.

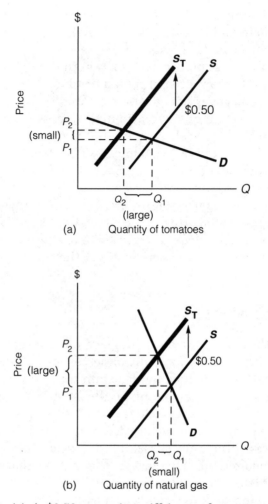

FIGURE 18-3 (a) A $0.50 per-unit tariff imposed on a product with a relatively elastic demand raises the import price slightly but curtails the quantity demanded by a large amount. (b) The same $0.50 per-unit tariff levied on a product with an inelastic demand raises the import price considerably but has little impact on the quantity demanded.

Perhaps of even greater concern to the domestic industry, which pushed for the tariff in the first place, is how the tariff affects the *quantity demanded* of an import. The "choking-off" effect on imports is obviously greater in the elastic tomato market than in the inelastic natural-gas market. Generally speaking, we can say that *the greater the demand elasticity, the more a tariff will help the domestic industry achieve its goal of keeping out foreign competition.*

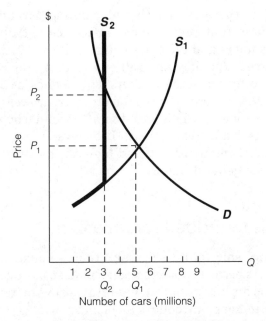

FIGURE 18-4 An imposed quota of 3 million cars fixes the supply curve in a vertical position at S_2 directly above the quota quantity. The equilibrium price after the quota is P_2. (Note that the free-market equilibrium price is P_1.)

When the tariff is not effective, however, a second, more extreme protectionist strategy, the import **quota,** can be used. Quotas simply limit the quantities of imports that are legally allowed to enter the country, so that cheap goods will not "flood" the domestic market. The impact of a **quota** can be seen in Figure 18-4.

Although economists do not favor any form of protectionist measure, they may dislike quotas most of all. At least with a tariff, it is possible to obtain an additional quantity of a product if the consumer is willing to pay the tax. But the quota is an *absolute barrier* once the legal limit has been reached. In Figure 18-4, the foreign quota was set at 3 million cars, but the normal trade equilibrium would have been 5 million cars. Also note that the restricted S_2 supply forces consumers who want to purchase the product to bid the price up from P_1 to P_2. When faced with quotas, some exporters simply *upgrade* their exported product by selling only the most expensive (and therefore most profitable) units, unfairly shutting out many lower-income families from the benefits of trade.

Indeed, if there is one thread running throughout this discussion, it is that protectionist measures usually hurt all types of consumers and ultimately diminish the efficient use of world resources. Yet they are still enforced. A major reason is the political influence of the workers and businesses affected by foreign competition (recall the Wisconsin citrus-growers example). However, it is sometimes difficult to understand why the *public itself* supports trade restrictions. Let's examine some of the arguments most frequently offered by both the vested interest groups and the general public.

Arguments for Trade Protectionism

A student once said (quite sincerely) that we ought to restrict foreign imports because it's important "to keep our money in our country." This argument has an irrefutable ring to it: how could we *not* want to keep our dollars at home?

On further reflection, however, this is actually a counterproductive argument. Again, we should recognize that trade is a "two-way street." For example, U.S. dollars that go to Japan for VCRs or Toyotas come back to our country when the Japanese buy our rice, soybeans, stocks and bonds, computers, and real estate or help to finance our public debt by purchasing securities from the U.S. Treasury. If there is a healthy trade arrangement between these two countries, our money *will* eventually return to us because the Japanese have no need to hold on to U.S. dollars at home.

Another argument we hear quite often is that our country ought to restrict imports because our workers cannot compete with "cheap foreign labor." This powerful, often emotionally charged issue—the claim that products from low-wage countries jeopardize American wage rates, American businesses, and, ultimately, American jobs—should not be dismissed lightly.

Proponents of this argument often overlook the fact that U.S. wages are higher than wages in other countries, primarily *because U.S. workers are generally more productive,* better educated, and more skilled. Often, American workers also use more advanced production techniques than foreign workers do. In fact, other less technologically advanced countries have sometimes argued for tariffs to protect *their* domestic industries from the "unfair competition" of the "highly productive" American industrial worker or farmer. In certain industries, of course, U.S. wage rates may be out of line with industry's general level of worker productivity. But why should the American consumer be forced, through protectionist import restrictions, to subsidize high U.S. wage rates that are not matched by corresponding productivity? Or, putting it slightly differently, why shouldn't U.S. consumers be allowed to *benefit* from inexpensive products made by low-wage workers? And, equally importantly, why shouldn't foreign consumers *benefit* from the output of our nation's most efficient industries?

If you scratch beneath the surface of the "cheap foreign labor" argument, you usually discover that it is an oblique admission that a particular U.S. industry is no longer efficient according to world standards. In certain cases, some of the producers may not have modernized their factories; in other industries, wages may be out of line with productivity or product design or quality may not have kept up with foreign competition. Indeed, it would be unusual if we didn't see some domestic industries (or individual companies) lose their competitive advantages over time.

Needless to say, if we begin to erect trade barriers based on the "cheap foreign labor" argument, there is no reason why other countries cannot *retaliate* with their own tariffs and quotas on U.S. producers. This would be the beginning of a destructive *trade-restriction war* that everybody would lose in the end. A good illustration of such short-sightedness, the enactment of the Smoot-Hawley tariffs in 1930, raised the average cost of goods imported to the United States by about 60 percent. Foreign retaliation ensued, and the inevitable cutback in world trade made the Great Depression of the 1930s just that much worse.

The popularity of such seemingly "logical" arguments should not mask the fact that they simply do not hold up under scrutiny. But perhaps you're wondering, "are there *any* conditions under which interference with free trade might be warranted?" The answer to this question is a qualified "maybe."

When a country is confronted with a violation of international morality, restrictions on both imports and exports may be justified on *ethical grounds*. The United States, for example, has, in the past, put trade restrictions on South Africa for their undemocratic, apartheid policies. In the late 1970s, President Jimmy Carter placed an embargo on grain exports to the Soviet Union after their invasion of Afghanistan; and, more recently, a United Nations–sanctioned trade embargo was placed on Iraq after Saddam Hussein's surprise invasion and takeover of Kuwait in August of 1990.

It has been argued that Third World countries should temporarily restrict imports to give their new domestic industries an opportunity to become established. This is usually referred to as the ***infant industry argument***. Its implications are that (1) it is desirable for less-developed countries to diversify their internal economies, and (2) temporary restrictions are needed so that the "infant" can have breathing space to "mature," to become efficient by world standards, without getting unduly hurt by existing international economic giants. For this argument to be valid, the domestic industry should be forewarned that the import protection will be cut off at some specific date. Otherwise, the "infants" will probably want to perpetuate their protected status. Like the proverbial son who refuses to leave home, some protected industries could resist confronting the real world indefinitely.

Finally, an argument can be made for temporary protectionist measures to prevent genuine "culture shock" in some developing countries. This is not so much an economic issue as it is an anthropological one that recognizes the potential for the destruction of traditional handicraft societies that a sudden, unexpected influx of machine-made goods can represent. When such an influx occurs, it frequently affects not only the economic livelihood but also the age-old cultural fabric of the community. Again, this is not an argument for permanent restrictions; it is simply an admission that it may be desirable to slow things down to give people in smaller, less-developed countries a chance to make economic adjustments.

But when the exceptions are noted and acknowledged, the fact remains that free trade is, more often than not, a worthwhile goal. Fortunately, the world's major trading partners generally recognize this fact. Since 1947, there have been significant attempts to reduce trade barriers through the General Agreements for Tariffs and Trade (GATT). By the early 1980s, various tariff-negotiation milestones (the so-called "Kennedy Round" in 1967 and the "Tokyo Round" in 1979) had reduced tariffs to historically low levels. Of course, there will always be domestic pressures to impose protective tariffs and quotas on foreign goods, so there will always be the threat of a worldwide trade-restriction war lurking in the background. We should be on guard.

But even without a trade war, periodic imbalances of trade still pose some knotty problems for any country. It's time to take a closer look at the age-old struggle of how countries balance their international payments.

Questions for Thought and Discussion

1. If trade is so good for all countries, then why shouldn't all tariffs and quotas be dropped?
2. Given a traditional economic system, what kinds of changes must be made in subsistence, agrarian societies to generate the necessary surpluses for trade to take place?
3. In the 1980s, many U.S. manufacturing jobs were lost to foreign competitors and plant modernizations. What can/should society do to assist these dislocated workers? Specify appropriate policies, costs, and benefits.
4. "Trade provides the same kinds of improvements in well-being that a country gains from having additional economic resources." Explain the reasoning behind this statement.

19

The Problems of International Trade

Remember the imaginary trade between Wisconsin and Florida back in Chapter 18? This example illustrates the key concept that the principles of specialization and comparative advantage apply equally to all forms of trade—between states, between regions, between countries. Then why does it seem to be more difficult to make trading arrangements in the international sphere than it does in the domestic sphere? The question leads us to one of the most interesting issues in economics—the *balance-of-payments problem.*

Let's return to our trading arrangement between Wisconsin and Florida. If Wisconsin imports more oranges from Florida than it exports dairy products to Florida, then we say that Wisconsin is experiencing an "unfavorable" balance of trade. However, neither state gets very excited about this trade imbalance. Why not? The answer is because the entire United States *uses the same currency.*

If Florida businesses collect a *surplus* of Wisconsin dollars, they can easily spend them in Florida—or, for that matter, anywhere in the United States. In contrast, if the United States experiences an unfavorable balance of trade with Japan, the Japanese will accumulate extra dollars that, generally speaking, cannot be spent in Japan. If this imbalance continues, the

Japanese will be faced with the problem of what to do with all their dollars. Thus, unlike trade between individual states, trade between countries ought to roughly "balance out" over time; otherwise, the surplus country will build up quantities of unwanted foreign currency while it sacrifices real goods and services.

What mechanisms or policies are available to bring imbalanced international trade back into balance? There have been three major approaches to dealing with this situation. One of the earliest mechanisms to help a country solve its trade imbalance was the *classical gold-flow model,* originally described by philosopher-economist David Hume in 1752. Let's begin by taking a look at this interesting idea.

Classical Gold Flow

For the classical model to work, David Hume assumed that all the countries involved in trade had to be on both *international* and *domestic* gold standards.

When trading countries go on an **international gold standard,** it means that traders from a foreign country who wind up with a surplus of, say, dollars have the right to trade those dollars for U.S. gold. If, on the other hand, traders from the United States wind up with a trade surplus, they have the right to obtain foreign gold for their surplus currencies.

To be on a **domestic gold standard** means that every dollar in circulation must be backed up by an equivalent amount of gold. A country's money supply therefore depends on how much gold it has. After losing some of its gold to a foreign country, for example, the United States will be forced to reduce its domestic money supply because it now has less gold with which to back it up. On the other hand, if U.S. gold holdings are enlarged, then the U.S. money supply will automatically increase.

Before this model can be used to solve a balance-of-payments problem, one further assumption needs to be spelled out: the linkage between money and prices through the so-called *quantity theory of money.* This theory can be summarized quite neatly as

$$MV = PQ$$

where M is the money supply, V is the **velocity of money** (the number of times an average dollar changes hands during the

Hi! I'm David Hume. I would like to show you how two small countries can solve an imbalance of trade when they are both on an international and a domestic gold standard.

The two islands of Chetek and Mondovi are always trading between themselves. Last year things were pretty much in balance; that is, imports roughly equalled exports.

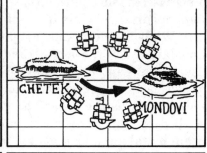

But this year Chetek imported twice as many goods from Mondovi as Mondovi imported from Chetek.

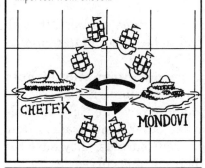

When Mondovi sells more goods, they get a surplus of Chetek currency which they trade for gold. The extra gold increases the money supply and soon pushes up Mondovi prices.

In Chetek just the opposite was happening. A loss of gold reduced their money supply and soon their prices began to go down.

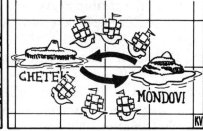

High Mondovi prices therefore discourage Chetekites from buying Mondovi imports, and low Chetek prices encourage Mondovians to purchase Chetek products. Soon trade is back into balance.

KV

year), P is the general price level, and Q is the physical volume of goods and services.

Classical economists like David Hume assumed that both V and Q remain relatively constant, *leaving* M *and* P *to rise or fall together*. Thus, if the U.S. money supply goes up, it drives prices up, too (inflation); if M goes down, it lowers the general price level P (deflation). Keep in mind that in our simplified, classical world, all prices are assumed to be completely flexible: to move downward or upward with equal ease.

The stage is now set for solving an imbalance problem. We'll assume that the United States suddenly finds itself in a serious trade deficit with Japan: U.S. imports to Japan are greater than U.S. exports from Japan. As a result, the Japanese receive more dollars than they can spend. Under the classical assumptions just outlined, Japanese traders exchange their surplus dollars for American gold, and the quantity of gold in the U.S. Treasury declines. This reduction in gold stock forces a reduction in the U.S. money supply, which is followed quickly by a decrease in our prices. Falling U.S. prices, in turn, make our products less expensive and therefore more attractive to Japanese consumers. As U.S. exports expand, we find ourselves moving toward a balance-of-payments equilibrium.

While all this is going on in the United States, Japan's growing gold stock enables more money to circulate in its economy. More money (given a fixed volume of goods and services) will create Japanese inflation. Finally, high Japanese prices will discourage the Japanese from importing goods to the United States and help to resolve the original imbalance of payments. A summary of the relevant linkages leading to this trade equilibrium are diagrammed in Figure 19-1.

Classical gold flow is a completely automatic and totally reliable system. This model operates like some self-regulating Newtonian machine, continually moving the system toward a favorable balance-of-payments equilibrium without messy maintenance or outside tinkering. So why isn't this system used in the United States today?

First, the United States is no longer on an international gold standard, nor is it on a domestic gold standard (the last vestige of gold backing disappeared in 1967). There is simply not enough gold to keep up with expanding domestic money supplies and the general growth of world trade.

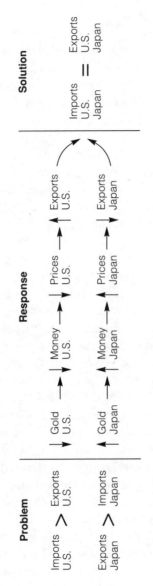

FIGURE 19-1 Classical Gold Flow model

More importantly, though, prices would probably not respond with the classical flexibility needed to make the system work even if the United States were still on the gold standard. Today, prices tend to go up and up and very rarely go down. In fact, the only time the United States has experienced general deflation in the twentieth century occurred during the Great Depression of the 1930s! If a depression is what it takes to get prices down, it's simply not worth it. There must be a better way to solve our international balance-of-payments problem. This brings us to our second method of solving international trade imbalance—a method that is even simpler than the classical model in many ways. It's called the ***flexible exchange-rate system.***

Flexible Exchange Rates

The key to understanding flexible exchange rates is to realize that world currencies are subject to supply and demand markets not unlike those markets for corn or soybeans. In theory, we can draw demand and supply curves for every country's currency. Perhaps it would be helpful to illustrate this point by choosing one specific currency—the German mark.

We begin by asking, "Why would Americans demand German marks?" There is basically one answer: marks are needed for American consumers to purchase German products and services. Thus, the U.S. demand for marks will reflect the demand for German imports. If American consumers suddenly want lots more German cars or cameras, they will need more marks, and the demand for marks will rise.

We then ask, "Why would the Germans want to supply us with marks?" Germany will supply the United States with marks in direct relation to its desire to purchase U.S. products and services. If Germans want a lot more American wheat or computers, for example, then the supply curve for marks will increase.

Assuming that there is an equilibrium between German and American trade, there will also be an equilibrium in the market for marks. This example is illustrated in Figure 19-2, where the "price" of a German mark (its ***exchange rate***) is $0.25. We are assuming that at the $0.25 price trade between the United States and Germany is in balance.

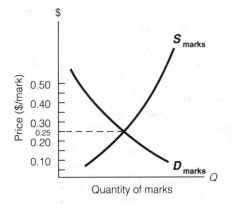

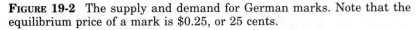

FIGURE 19-2 The supply and demand for German marks. Note that the equilibrium price of a mark is $0.25, or 25 cents.

Now let's see what happens when American consumers suddenly want a lot more German products or decide to travel more in Germany. They might also be interested in building U.S.-owned factories in Germany or investing in the German Stock Exchange. Each of these measures will contribute to a short-run U.S. *balance-of-payments deficit;* each of these activities will also increase the U.S. demand for German marks. We will assume that Germany is not particularly interested in purchasing any more American products, so that their willingness to supply marks remains constant. The market for marks is then altered, as demand increases in relation to a constant supply curve.

This change is shown in Figure 19-3. What is happening, of course, is that those who want additional marks *must bid up the price* to get them. This is reflected by a new equilibrium price of $0.40 (versus the old price of $0.25). As the price for marks goes up, we say the dollar is being *depreciated;* U.S. dollars are now worth less in relation to German marks.

In the word "depreciation," we discover the real key to the flexible exchange-rate system. Since the dollar is now worth less, it will take *more* dollars to buy a given amount of German goods and services. If a bottle of German beer costs 1 mark, for example, then Americans must pay $0.40 for that bottle of beer, in contrast with the former price of $0.25 a bottle. Virtually every economic dealing with Germany will cost proportionately more: buying a Mercedes Benz, traveling to Bonn, building a soap factory in Cologne, or buying a share of stock in a German company. As dollars depreciate relative to the mark, most

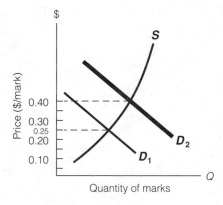

FIGURE 19-3 Assuming that U.S. citizens want to buy more German imports, to travel to Germany, or to make investments directly within the German economy, they will need (demand) more German marks than they did before. Graphically, this development will shift the demand curve to the right from D_1 to D_2. Note that this shift in demand increases the price of a mark from $0.25 to $0.40.

Americans will begin to cut back their German purchases and travel plans, which will tend to bring trade back into balance.

Note that the change in the currency's equilibrium price represents not only **depreciation** for the U.S. dollar but also **appreciation** for the German mark. Germany now sees U.S. exports as less expensive (1 mark, for example, will buy $0.40 worth of U.S. goods instead of $0.25 worth) and therefore begin to *increase* their purchase of American products. They may also start to set up factories in, and travel more to, the United States. All of these activities should help to restore the original trade balance.

Now assume for a moment that you are planning to travel to a foreign country. How do you find out what it will cost you to purchase the foreign currency you will need? Check the business section of most major newspapers, and you will find a table listing the value of most world currencies in relationship to the dollar. Using Table 19-1, see if you can determine how much it cost in U.S. dollars to purchase a Swiss franc on April 10, 1990.

According to the table, a Swiss franc would cost you about $0.67 ($0.6748). Also, in the column "Currency per U.S. $," note that $1 will purchase 1.4820 Swiss francs. Of course, international currencies rise or fall in value according to shifts in supply and demand. For example, in early 1985, that same Swiss franc was worth about $0.37, which means that this particular currency

TABLE 19-1 Abbreviated Exchange-Rate Table (Tuesday, April 10, 1990)

COUNTRY	U.S. $ EQUIV.	CURRENCY PER U.S. $
Argentina (Austral)	.0002174	4600.03
Austria (Schilling)	.08476	11.80
Bahrain (Dinar)	2.6522	.3771
Britain (Pound)	1.6450	.6079
Canada (Dollar)	.8623	1.1597
China (Yuan)	.211640	4.7250
France (Franc)	.17773	5.6265
India (Rupee)	.05834	17.14
Ireland (Punt)	1.5885	.6295
Israel (Shekel)	.5008	1.9968
Italy (Lira)	.0008112	1232.76
Japan (Yen)	.006343	157.65
Mexico (Peso)	.0003598	2779.01
Netherland (Guilder)	.5297	1.8880
Pakistan (Rupee)	.0472	21.18
Philippines (Peso)	.04502	22.21
South Korea (Won)	.0014245	702.00
Spain (Peseta)	.009390	106.50
Sweden (Krona)	.1637	6.1100
Switzerland (Franc)	.6748	1.482
Taiwan (Dollar)	.038168	26.20
W. Germany (Mark)	.5972	1.6745

has nearly doubled in dollar price between 1985 and 1990. This change implies that imported Swiss products or the cost of touring Switzerland will be noticeably more expensive in the early 1990s in contrast to their prices in the mid-1980s.

If we were to compare the U.S. dollar to an *average value* of other currencies as a whole, we would see a considerable "flip-flop" in its value since the early 1970s: first, a long drift downward (dollar depreciation) during the 1970s; then a steep climb of approximately 60 percent from 1980 to 1985. This trend made U.S. consumers and travelers smile but, at the same time, created headaches for American export industries because U.S. products were generally more expensive in the eyes of foreign buyers. American farmers and heavy-equipment manufacturers were among those especially hurt by the 1980–1985 increase in the value of the U.S. dollar. After 1985, however, another dollar depreciation in effect reversed the respective groups who benefit (U.S. exporters) and who pay more (U.S. consumers).

The peaks and troughs of the ever-changing exchange rates are, needless to say, difficult to predict. Sometimes the speed of a currency's ascent or descent makes many exporters and central bankers uneasy, not unlike experiencing the ups and downs of a roller-coaster ride.

Still, it is this flexible exchange-rate system—with some modifications and central-bank interventions—that is working to help realign currencies throughout the world today. Before we discuss recent policies, however, we need to take a brief look at the third method of dealing with world balance-of-payments problems: the *modified gold/fixed exchange-rate system,* which dominated the international scene for almost 30 years (1944–1971). How did this system differ from the classical gold-flow model or the flexible exchange-rate system? Let's take a look.

Modified Gold/Fixed Exchange-Rate System

The system of fixed exchange began in a specific location at a specific time. It's birthplace was Bretton Woods, New Hampshire, and the year was 1944. World War II—the war that had devastated much of Europe and almost all of Japan—was coming to a close. Entire economic infrastructures (factories, roads, power plants, etc.) had literally been blown apart.

The United States, however, was stronger than ever. Its economic infrastructure remained intact; its work force was basically unharmed. It was not surprising that the major industrial countries of the world looked to the United States for postwar assistance and leadership.

U.S. assistance was offered in the form of the *Marshall Plan* and the *International Bank for Reconstruction and Development.* Both of these programs poured billions of dollars into European reconstruction. In terms of international leadership, it was agreed at the 1944 Bretton Woods Conference that the world was henceforth to be on a *fixed exchange-rate system,* using the dollar as the centerpiece currency. All other major world currencies would be pegged at fixed values in relation to the dollar; the dollar, in turn, would be pegged at a fixed rate of $35 per ounce of gold. Thus, the world nations were on

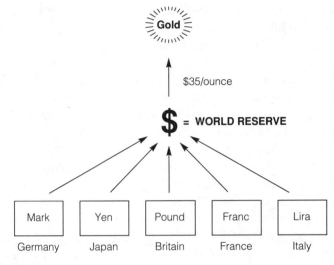

Figure 19-4

an international gold standard: countries with a surplus of dollars could, if they wished, trade them for U.S. gold. However, most countries chose to keep their dollars as reserves in their international "checking accounts." Dollars therefore became a kind of world "legal tender." These monetary relationships are diagrammed in Figure 19-4.

Fixed exchange rates had the virtue of being resolutely stable; at the time, they were backed by gold, a strong dollar, and an unrivaled American economy. The chance, however, that a country might experience balance-of-payment difficulties still existed. Anticipating such problems, Bretton Woods officials agreed to set up an institution that could loan deficit countries the requisite amount of dollars (or other currencies) as their needs arose. The chief purpose of this *International Monetary Fund* (IMF) was to help make these short-term loans and perhaps some long-term readjustments in a country's basic exchange rate.

Suppose that some country (for example, Great Britain) kept running chronic balance-of-payments deficits. The British pound would then be "overvalued" in relation to other currencies and would eventually have to be devalued. How would Britain devalue the pound? British bankers would approach the IMF and *request* a new (lower) exchange rate for the pound in relation to the dollar; instead of $2.60 per pound, they might want to go down to, say, $2.00.

Devaluation may sound like a case of depreciation under a flexible exchange-rate system (discussed in the last section), but there are a couple of important differences. First, the *flexible* exchange-rate system adjusts *automatically* to short-run changes in the supply of, and demand for, a currency. In the case of the devaluation of the pound under the *fixed* system, the British *have to ask the IMF for permission* to adjust the exchange rate. The IMF Board of Directors thus ensures orderly readjustments in world exchange rates.

The second difference is perhaps more subtle. After devaluation, the British pound is worth less not only in relation to the U.S. dollar but also to *all* other currencies valued in relation to the dollar (see Figure 19-4). To review, *depreciation* is the reduction of the value of a currency in relation to the value of *one* other currency; *devaluation* is the reduction of the value of a currency in relation to *all* other currencies.

In general, the fixed exchange-rate system worked reasonably well, but it had one overriding flaw: *an overwhelming reliance on the dollar.* For example, what would happen if the United States began to experience its *own* chronic balance-of-payments deficits—if the dollar itself became overvalued? How would you like to be holding millions of dollars in your international "checking account," believing these dollars would always be worth a certain amount in terms of other currencies (as well as gold), and then, unexpectedly have the United States devalue the dollar? This could be done by simply raising the dollar's par value with gold from $35 per ounce to some higher amount. If, for example, the United States raised the price of gold to, say, $70 per ounce, then the value of your foreign-held dollars (which you've retained because you have faith in the stability of the fixed exchange-rate system) would be cut in half! The fixed exchange-rate system had a structural inability to effectively deal with the possible devaluation of the dollar.

For a long time, however, it wasn't necessary to devalue the dollar. Postwar Europe, hungry for U.S. consumer goods and industrial products, demanded lots of U.S. dollars. However, beginning in the mid-1950s and continuing into the 1960s, problematic U.S. trade deficits occurred year after year.

One quite predictable reason for this was that the Europeans and Japanese eventually began to close the postwar "productivity gap." Their bombed-out infrastructures were replaced with the most modern facilities available. Also, the U.S. productivity growth rate fell from a relatively high 3 percent increase per year (the average rate from 1948 to 1966) down to 2 percent per year (from 1966 to 1973); for the rest of the 1970s, it averaged only about 1 percent per year! Not only did Japanese and German productivity increase more rapidly than U.S. productivity, but other energetic Asian economies, including Taiwan, South Korea, and Hong Kong, began to expand their own export production and to make significant inroads into U.S. markets.

An additional problem—the relatively high U.S. inflation rate—worsened during the mid-1960s. Higher U.S. prices discouraged foreign buyers and hurt the U.S. balance of payments. The American military presence overseas represented another net outflow of dollars. In addition, the costly Vietnam War undoubtedly contributed to U.S. inflation and trade deficits as well.

Another development that diminished U.S. exports was the formation of the **European Economic Community,** or the *Common Market,* which promoted free trade within its borders but often set up barriers to trade with the rest of the world, including the United States. To compete effectively within Common Market countries, U.S. corporations often had to make *direct investments* within the represented countries by setting up American factories on European soil. These direct investments again contributed to a net outflow of dollars and—in the short run, at least—hurt the U.S. balance of payments.

Each new problem enlarged U.S. deficits more and more. Of course, the modified gold/fixed exchange-rate system did provide some techniques (short of devaluation) for coping with this increasing deficit. First, it was possible to exchange gold for surplus dollars, as originally intended under the Bretton Woods agreement. Recall that the United States agreed to sell gold to foreign monetary authorities at the fixed rate of $35 per ounce. Indeed, countries like France and Austria often insisted on exchanging their surplus dollars for gold. Exchanging gold, however, had its drawbacks: the U.S. gold stock was unlimited. Originally worth some $25 billion right after World War II, U.S. gold reserves had shrunk to less than 50 percent of that amount two decades later.

Members of the U.S. Congress were tempted to solve the imbalance problem by restricting foreign goods. In Chapter 18, we found that such protectionist policies are self-defeating and can easily set off a restrictive trade war. Fortunately, the protectionists didn't get very far. Legislators did pass laws that helped to a certain degree. Efforts to "tie" foreign aid (require that the recipient country purchase U.S. products) were instituted. Restrictions were also placed on the amount of imported goods that an American tourist could bring back duty free. But these and other legislative efforts did not really solve the basic problem of an overvalued dollar. Still, the United States didn't want to devalue its currency unless it was absolutely necessary.

Perhaps the easiest way to deal with the U.S. deficit was to *convince foreign monetary authorities to hold onto their surplus dollars.* Many countries kept dollars strictly for legal tender; others wanted interest-bearing dollar assets. If U.S. interest rates were relatively high compared to interest rates on alternative investments, then foreigners might be in no hurry to make gold exchanges.

These techniques, in addition to selling gold and arranging for assistance from the IMF, helped the United States to hang on to the Bretton Woods system through the 1960s. But by the early 1970s, foreign dollar claims were skyrocketing, the U.S. gold supply was dwindling to an all-time low, and U.S. balance-of-payments deficits continued to grow. Something had to be done to avert an international dollar crisis. The Bretton Woods fixed exchange-rate system was simply not compatible with the realities of current international trade.

The dramatic moment finally came on August 15, 1971, when President Richard Nixon suspended all gold transactions. In effect, the old system of gold convertibility "went out the window." The dollar was now allowed to float; its future value was to be determined primarily by the forces of supply and demand. By 1973, the dollar had depreciated significantly compared to most of the world's major currencies. The prices of many imports—from German Volkswagons to Japanese Datsuns, from Middle Eastern oil to Swiss watches—went up accordingly. A new economic era had arrived.

Of course, the flexible exchange-rate system of the 1970s and 1980s didn't solve all U.S. balance-of-payments problems. Various governments (including the U.S. government) were not shy about intervening against speculators and other "threats" to their currencies, at times preventing proper currency realignments. The United States also found itself hurt by the emergence of an effective world oil cartel (OPEC) that created a sudden increase in the price of crude oil in the 1970s, contributing to a large net outflow of U.S. dollars. In the first half of the 1980s, the United States witnessed something new (and, to a large degree, unanticipated)—a phenomenal *increase* in the dollar's average exchange value against most major foreign currencies. Economists attribute this development to a strong foreign-dollar demand for *investments* in the United States. Why did this take place?

For one thing, the United States appeared to be a "safe haven" in a world of political uncertainty. Also, foreigners felt that the United States had good investment opportunities, especially in the years of a relatively high gross national product (GNP). And finally, high real-interest rates (due to ebbing U.S. inflation) made many American investments that much more attractive. Unfortunately, this increase in the dollar's international value hurt many traditional U.S. exporting industries and contributed to additional deficits in U.S. balance-of-payment merchandise accounts.

The United States as a Debtor Nation

Perhaps the most dramatic outcome of these developments was the fact that the United States officially became a net "debtor nation" in 1985, meaning that the value of foreign investments (stocks, bonds, government securities, real estate, bank deposits, etc.) in the United States exceeded its total investments in other countries. These foreign investments could put the United States in a potentially more vulnerable economic position, especially if this "debtor" status worsens progressively. Some analysts fear that such a trend might increase the possibility (perhaps the probability) of large, even violent, currency readjustments that would be beyond the nation's control. Sudden currency adjustments could, in turn, dramatically and adversely impact on inflation and even jeopardize real growth and employment.

Historian Arthur Schlesinger, Jr., for one, is concerned about what he sees as a parallel with the decline of the British Empire. In his view, the United States is suffering from the slow, but steady, erosion of its financial and, possibly, its military independence. In an editorial in *The Wall Street Journal* (December 22, 1989), Schlesinger writes:

> Consider . . . the national security implications if our creditors should register disapproval of government policies by dumping

Treasury securities and other holdings on the market. . . . Never before in American history has the United States been so much at the mercy of decisions made by foreigners. As a creditor nation in the nineteenth century, Britain ruled the waves; as a debtor nation in the twentieth century, it began to sink beneath them. . . . Now we are approaching Britain's condition of economic vulnerability. . . .

In the same editorial, Schlesinger quotes Robert Gilpin, political science analyst at Princeton: "It would be very difficult for the United States to fight another war on the same scale as the Korean or Vietnamese conflicts without Japanese permission and financial support of the dollar. . . . "

These comments may constitute an extreme position on America's international economic vulnerability. Other observers are not nearly as concerned. Princeton economist William J. Baumol reminds *Wall Street Journal* readers that the United States continues to have the highest absolute productivity level in the world, and he is also impressed to note that some U.S. industries, like steel, "rise from the dead"[47] with new and efficient "mini-mills." Economist Herbert Stein goes one step further, quoting the results of recent studies that claim the United States still has a healthy lead in per-capita standard of living and ending his article, "Who's Number One? Who Cares?" in *The Wall Street Journal* (March 1, 1990), with an unconventional view:

> Our real problem . . . is not to get richer than someone else or to get richer faster than someone else but to be as good as we can be, and better than we have been, in areas of our serious deficiencies, such as homelessness, poverty, ignorance, and crime.

Keep in mind, too, that unlike the economies of some European and Asian countries, the U.S. economy is not quite as dependent on its foreign-trade sector because the United States produces 85–90 percent of its domestically consumed goods and services within its own borders. Even in the vulnerable area of petroleum, the United States demonstrated a surprising adaptability to the conservation of oil and the development of alternative energy strategies under the heat of rapidly rising oil prices during the 1970s. At that time, you could hardly pick up a popular magazine without seeing articles on energy conservation, superinsulation, earth-sheltered homes, fuel-efficient cars, and the like.

Also, the United States is still generally competitive in many of its traditional export industries, including chemicals, hotels and restaurants, soft drinks, paper products, aircraft, telecommunications, food and fiber, insurance, office machines, banking, farm machinery, computers, TV sit-coms, and sports programming, just to name a few. Finally, we should recognize that even though the U.S. productivity growth rate has slowed significantly, the American output per worker hour (in absolute terms) is still higher than it is in most other industrialized countries.

In summary, the United States will continue to face various international trade problems in the future and, if certain trends (such as deficits and low productivity growth) become chronic problems, will be courting economic trouble in future decades. Yet in relation to the majority of the world's people, who live in the less-developed Third World countries, Americans are still very well off indeed. Perhaps now it is time to leave U.S. shores behind and journey to these struggling nations. What is life like in the developing countries? More importantly, what does the future hold in store for them?

QUESTIONS FOR THOUGHT AND DISCUSSION

1. Why don't all countries adopt the same currency in order to solve the balance-of-payments problem?

2. What would happen if all countries devalued their currencies by the same percentage?

3. What would happen to the quantity theory of money if the velocity of money V and the physical volume of goods and services Q were not held constant?

4. During the early 1980s, spokespersons for U.S. export industries argued that high U.S. interest rates were partially responsible for their weakened competitive positions in world markets. Explain how this might be possible.

20

World Development:
Prospects and Consequences

In the summer of 1974, well-fed Americans didn't seem quite so hostile to high food prices as they had been the previous year. One explanation might have been the depressing stories in major newsmagazines and on television—not stories of high food prices, but stories of no food at all. During that summer, there was very little food for millions of North Africans as they suffered through their sixth straight year of drought. A half-million men, women, and children were already dead, and an estimated 10 million more were living at near-starvation levels throughout the North African famine belt.

Some rain did finally fall on North Africa, but these horrifying statistics were repeated with grimly cyclic regularity in the mid-1980s and again in early 1990, exposing the developed world to its first close-up coverage of the frightening realities of mass starvation. That world could no longer ignore the suffering: the catastrophe was simply too large.

Of course, these crises would pass, as many others had for centuries before them. Yet the uneasy feeling around the world could not be forgotten as national leaders discussed the possibility that famine might eventually affect not just millions, but billions of people in low-income countries.

There is no doubt that Americans will have enough food for years to come. Even under the worst economic conditions, most people in the "over-developed" countries will continue to eat luxuriously[48] and even to feed protein-rich food to their pets. They have the income and can generate effective demand.

But what about the approximately 3 billion people in the less-developed Third World countries? What are their chances for widespread economic development? The problem of mass poverty must be considered one of the major global issues of our time.

Regions under consideration include most of Asia (except Japan, South Korea, and Taiwan), most of black Africa, and Latin America. Although some of these countries are monetarily "better off" than others, we are essentially talking about roughly two-thirds of the world's current population. Let's take a moment to examine some of the general characteristics common to many of these poorer countries.

Education and Nutrition

Certainly one common element in most low-income countries is the problem of *mass illiteracy*. Scarce resources often go toward the education of elite classes, who are taught an outmoded, colonial curriculum in schools that deemphasize the skills needed for economic development. For prestigious reasons, students often choose "literate" professions or civil-service training instead of business, farming, trades, or engineering. These new workers move into a world of bureaucratic desks and white shirts, rather than one of farms and factories.

Other students come to the United States, England, or France to receive legal or other professional training in order to eventually serve an upper-class clientele. Some never return to their homelands. Not only does this kind of investment use of scarce public money that could fund adult literacy classes and basic mechanical, agricultural, and paramedic training, but it also tends to reinforce class consciousness and widen income differentials.

Nutrition is also often a problem. Even without famine conditions, poor countries have always had difficulty obtaining food with adequate protein. Protein deficiency, in turn, may eventually result in the crippling disease known as kwashiorkor.

The victims, almost always children, are seen in photographs with large, protruding bellies and thin, reddish hair. Another nutritional disease, xerophthalmia, the result of a deficiency in vitamin A, exposes millions of people to a bacterial eye infection that can lead to permanent blindness. Many other diseases resulting from nutritional deficiencies impair mental and physical performance in one way or another.

Do these nutritional problems mean that industrialized countries ought to supply poorer countries with free food? This generosity would, ironically, probably do more harm than good (at least in the long run) because it would *obstruct the evolution of agricultural industries* in less-developed nations. To illustrate this point, imagine the impact of some "benevolent" country giving free milk to everyone in the United States. In a short period of time, much of the U.S. dairy industry would be forced into bankruptcy, and all Americans would be unnecessarily dependent on the charity of this benefactor.

What the Third World farmer needs is really no different from what other successful farmers require to be productive: *positive economic incentives,* such as reasonably high, stable

commodity prices, access to land, credit, marketing coopera-
tives, and appropriate farm technology.[49] Frequently, a successful agricultural industry can get under way by simply
eliminating obstacles that already exist, including elitist land-
tenure arrangements and artificially low prices imposed by the
government to placate urban workers. Indeed, a successful
agrarian base is often the best method of providing food to the
masses and upgrading nutritional levels.

Capital and Productivity

In general, Third World countries lack *productive capital,* which
includes productive tools, machines, and factories (among other
things). Indeed, the average African or Asian peasant does use
a certain amount of low-level capital goods—hoes, wooden plows,
manual systems for irrigation, and so forth—but some capital is
extremely unproductive.

The key word here is "productivity." The growth process in
capital-intensive countries goes something like this. First, highly
productive labor generates a large amount of output, which
translates into relatively high incomes for workers. High wage
rates increase production costs, forcing producers to mechanize
even more. Increased mechanization, in turn, increases productivity, and the growth sequence begins all over again.

On the other hand, less-developed countries cannot generate
high incomes because their capital resources generate extremely
low productivity. The result is a "vicious circle" of poverty and
underdevelopment in the form of low productivity, low incomes,
and low consumption levels. The overall productivity level in
most poor countries is so low that a large percentage of the
people live at the subsistence level, producing so little that they
are forced to exist not much above the survival line.

Living near the margin of survival without the expectation
of upward mobility distinguishes the poor of the Third World
countries from the poor of the industrialized countries:

> Living poor is like being sentenced to exist in a stormy sea in a
> battered canoe, requiring all your strength simply to keep afloat;
> there is never any question of reaching a destination. True pov-
> erty is a state of perpetual crisis, and one wave just a little bigger
> or coming from an unexpected direction can and usually does
> wreck things. Some benevolent ignorance denies a poor man the

ability to see the squalid sequence of his life, except very rarely;
he views it rather as a disconnected string of unfortunate sadness. Never having paddled on a calm sea, he is unable to imagine
one. I think if he could connect the chronic hunger, the sickness,
the death of his children, the almost unrelieved physical and
emotional tension into the pattern that his life inevitably takes,
he would kill himself.[50]

Thus, the poor in the developing countries live with uncertainty under substandard conditions. Illiteracy, poor physical
and mental health, and hunger are combined with a traditional
economic system based on unskilled labor and low-productivity
tools.

Institutional Barriers

One much less visible element of underdevelopment may be
even more harmful to developmental efforts than a lack of
productive resources. Economists call this area *institutional
barriers to change.* It includes adverse power relationships,
elitist political systems, cultural traditions, tribalism, graft and
corruption, and the impact of foreign values. Relevant questions
pertaining to institutional problems might include:

- How do traditional cultural practices affect developmental efforts?
- How equal or unequal is the distribution of wealth and
  income?
- What percentage of agricultural workers own no land?
- What role do foreign values and economic interests play
  in Third World development?
- How strong is national cohesiveness? How do the loyalties of citizens to the nation state (to its laws, taxes,
  language, etc.) compare to tribal or traditional religious
  loyalties?

Population

Let's begin with the question of traditional culture and its effect
on economic development. Many economists feel that the major
obstacle to economic betterment is the simple desire to have a

large family. Among low-income, traditional communities, we find a high degree of social status (as well as future "social security") given to parents who have many surviving children. Yet such a simple cultural value can create social and economic problems. A growth rate of 2 percent, for example, can double a population in about 35 years. Although some Third World countries exceed this 2-percent figure, the average growth rate for the world as a whole is about 1.7 percent. Still, there will probably be more than 6 billion people in our world by the year 2000—1 billion more than today's figure.

These numbers may be more meaningful when we put them into historical perspective. It took about 2 million years for the human species to bring the world population up to its first billion people. The second billion were added in about 100 years; the third billion, in just 30 years; the fourth, in only 15. The fifth billion was added within fairly recent history—from 1974 to 1987, or in roughly thirteen years! If the 1.7-percent population growth rate figure holds, approximately 8 billion people will be living in this world by the year 2015, and 16 billion will be living here only one generation later (by the year 2055). Most of these increases will be in the populations of less-developed countries.

These figures are staggering indeed. Such large numbers will probably be modified, either by rising overall death rates (due to possible starvation, military conflicts, a pandemic, etc.) or, more humanely, declining overall birth rates. Indeed, population experts have pointed out that much more can still be done in the area of birth control and family planning. It is interesting to note that the countries that are currently most successful at controlling their growth rates are either authoritarian (mainland China, for example) or have demonstrated rapid economic growth at some time (as Taiwan, Singapore, and Hong Kong have). Ironically, the best and least-repressive method of reversing attitudes about family size is through the process of community development: helping children to survive by offering them better health care and equally important, by providing women with alternatives to childbearing in the form of outside work opportunities. Indeed, after years of traveling, researching, and evaluating family-planning programs, writer Pranay Gupta, in his book *The Crowded Earth,* put the greatest emphasis on the importance of upgrading the economic status of women:

I found during my travels that more and more women also seem to want to get out of their homes to involve themselves in economic activities, a situation that could eventually lead to even more women producing fewer children and thus bring down Asian nations' annual population growth rates. The experience of places such as Bali, Sri Lanka, South Korea, and the southern Indian state of Kerela has shown that, where women were brought into the economic mainstream through increased female education and employment, there was not only an overall decline in the population growth rate but also an improvement in the content and pace of development and in the general quality of life of the entire community.[51]

Yet for many of the poorest Third World countries, economic opportunities, health-care resources, and other fruits of economic development are often beyond the reach of individuals, families, and communities caught in the vicious circle of poverty. On the one hand, high population growth rates stifle the potential for economic development; on the other hand, women want fewer children only when they have access to greater opportunities and are assured that their children have a high probability of survival. Can anything be done about this dilemma?

Perhaps one answer is economic assistance from the developed countries, but it should not be the typical kind of aid that finances such impressive, capital-intensive projects as dams, army installations, airports, and luxury hotels. Instead, it should be in the form of financial and technical assistance to promote local projects that offer widespread benefits in nutrition, health, education, clean water, housing, small-scale rural technologies, and where requested, assistance in family-planning projects. It's doubtful that these "people-oriented" investments will increase the Gross National Product as much as a new steel mill or a hydroelectric plant would, but a more equal distribution of income and the possible reduction of population rates may prove to be far more beneficial in the long run.

Wealth and Income Distribution

Another major obstacle to Third World development is the *uneven concentration of power, wealth, and income*. To understand the distribution of wealth and power in underdeveloped countries, we must first grasp the importance of land ownership. Poor countries are often agrarian societies in which more than

75 percent of the population works and lives in rural areas (compared to 5 percent of the population of the United States, for example.

In such communities, prestige, wealth, and power are measured not so much by capital, money, or material goods but by the amount of land a person controls. Think, for example, of the Philippines—a country that has shown some economic growth but little widespread development—where well over 50 percent of all agricultural workers are landless. Or we could journey to Latin America, where magnificent estates, each tens of thousands of acres, are owned by only a few families. We could also find many great plantations extending for miles throughout the fertile regions of Africa and Asia.

These vast acreages and plantations produce tremendous riches for their owners but usually continued poverty and dependence for the people who work or rent the land:

> In South America, the poor man is an ignorant man, unaware of the forces that shape his destiny. The shattering truth—that he is kept poor and ignorant as the principal and unspoken component of national policy—escapes him. He cries for land reform, a system of farm loans that will carry him along between crops, unaware that the national economy in almost every country sustained by a one-crop export commodity depends for its success on an unlimited supply of cheap labor. Ecuador needs poor men to compete in the world banana market; Brazil needs poverty to sell its coffee; and so on.[52]

Concentrated wealth, however is not limited to local landlords and the traditional elite classes. Some foreigners, particularly former colonists who continue to live in underdeveloped countries, own immense parcels of property. Also, foreign interests frequently dominate the mining sectors that extract large amounts of raw materials from beneath the earth's surface: tin from Bolivia, petroleum from Nigeria and Mexico, tropical hardwoods from Central America, copper from Zambia and Chile, aluminum ore from Jamaica and Guinea. The list of foreign investments is extensive. Although they may bring some economic advantages to local workers, the long-run benefits to the poor of such investments are questionable in view of the exported profits, the all-too-frequent environmental damage caused by such operations as deforestation and open-pit mining, the continued dependence on foreign business, the strain created by unequal growth, and the tremendous reliance on a minimal number of exports to earn foreign exchange.

This last point takes on even greater significance when we learn that about 50 percent of the foreign exchange for a sizable group of developing countries is earned by the export of only one or two raw materials. For example, this means that Bolivia's ability to purchase imports (capital goods, food, consumer products, and so on) is largely dependent on how much foreign exchange the country can earn from exporting tin. Under these conditions, a small drop in tin prices could bring tremendous financial problems to Bolivia. Its foreign exchange earnings would drop significantly, its consumption of imports would be curtailed, its balance of payments would take a turn for the worse, and its major developmental projects might have to be cut back—all because of a relatively small drop in the price of tin.

Manufacturing industries are frequently dominated by foreign interests, too. Indeed, our journey to typical Third World countries would not be complete without a visit to the industrial parks on the fringes of major capital cities, where Westerners would feel quite at home in the presence of such familiar corporations as Coca-Cola, Ford, Union Carbide, and Texaco, not to mention branch factories of British, Japanese, German, French, and Dutch firms. These *multinational corporations* manufacture everything from soaps, shoes, and ballpoint pens to bicycles and portable radios. Domestic manufacturing, in turn, may be stifled because small-scale local operations usually cannot compete with these giant foreign companies.

The lopsided distribution of wealth and the dominance of foreign interests in the Third World countries can erode the incentive for local economic development. Why build up a rural homestead if you don't own the land and can't benefit from your labors? Why attempt to compete with giant corporations when you are at a disadvantage in all phases of operation, from obtaining raw materials to marketing the product? In summary, institutional barriers can deaden economic incentives.

What can be done about institutional problems in underdeveloped nations? Some economists believe that, over time, powerful governments can force the necessary reforms and remove the obstacles to economic betterment. The centralized authorities must have the means and the will to radically alter land-tenure relationships, to reduce the enormous economic and social inequalities, and to evolve an effective program of population control combined with mass health and hygienic improvements.

Governments must also facilitate the emergence of local entrepreneurs and create economic environments, particularly around cities, that are conducive to the critical process of import replacement.[53] They must encourage national savings, so that financial capital is available for business loans and essential public services. Equally importantly, they need to safeguard traditional communities that want to achieve economic self-reliance in their own ways. Governments must learn to recognize when it is better to keep out of economic affairs and when it is correct to step in.

Indeed, these are difficult tasks for the world's young nation states. Many poor countries presently lack the sense of national legitimacy, unity, and long-term stability needed to institute such far-reaching economic and social changes. Some governments will continue to be corrupt and unresponsive to national economic needs. Others will promote economic and political democracy and try to find the right balance between government intervention and the encouragement of independent action and private incentives.

Thus, one of the major problems in economics today is how highly developed countries can help bring about the changes necessary to increase the economic well-being of less-developed countries. A sharing of resources and know-how and a willingness to make some sacrifices will help to reduce the world's gross economic imbalances.

However, if economic equality is achieved in terms of successful development—especially if that development replicates Western industrial growth—then a new irony will arise, an irony that is both disturbing and, from a political viewpoint, perplexing. That subject, our final topic in this book, is the relationship between world development and global pollution.

World Development and Global Pollution

The air you breathe may seem clean to you. Of course in some notorious metropolitan areas, such as Los Angeles; Mexico City; Lagos, Nigeria; and Krakow, Poland, there is more often than not, a disagreeable smog which we know causes respiratory and

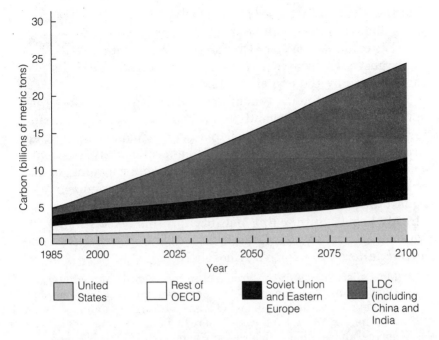

FIGURE 20-1   Carbon-dioxide emissions by region. The less-developed countries' (LDC's) share of CO_2 emissions is projected to grow rapidly; the relative U.S. share is projected to decline.

other well-documented health problems. But even in small towns and villages, you will find air pollutants derived from a variety of sources. In one test of air quality, biologists look for the presence or absence of lichens—the lovely, colorful, scale-like growths that cling to rocks and trees in noncity environments. But the sensitivity of lichens to even low levels of air pollution makes them a rare sight in populated areas. Even more subtle, invisible air contaminants are, unfortunately, becoming more and more prevalent *no matter where on earth measurements are made.*

Traces of synthetic chemicals plus carbon and sulfur dioxide (both byproducts of fossil-fuel combustion) are intermixing throughout the global atmosphere. These emissions are mainly the result of human activities connected with industrialization and economic development. Indeed, the President's *Economic Report to Congress* (1990) expresses great concern about the levels of current and projected future emissions; its conclusion makes no pretense that the solution to reducing these gases will be a simple one. In one chart (Figure 20-1), the *Report* indicates that the greatest increases in carbon dioxide (CO_2) between the years 2000 and 2100 will be in Third World countries.

For example, consider China—a country that currently has the largest coal reserves in the world and plans to *double* its coal consumption by the end of the 1990s!

Yet, even without *any* additional CO_2 releases, we know that since the Industrial Revolution, economic activity has already increased the concentration of this gas by roughly 25 percent (from 280 parts per million (ppm)[*] to approximately 360 ppm). The result is the very real possibility of global warming, or the so-called "greenhouse effect." Setting aside for a moment the honest differences of climatologists as to whether warming has already begun, author Bill McKibben, in his book *The End of Nature,* asks us to pause and reflect on the fact that we have *already* altered the earth's atmosphere:

> Most discussions of the greenhouse gases rush immediately to their future consequences—is the sea going to rise?—without pausing to let the simple fact of what has already happened sink in. The air around us, even where it is clean, and smells like spring, and is filled with birds, is *different,* significantly changed.[54]

Global warming, according to theorists, begins with an increase in carbon dioxide and other greenhouse gases, such as methane, chlorofluorocarbons (CFCs), and nitrous oxide. The altered atmosphere then traps *additional heat,* which in time increases oceanic evaporation and, hence, atmospheric water vapor. Water vapor, in turn, is an efficient greenhouse gas itself and invites further warming in a "looping" feedback process that may be difficult to reverse. Possible increases in average temperature range between a conservative 2°F and a relatively large 8°F. Temperatures in the higher range would probably be great enough to begin to melt the polar ice caps. Along with such projections, some scientists argue that the earth may have some positive, self-regulative abilities, such as the absorption of excessive CO_2 by the oceans or the possible formation of protective cumulus-type cloud covers.

Thus, like a football player subjected to continual bumping, bending, and bruising, the earth is also under stresses initiated by human activities and technologies and fueled by economic

---

[*]Preindustrial levels of CO_2 have been measured in polar ice-core samples, which contain pockets of air trapped from earlier eras.

development. What we don't know is whether the earth's "body" can absorb these physical insults and—like a young, well-conditioned athlete—demonstrate a surprising resiliency, bouncing back without injury when the stress lets up.

Or is our planet more like a middle-aged, weekend player, whose nasty bruise to the knee or shoulder may be more or less permanently disabling. Environmental pessimists, looking at the ominous trends of future pollution, might remind us that even the most resilient athlete who experiences repeated traumas can be permanently injured and face severely diminished health and life processes. The precise metaphor is currently unclear, but its configuration in relation to climatic change will probably come into focus within the next 10–50 years.

Other concerns related to developmental activity include the ongoing destruction of tropical rain forests. When a tract of forest is cut and burned to accommodate cattle ranches or small farms or to harvest tropical woods, it compounds the greenhouse effect by reducing plant photosynthesis, which absorbs CO_2, and by releasing additional CO_2 into the atmosphere when wood is burned. It is estimated that rain-forest destruction contributes roughly 20 percent of the CO_2 buildup that climatologists have been measuring in recent decades.

Another concern related to the destruction of tropical rain forests is the *extinction of entire animal and plant species*. In addition to their intrinsic ecological value, the disappearance of biological diversity also has serious economic and potential health implications for human beings:

> The fact that many medicines contain active ingredients obtained from substances in plants and animals, especially those in the tropics, suggests that a reduction in diversity could represent a significant economic loss.[55]

Peter Raven, Director of the Missouri Botanical Garden, estimates that approximately one-fifth of all plant and animal organisms are "at risk" of becoming extinct during the next 30 years.[56]

A further complication of rain-forest loss combined with climatic change is the possibility of extreme weather events. Indeed, James Lovelock, originator of the **Gaia theory** (which regards the planet as a self-regulating system that behaves as if it were a living organism) feels that the increased frequency of violent weather—superhurricanes, tornadoes, tidal waves, and record high and low temperatures—ought to be one of our main concerns:

> The destruction of the tropical rain forests and the greenhouse effect are so serious—they're not just the doom stories of scientists. . . . They will come in the form of surprises: storms of vastly greater severity than anything we've ever experienced before.[57]

Ozone depletion and acid rain are further destructive side effects of worldwide atmospheric pollution. In these areas, however, there may be greater possibilities for clean-up through the use of alternative technologies for coal-fired burning (the major cause of acid rain) or substitutes for known ozone-damaging chemicals (such as chlorofluorocarbons).

In summation, world development has produced—and probably will continue to produce—problematic environmental side effects, the most serious of which could have an adverse impact on the earth's climatic balance. Many economists point out that additional research is needed and that the costs (especially before all the relevant data is in) may simply be too high, given the uncertainties. Consider, for example, all the individual workers and industry-energy related businesses (including coal mining, electric utilities, automobile manufacturers, ore and metal companies, and airlines, to name a few) that would be adversely affected by a sudden or even a slow shift away from oil and coal usage.

Other economists say that we had better not wait: if we err, we should, as the saying goes, "err on the side of caution." Rushworth M. Kidder addresses this issue in his essay "Let's Not Wait for 'Proof' on Warning of Global Warming," when he argues that we should not evaluate clean-up costs based on certainties; instead, we should view them as costs or premiums paid on a global health-insurance policy:

> We need to change our metaphor. We need to stop looking at environmental issues as though they were court cases. We need, instead, to think of ourselves as homeowners buying insurance. You don't insure against the absolutely predictable. You protect against the possible. . . . You defend yourself against large and irreversible damages.[58]

In fact, some progress has already been made within the developed countries. The United States has initiated a reforestation plan, and some electric utilities have committed company resources to planting trees.[59] In addition, Sweden has taken the important first step of levying a CO_2-emissions tax. Also, in the Montreal Protocol—a 24-nation treaty signed in 1987—the representative countries pledged to reduce ozone-depleting CFC emissions by 50 percent by the year 2000. In the summer of 1990, this directive was strengthened to include 59 countries, which established the more ambitious goal of achieving a 100-percent reduction in CFC emissions by 2000. Indeed, many environmental groups see the Montreal Protocol as a model for future negotiations that will address even more complex environmental problems, such as atmospheric warming, on an international scale.[60]

Economists are beginning to rethink developmental strategies for the Third World countries that are compatible *both* with planetary health and with the betterment of living standards for the world's poorest nations. Working out such short- and long-term policies will be the great challenge of the coming decade and the early part of the next century. Given the complexity of these issues, economists would be well-served not only to have a grounding in politics (the traditional science of political economy) but also to synthesize their discipline with ecology as well. Indeed, the words "economics" and "ecology" have the same root (*eco*-household), implying a knowledge of, and a concern for, the human "household" and nature's "household." We now know that these households are interdependent and intimately linked.

For government officials, this same approach is equally valuable. Considering the enormous implications of today's decisions for tomorrow's generation and the next—in both the developed and the developing worlds—our leaders might well heed the advice of Lao Tzu, written in the fourth century B.C. Toward the end of his little book, *The Way of Life*, dedicated in part to helping the ruling class of his era, Lao Tzu writes:

> Solve the small problem before it becomes big.
> The most involved fact in the world
> Could have been faced when it was simple
> The biggest problem in the world
> Could have been solved when it was small.[61]

When we consider human impact, world economics, global population, and the environment, such advice is as solid, wise, and true today as ever.

QUESTIONS FOR THOUGHT AND DISCUSSION

1. Should all countries be developed in the pattern of industrialized Western societies?

2. In what ways is an Indian reservation in the American West like a less-developed country?

3. Why can't most people in less-developed countries "pull themselves up by their boot straps" and take care of their own economic problems?

4. Consider for a moment *how* you did your laundry last week (i.e., did you use hot water or cold water; did you dry by the sun or by machine; did you use a phosphate or a non-phosphate detergent, etc.). How does the way you did your laundry relate to the regional, national, and global environments? Be specific.

Notes

1. See, for example Bernd Heinrich's book *Bumblebee Economics* (Harvard, 1979) where the author examines the bumblebee's economic problem primarily in terms of energy efficiency. Another related book is Donald Worster's *Nature's Economy* (Anchor, 1979), and his title derived from the early naturalist's concept of what is today called "ecology." Note the word "ecology" has the same root as the word "economics": *oikos* (Greek for household). Thus the natural world also has cooperation, competition, inputs and outputs, maximization, etc., as nature attempts to maintain its "household." Its "management" is not a matter of consciously choosing alternatives (as we do) but is primarily genetic, adaptive, and evolutionary. Incidently, Darwin's great insight of natural selection came to him while reading the great 18th century economists including Adam Smith and even more importantly, Thomas Malthus, whose essay *On Population* led Darwin to the idea of nature's "struggle for existence." (See *Charles Darwin's Autobiography,* Henry Schuman, 1950, p. 54.)

2. See Vernon Carter and Tom Dale, *Topsoil and Civilization,* (Norman, OK: University of Oklahoma Press, 1974). This is perhaps the best reference I have seen that puts the depletion of the world's topsoil in a historical context.

3. Henry David Thoreau, *Walden*, p. 29–30, Bramhall House, New York.

4. North Country Anvil, #4 (Box 37, Millville, MN 55957)

5. George B. Leonard, "Winning Isn't Everything, It's Nothing," *Intellectual Digest* (1973): 47.

6. Milton Friedman, "The Voucher Idea," *New York Times Magazine* (1973): 23. See also John Coons and Stephen Sugerman, *Educations by Choice: The Case for Family Control* (Berkeley, CA: University of California Press, 1978). In a modification of the public school voucher idea, Harvard economist Lester Thurow has proposed a "skill voucher" for those who do not choose to go to college. Thurow suggests such a voucher would be worth $12,000 or an amount equal to the average subsidy currently received by college students. (See *The Zero Sum Solution,* p. 205, Simon & Schuster, 1985.)

7. For an appraisal of the financial success (or failure) of the largest mergers and LBO acquisition of the 1980s see *Business Week,* Jan. 15, 1990.

8. Maurice Zietlin, ed., *American Society, Inc.,* (Chicago: Markham Publishing Co., 1970), pp. 513–514.

9. From *The Retreat from Riches* by Peter Passell and Leonard Ross, (New York: Viking Press, New York: 1971), p. 36.

10. George F. Will, "Unpadding the 'Padded Society,'" *Newsweek* (1981): 100.

11. The attempts to increase productivity in some professions—high-speed drills for dentists, clinics for doctors, TV courses for educators—have undoubtedly kept costs and prices from rising higher than they would have without the productivity gain.

12. See Milton Friedman, *Capitalism and Freedom* (Chicago: University of Chicago Press, 1962), p. 150. In his chapter "Occupational Licensure" Friedman suggests that all professional licensing (including medical licensing) should be abolished in favor of a more free entry into the occupations. According to Friedman, this would ultimately lower the cost of professional services for the consumer.

13. Arthur Schlesinger, Jr., "Neo-Conservatism and the Class Struggle," *Wall Street Journal* (1981).

14. Saul Pett, "The Bloated Bureaucracy," *St. Paul Pioneer Press* (1981): 4.

15. See *The Eight Myths of Poverty,* by William O'Hare, *American Demographics,* May 1986, p. 24.

16. This data was taken from Greg Duncan's book, *Years of Poverty, Years of Plenty* (Institute for Social Research, Ann Arbor, 1984).

17. Op. cit. (O'Hare) p. 25.

18. Michael Harrington, *The Other America* (New York: Macmillan, 1962), p. 13.

19. See Michael Harrington's more recent book, *The New American Poverty* (Holt, Rinehart & Winston, 1984), p. 690.

20. Op. cit. (Thoreau) p. 89.

21. See footnote 6.

22. Leopold Kohr, *Overdeveloped Nations* (New York: Schocken Books, 1978), p. 39.

23. Wade Green and Soma Golden, "Luddites Were Not all Wrong," *New York Times Magazine.* The most extreme position I have seen concerning economic growth and man's ecological destructiveness is in the poetry by the late California poet Robinson Jeffers. Many readers have interpreted his poetry to essentially say that "the human race is, in fact, not needed." See Gilbert Highet, *The Powers of Poetry* (New York: Oxford University Press, 1960), pp. 133–134.

24. Irving Kristol, "The Worst Is Yet to Come," *Wall Street Journal* (Nov. 26, 1979, p. 24).

25. Mel Ellis, "The Good Earth," *Milwaukee Journal* (1974).

26. E. B. White, *The Points of My Compass* (New York: Harper and Row, 1962), p. 67.

27. Henry Caudill, *My Land Is Dying* (New York: Dutton, 1971), p. 104.

28. *The Quality of Life*; James A. Michener (Lippincott, 1970), p. 86–87.

29. *The Making of the President, 1964*; Theodore H. White (Atheneum, 1965), p. 322.

30. The highly respected forecasting newsletter, *Blue Chip Economic Indicators* (which uses a "consensus" approach of averaging the projections form approximately 50 economists), projected in March 1982 an inflation rate of 6.9% for '83, 6.6% for '84, and 6.4% for '85. In contrast, the actual rates (GNP Price

Deflator) was 3.8% in '83, 4.1% in '84, and only 3.3% in '85. (Sources: *Blue Chip Economic Indicators,* Sedona, AZ, March 10, 1982, p. 7, and *The Economic Report of the President,* Feb. 1986, Washington, D.C., p. 257.)

31. See John Galbraith, *The Great Crash* (Boston: Houghton Mifflin, 1961) for a fascinating account of 1929's "Black Tuesday" and the early days of the depression.

32. James R. Adams, "Supply-Side Roots of the Founding Fathers," *Wall Street Journal* (1981): (Nov. 17, 1981, p. 26).

33. Henry Clay Lindgren, *Great Expectations, the Psychology of Money* (William Kaufmann, 1980), p. 19.

34. Walter W. Haines, *Money, Prices and Policy* (New York: McGraw-Hill, 1958), pp. 24–25.

35. Kristen Anundsen and Michael Phillips, "Fun in Business," *Briarpatch Review,* a Journal of Right Livelihood and Simple Living (1977): 30.

36. E. F. Schumacher, *Small Is Beautiful* (New York: Harper & Row, 1973), pp. 54–55.

37. Harold Stewart, trans., *A Net of Fireflies* (Rutland, Vermont: Charles Tuttle Co., 1960), p. 18.

38. Some textbooks call the *consumption effect* the *substitution effect* and use the term *income effect* for what is called here the *leisure effect.* The change was made to eliminate confusion with the use of *income effect* and *substitution effect* in the supply and demand chapter (Chap. 3).

39. Adam Smith, *Inquiry Into the Nature and Causes of the Wealth of Nations,* Volume 1 (New York: Dutton, 1910), p. 108.

40. Ibid., p. 110.

41. Ibid., Smith, p. 8.

42. Ivan Illich, *Tools for Conviviality* (New York: Harper & Row, 1973), p. 55.

43. See Michael Maccoby, *The Gamesman* (New York: Harper & Row, 1973), p. 55.

44. For more information on these cartels, see "The Incredible Electrical Conspiracy," *Fortune* (April and May, 1961) and also "Cozy Competitors," *The Wall Street Journal,* May 4, 1978, p. 1.

45. Quoted from *The Arizona Republic,* Jan. 4, 1986, p. 1E.

46. "Angry Workers Desecrate Flag in Milwaukee," *St. Paul Pioneer Press* (1981): 1.

47. William J. Baumol, "U.S. Industry's Lead Gets Bigger," *The Wall Street Journal,* March 21, 1990.

48. See Frances Moore Lappe, *Diet for a Small Planet* (New York: Ballantine Books, 1975).

49. It should be noted that a growing number of economists are concerned that the less developed countries are adopting large-scale technology. This is happening because they want to emulate developed countries' production techniques, and because middle or "intermediate" technology is simply not available. One economist who not only described the problem but also started "intermediate technology groups" to develop tools and equipment more suited for poor, labor intensive countries is the late E. F. Schumacher. See E. F. Schumacher, *Small Is Beautiful,* and the follow-up book, George McRobie, *Small Is Possible* (New York: Harper & Row, 1981).

50. Mortz Thomsen, *Living Poor: A Peace Corps Chronicle* (University of Washington Press, 1969).

51. Pranay Gupta, *The Crowded Earth,* (Norton, 1984): p. 109.

52. Op. cit. (Thomsen) p. 173.

53. For an innovative analysis on the importance of cities and the process of important substitution, see Jane Jacob's book, *Cities and the Wealth of Nations* (Random House, 1984).

54. Bill McKibben, *The End of Nature,* (New York, Random House, 1989), p. 18.

55. *Economic Report of the President* (1990), p. 221.

56. Peter Raven, "One-Fifth of Earth's Species Face Extinction," *U.S.A. Today*, June 6, 1986, p. 5.

57. James Lovelock, "Only Man's Presence Can Save Nature," *Harper's Magazine,* April, 1990, p. 47.

58. Rushworth M. Kidder, "Let's Not Wait for 'Proof' on Warning of Global Warming," *The Christian Science Monitor,* June 27, 1988.

59. Janet Raloff, "CO_2: How Will We Spell Relief?" (*Science News,* Dec. 24 & 31, 1988). For example, the utility Applied Energy Services of Arlington, VA, is helping to finance the planting of 50 million trees in Guatemala, p. 133.

60. Janet Raloff, "Governments Warm to Greenhouse Action," *Science News,* Dec. 16, 1989, p. 394.

61. Lao Tzu, *The Way of Life* (Tran. by Witter Bynner), New York, Capricorn Books, 1944, p. 65.

Index

Bold page numbers refer to key terms and concepts presented in the text.